Malachite Eyes

Dan Wallace

Wylisc Press
Silver Spring, MD

© Copyright © 2024 by Daniel C. Wallace
Published 2024 by Wylisc Press

This book is a work of fiction. Names, characters, places, and incidents are the products of the author's imagination or are used factiously. Any resemblance to actual events, locales, or persons, living or dead is entirely coincidental.

All rights reserved. Printed in the United States of America. No part of this book may be used or reproduced in any manner whatsoever without written permission except in the case of brief quotations embodied in critical articles and reviews. For information, contact Wylisc Press (wyliscpress1@gmail.com).

Malachite Eyes
Dan Wallace
ISBN 97817353006-6-5 Trade Paperback
ISBN 97817353006-7-2 E-Book
6 x 9
303 pages
Publication Date: September 2024
Cover design by Molly A. Wallace

Wylisc Press
Silver Spring, MD 20901-1205
wyliscpress1@gmail.com

To Ellen,
Wonderful Sister,
Defender of the People,
And Fabulous Raconteur

One

She dropped her clothes where she shed them and before he had a chance to pick them up, she drew him into the bed. Looking down at her wonderfully naked body squirming in anticipation of a new lover, he concentrated on those new old road signs, her hard-nippled breasts, perfectly round as if from a boob job, though he couldn't see any telltale lines beneath her lower half-moons. She had terrific skin, too, not an ounce of extra fat. Muscles in fact, rippling a bit at her midriff as she rolled, even her navel taut, tribute to aerobic devotion. Her legs twitched back and forth, knees up and down, open then closed pinning his hips, first a glance of her muff, a grand tight thing, neat and unready for the joy of love to come.

As he fell onto her, he marveled at the wreath of red hair around her head, a spray of root beer framing a delicate oval, angelic face. He plunged his mouth on hers and began to slip his hands around her body. She was perfect, like ten thousand other girls he had laid over the years. No matter, he worked hard to make her happy, a surprise to her, it seemed, from the little startled cries she made.

"Jesus!"

He kneaded her shoulders as he nuzzled her neck, licking, flicking his tongue, then slowing it to caress the bump of her collarbone. His hands worked down her arms as his head dropped lower between her breasts. He pressed his nose against her sternum, shifting to rub her chest with his cheek as he reached a nipple with the tip of his tongue. He twirled his tongue around it, moving his head to mouth it, laving it lavishly at the same time running his hands down her rib cage to press her waist. He switched to her other nipple as his hands slipped under her to cup and squeeze her ass cheeks.

"Oh my God," she grunted.

He continued to drop lower, running his tongue down the cavern between her ribs into the hollow of her stomach, she laughing, tickled. Finally, he slid his tongue tip down to her mound, parting the soft hair there until he reached her nether lips, parting them too, gently, until he'd reached the point that made her gasp, groaning, "Ohh—"

There he stayed until she climaxed, once, twice, again, and again. He rolled her over gently, then licked her from behind until she came again, all the while massaging her rump or cupping her breasts.

He kept going until she said, "My God, I can't believe you're doing this. I've almost had enough!"

She came again, becoming almost comatose afterwards, lying trancelike on the bed, utterly oblivious. He entered her.

"Oh, fuck!" she said, wrapping her legs around him. He pumped for a while, climaxed, then fell off to the side.

They lay in the bed, Tom musing aimlessly about what his best bud Don would call refracting. Except only men needed to refract, he thought.

After a time, she said, "Do you do that with all your one-night stands?"

Startled, he said, "I try."

She said, "My God. I'm amazed. You don't fit the rock star cliche at all."

"Oh," he said, dismayed. He rolled over away from her. "I prefer musician, rock musician, if you must. Anyway, I haven't been a rock star," he exaggerated the words, "for more than twenty years."

"Yeah, I guess so," she said, and he winced silently. "But still," she went on, "I recognized you."

He turned back to her, "Oh, yeah?"

"Sure," she said, "I saw a picture of you in a *People* article 'Where Are They Now?'"

"Yeah, right," he said, "where am I now?"

She leaned over to hug him, "Why, with me, Baby. Hey, I don't bounce from an A-list party to fuck just anybody, you know."

"Uh huh," he murmured.

"I'm no groupie, I wouldn't do it with Michael Stipe or Hootie."

"Maybe you're an oldies groupie," he said.

"No way. You couldn't get me anywhere near Tom Petty, or that weird hair guy, Lyle Lovett. Whatever did Julia Roberts see in him anyway?"

"He's a real nice guy," he said sincerely. "He also can play and write songs."

"Yeah, well," she said, trailing off.

"Yup," he said.

The quiet lengthened until it baldly pointed out that their conversation was failing, maybe had already failed.

"Well, anyway," she said, punching his shoulder, "you still do all right, I'll bet. You don't do what you did to me without a lot of practice. I'll bet a lot of girls remember you and fall all over you."

He closed his eyes, smiling. "Okay," he said, "so what's my name?" He waited for her to answer. When she didn't, he opened his eyes. She pounced.

"Ted Weatherly! See, I knew it!"

"Tom," he said softly.

"Oh." She paused, then said, "Well, I was close, right? And I got your last name right, right?"

"Pretty much," he said, "but you misspelled it."

"Oh?" She frowned, then smiled slowly, "Hey," and punched his shoulder again.

He eyed her again, watching the utterly unselfconscious way that she moved, completely at ease naked, her striking pert breasts bouncing as she reached over to hit him, he found himself endeared again.

He reached for her, but she held him off.

"Okay," she said, "so what's my name?"

"Martha," he said at once.

"Oh," she said, disappointed, "that's right."

He moved to grab her, but she stopped him again. "Okay, what about my last name?"

He froze. "You didn't tell me," he lied.

"Oh," she said, "I didn't?"

"Come here," he said, "who needs names when we've known each for so long?"

At four a.m., Tom arose and dressed except for his shoes. He padded around the room, picking up her clothes quietly, every now and then glancing over to the bed to see if he was waking her. She slept on, her face covered by that wonderfully burnished brown hair.

He folded her clothes neatly and put them on an easy chair next to the bed. He then padded over to the chair in front of the desk and slipped on his socks and shoes. He left the hotel key on the dresser and started to leave a couple of bills for the housekeeping staff but decided that Martha might misunderstand. He slipped out the door, easing it closed to keep it from making any noise.

Downstairs, he strolled over to the registration desk.

"Hi, I'm checking out of 601. My guest hasn't left yet, though. If she leaves late, just put it on my bill."

While he waited, he glanced around the lobby at the pink marbled fountains filled with faux green seawater, flanked by aqua colored sofas and chairs. Escalators in the middle broke the vast unrelieved expanse of the foyer, also curtailed by the phalanxes of cylindrical glass elevators that afforded a view of the atrium as they shot up to the rooms. Tom thought they looked like giant pneumatic tubes for humans, swooping them up like living messages for deposit in some indistinct communication center, or maybe a bank, a human bank.

"Thank you, Mr. Weatherly," said the night clerk. "Is there anything else I can do for you?"

"Yes, could you please call a limo for the airport."

"Yes sir, at once. Shall I get a bellman for your luggage?"

Tom shook his head, "Don't have any. This was an unscheduled stop."

"Fine," and the clerk turned to the phone as Tom continued his idle once-over of the hotel.

He liked these architectural extravaganzas, even though they were kind of sterile. The anonymity of them was a comfort, everyone kept at a distance by the vastness of the structures. He'd spent a lot of time in these kinds of places over the years, usually holed up in his room until his fame faded. Then he could plop himself down in the middle of the sweeping resort grandeur without being bothered much. Except every now and then, when someone wanted to know why he looked so vaguely familiar. The answer seemed more about the relief of the feeling nagging them rather than joy at seeing an old-time idol. He really didn't miss the crush much, though.

These space colonies on the ground were a far cry from the dumps he'd stayed at when first coming up. The famous British music invasion also heralded the arrival of their unfailing sense for finding funky hotels, the driving operative being that they were cheap. In the Cheshire, for example, they shared the bathrooms down the hall with drag queens who promenaded long before it became fashionable. They were a howl, he recalled, and the band learned a lot from them, especially about fronting. Passing the old jazz players in the hallways, too, nodding away as they did.

Jesus Christ, it had been hard to sleep in those days. Every kind of band played until two then breakfasted until six. And then, for some unknown reason, some poor son of a bitch aired out his misery on his horn at high noon. "What the hell was he thinking?" Tom once asked. "Not thinking," his fellow troubadour Don would say, "feeling." "Yeah sure, but how can you feel without sleep?" Tom asked back.

He always liked hotels even in those bad old days when they stayed at the fleabags favored by the Brit bands. As bad as they might have been, they always had something fascinating about them, some detail or amenity from a time past when the proprietors aspired to a social station that either never arrived or passed by too quickly. Or was it a train that had passed, like in the night? Whatever, he'd find himself staring at the beautiful carved paneling, real African mahogany, or the fireplaces in each room, plugged up of course. Even so, every now and then some whacked-out drummer would start a fire in one anyway, raising hell with the sprinkler system and fire alarms, clearing the entire building. Firefighters dressed like stormtroopers wearing fifty pounds of gear would smash their way into the player's smoky room and smother the burning newspaper stuffed in the grating with foam, the drummer saying all the while between hacking from the fumes, "Hey, man, what're you doing? I was freezing in here."

"Your limousine is ready, Mr. Weatherly."

"Yeah, thanks," said Tom. He passed a Canadian twenty to the clerk, "This is for you, okay? But you gotta make sure that this," he handed him another folded bill, "goes to the housekeeper for my room, right? Room 601, remember, after my guess leaves? I'm counting on you, man, really. Right?"

The clerk, a handsome twenty-year old, gave him a surprised look. A small smile flickered at the corners, then disappeared. "I sure will sir, I promise," he said sincerely. "I'll walk it up myself."

"Yeah, that's good. Okay, thanks."

"Be sure to stay with us again, Mr. Weatherly."

"You bet," Tom said. He turned around, located the driver, then started for the large brass doors.

"A beautiful day, cool but sunny."

"Yessir," the driver said, holding the car door. "Cooler than most August days here."

"Oh, but you should spend time in New York. Hot, hot, hot, believe me."

In the car, he sat quietly. *People* magazine. They must have used an old archive photo, which made him wonder how Martha had recognized him. Still, he was the same height, just under average, and the same weight, 156 pounds, give or take a beer. His skin was the same, nightlife pasty, but his light brown hair— wheat brown, Christine used to call it—was a bit lighter around the temples, sun-bleached some would say, but he knew the truth. And there were other signs you couldn't put your finger on until you looked at an old photograph. Then, though indescribable, it was obvious. He looked younger only compared to being older.

He lifted the phone up to his ear while dialing.

"You are a nervy toad to violate my privacy with your capricious phone jones," a deep basso profundo said, "and I must have you corrected, pummeled, and neutered. Leave your name, number, and the time you called so that my bully boys don't have to track you down like the yellow running dog that you are it'll go easier for you. Wait for the tone and have a nice day."

"Pick up, Don," Tom said when the machine ding-donged, "you sick fuck."

"Who's sick?" the bass said, even deeper and more ragged than the voice on the tape, "I'm not calling in the dead of night to roust an innocent citizen with fear and loathing. It isn't me who's the poster boy for a South American death squad."

"It's seven in the morning, for Christ' sake. The sun's been up for an hour."

"Yeah, sure, maybe in Toronto, but not New York."

Tom did a double take. Dark in New York with sunup two hours earlier than Toronto? They're in the same time zone.

Don continued, "Anyway, what are you doing up this early yourself, or should I guess?"

Tom shook his head as if they were in the room together. "Don't."

"Okay," Don said, drawing out the word. "So, how was Toronto?"

"Not much. They want all the old stuff, none of the new."

"Oh." After a brief pause, he said, "Sorry."

"Yeah, well . . .," Tom trailed off. He waited, then thought how silence seemed heavier between people when talking on the phone.

Don said in a cheerful voice, "Disco is back, buddy."

"We never did disco," Tom snapped, then quietly, "except that one time. And that was a ballad."

"Yeah, but that one-off disco ballad made us rich. Or made you rich, you capitalist prick."

"It improved your health, too, pal. Don't forget, you live in New York."

"Yeah, but it wasn't the Don Vasser Experience, was it? And I didn't have Gordon Gekko for a brother, either, turning my modest earnings into more filthy lucre than Uncle Scrooge dives into in his money bin."

Exasperated, Tom said, "Joe offered to handle your portfolio, but you said no thanks."

"Oh, 'portfolio,' is it? No thanks," Don said, "one sell-out's enough."

"Uh huh," Tom said, "I know, I'm the asshole in this piece. Can we move on, now?"

"Sure, sure, okay," Don sniffed, "So, what do you want?"

"I'll be back in about three hours. Call the guys and see if they all can make it over tonight."

"Oh? We're pressing on, even after this latest disappointment?"

"Screw you," Tom said. "So, are you going to do it or what?"

"Of course," Don said, "I'll call them, but not until daylight if that's all right with you."

"Whatever."

"You want me to pick you up?"

"No, I'll take a cab."

"One with a phone? Still flaunting it, huh?"

"Well, you said it, I'm a big wheel now."

He ground his fists into his eyes on the flight home, wishing he could sleep, sleep, sleep. They say that people sleep fewer hours as they grow older, but he didn't sleep at all. It seemed that way, anyway. He wondered why? His life was okay, he was still writing even though the old group hadn't played out for years. And for all of Don's bullshit, when they practiced with the new players, he was serious about putting it together, focused. That must be a good sign. Don wouldn't do it if he thought the music sucked, and he'd be clear about that, too. But maybe Don couldn't tell anymore either. He'd hated *Malachite Eyes*, the little toss-off they'd done that had gone ballistic, made them all super famous and rich enough to forget about it. Don always rode him about loving the gushing crowds, the threads, the chicks, the booze, and the drugs more than the music. There was some truth there, Tom admitted, some guilt. Not that much had changed either, except he'd dropped the drugs. He still liked clothes, he could afford them, and he wore them.

The flight attendant came to his seat, leaned down, and smiled as she asked him if he'd like something to drink.

"Scotch and soda," he said, "Dewars." She blinked and he followed with, "I'm on European time. Weird connecting flight, you know?"

She smiled again as she straightened up, but by the time she got back with the drink, he was long gone asleep.

Two

For breaking a two-by-four over the head of Marcella Stephen's husband, Norah Kealy had been urged by her boss to consider a career change. Maybe stop working with battered women, get into some other branch of social work.

"That's rich, Teddy. I know what. I could counsel abusive men, ask them how they feel about beating their wives or girlfriends half to death, then encourage them not to do it ever again."

Dark-haired and hazel-eyed, she was a woman who could be stunningly attractive if she cared about that sort of thing. But she dressed for her work, which meant flannel and denim in layers dictated by the weather and whether she felt fat. Her high energy level kept the latter concern a cultural illusion, even though she never exercised. As far as Teddy knew, she was always at the Center.

"Come on, Norah," he said. "You're too close to it. You need to move on to something that you can be more effective at."

Teddy filled a wheeled wooden captain's chair, his elbows comfortably resting on the curved arms, his hands spread out over his considerable paunch. He and Norah had been friends for a long time, but he was beginning to seriously piss her off.

"Damn, Teddy, I've been doing this effectively for ten years."

"Yeah, and this isn't the first time you bopped one of our clients' boyfriends on the noggin. It's not quite the nonviolent example we're looking for here."

"Very goddamn funny. If the schmucks didn't turn up like they do, with their BMF attitudes, they'd have nothing to worry about."

"Norah," Teddy said half-plaintively, half annoyed, "some of them are their husbands, the fathers of their children. Yes, these women don't have to put up with the abuse, but they do have to deal with them about matters such as alimony, child support, and other domestic issues. The men have a legal right to discuss these matters."

"As long as they don't behave like the shitheads they are. And that's bullshit anyway. When in your lifetime did you ever hear of any of these assholes paying child support or alimony?"

Teddy closed his eyes for a moment to rest, and she remembered days past when she imagined the pale shade of his eyelids the result of the bushy red overhang of his eyebrows. Now, after so many years of frustration, endurance, and redundant pain, gray had crept into that last bastion of his fading youth.

"This is all beside the point," he said finally, opening his eyes again and leaning forward on his desk. "You're burnt, Norah, you're toast. You give these shits actionable grounds and it inevitably makes it worse for the ladies. You need to get out for your own good—you need a new gig."

"Teddy, I like what I'm doing, it's my fucking life!"

"Yeah, well, I don't know how to tell you this," he said, "but, you're out. The board says so."

She sat back, stunned. Without thinking, she reached up and began to pull on a dart of the black hair framing her face, at the same time twisting her lip to chew on it, practices of hers at times like this. Seeing her do it again, Teddy softened. "Norah. You're beautiful, a beautiful woman and a beautiful person. You need a better life than this."

"Oh, really, Teddy, you mean like yours? How's your wife, how's your family?"

Teddy mugged a broad wince as he said, "Yeah, but I'm different, Norah, I'm basically stupid. You're not."

"Please, Teddy, spare me."

He nodded, "Okay, okay." He paused, then picked up a sheaf of papers and leaned over, gently placing them in front of her. Norah stared past the papers at the desk's badly scratched and cracked varnish, noticing it for the first time—the last time.

"I did a little calling around and found this place looking for a first-class counselor for kids who become wards of the state. It's not a live-in, though there is periodic weekend duty. The director is an old friend of mine from Wisconsin. She says the kids are great and that they really could use somebody with a little imagination to come in."

Norah read the top page of the bundle as she listened.

"The other stuff is what's available elsewhere which I thought looked pretty good."

Norah gazed up at Teddy, "This is in New York! You're sending me to the other side of the Earth! Man, you really do want to get rid of me."

"Now, Norah, that's not true. First, it's in Syossett, Nassau County, Long Island. I honestly had in mind what I thought you might like the best. It's kids, for Chrissake! You like kids. You'll be helping them without having to deal with the jackasses who left them there."

"Yeah, but there are kids in Oakland, too."

"Not in any agencies with any openings," he said.

"You mean not in any that will have me," Norah said bitingly.

He sighed, exasperated. "That's not it. There really aren't any openings, really. If you want to stick around until there are, that's fine, that's your decision. You know you'll get the best recommendation from me." He dropped his eyes to his hands, mumbling, "This is the board's idea, not mine."

Norah's anger suddenly fled. She reached her own hand over and covered Teddy's, dry and soft.

"Jesus, Teddy, I'm sorry. I know you don't want to see me gone. Thanks, really, for all you've done. You're still my best pal, you know that?"

He smiled sadly into his breast, "Yeah, Norah, you're my little sis."

"Keep telling Betty that," she said. "She'll never suspect a thing, and I can fly in on weekends."

He laughed, getting up, "Yeah, and there's always vacations."

"Right, bring the kids."

They hugged, and Norah went upstairs to clean out the few things of her own she kept in her desk.

At home, she cried until she heard Marilyn's key in the door.

"Guess what? I've been canned," she announced.

Marilyn rushed over to wrap her arms around her. "Oh, Honey, I'm so sorry."

"Yeah," said Norah, beginning to cry again, "Me too."

"Oh, don't cry, Norah," Marilyn said, weeping herself, "Don't cry. Damn. Now look at me."

They both laughed through their tears.

Norah took a deep breath. "Yep, I'm outta here."

Marilyn leaned back, looking at her so sorrowfully with those remarkable brown eyes set in that rich, almond face. Norah had to wonder how anyone could want to hit them until they were closed, skin-tight. That's how she'd first met her, at the Center, six years ago as a client. Now Marilyn was divorced, through school, and a counselor herself. They'd moved in together after her split up. She remembered how Marilyn looked when they'd first met, compared to now, a reconstructed, fully realized woman. Yet, she would always be damaged to some degree, a fact that simply intensified Norah's fury at men who knocked women back to square one and behind. Thoughts of their lost potential just drove her mad.

Norah often wondered why she felt so passionate about her work, given her own ordinary experience. She had dumped her own worthless lump of a husband, quintessential 80s man that he was, but he had never abused her physically, just her intelligence. She figured it had to do with her father, who had ignored her most of her childhood except when he put her down verbally for complaining about not being treated fairly, never equal to her brothers. The old man was a master at destroying a kid's confidence and self-image.

So, maybe working with kids wasn't a terrible idea.

"What are you going to do?" Marilyn asked.

"Do? Believe it or not, Marilyn, I think I'm moving to New York."

"Really? All that way? Oh, Norah, I'll miss you so!"

The tears started again, and they hugged each other tightly.

On the plane, Norah asked herself again if she was doing the right thing. Moving East meant being near her family, thereby risking potential obligation. She thought of Vonnegut's description in *Cat's Cradle* of the phony loyalties that people created and treasured—Granfalloons, he called them. She laughed thinking that he might be surprised to learn that some people thought of their own families as Granfalloons. Or maybe not surprised.

Winter again, also, she thought, shuddering. But the Bay Area got cold, too.

She admitted to herself that none of that actually scared her. The new job was the thing that really frightened her, the idea of facing those kids, innocents no more most likely, but more innocent than she could ever be again. They' know just looking at her because she carried the original sin that all adults did, the sin of being older and thereby undeservedly empowered over every one of them. These children would look at her out of the only experience they had with their parents, abuse of that power in the most fundamental ways. Such sin, she thought, bowing her head, pressing her temples with her thumbs and index fingers.

Gertrude Weintraub met her at the front door and welcomed her in, saying, "I hear you're a feisty one." At 5'6", Norah towered over this soft, plump woman. "Good," she said," we could use a ninja warrior around here. This is Marbury, after all, spitting distance away from the City."

"I'm not proud of losing my shit," mumbled Norah.

Gertrude turned her eyes on her, "Sure. But if you channel that kind of fury in the right place, you can do a lot of good things." Seeing Norah's head lift in surprise, Gertrude smiled slightly, "Oh, yeah, I know all that cosmic psycho-feel-good BS. Long Island's in the East; we read books here too, you know."

"I know," said Norah, "I came from Cherry Hill originally."

"No kidding?" said Gertrude, her turn to be surprised. "You should feel right at home."

Just then, a line of children came out of a door at the end of the hall, and headed in their direction, veering off to enter another doorway. Norah gazed at them, boys and girls, brown and black, four to ten years old, clean and healthy looking in clean though well-worn clothes. They stared back at her, wondering who she was. But she saw something else, too, a question, a guarded hope maybe, something bright in the clear white around their lyrical brown and black eyes, a possibility reflected in her being new. She melted, she could stop them and hug them all, each one by one. She could love them all.

"Yes," she said, "could be."

Three

When Tom returned home, his housekeeper Mary opened the windows and doors to air the place out. Leaning against the patio door, he watched the groundskeeper Felix Orujo ride the John Deere in concentric circles around the flower beds. Like it was his jet ski on a lush green sea, Tom thought. The sky was clear now, but if a thunderhead cropped up, he and Mary would be half an hour closing all the windows. Felix would never make it back in time. Don't try it, Felix; abandon the mower and lie flat on the ground. No, no, don't crouch under that peach tree, don't! Too late; Felix peach cobbler.

He turned back to Mary, who was dusting the blond wooden bookcase situated against the interior wall. She even opened the doors and started to wipe down the sound system inside, which he hardly used. When he'd had the place built, he insisted on individual sound systems for every room, even the guest rooms, upon his conviction that every visitor should have the right to listen to the music of their choice. Of course, he chose the music in the common rooms—Lord of the Manure.

"Mary, time to go."

"Excuse, me, Mr. Tom?"

She had adopted this form of address years ago when she insisted on calling him Mr. Weatherly while he insisted on being called by his first name. He swallowed an internal grimace and said, "You need to go home, Ms. Mary."

"But there's so much to do!" she said, alarmed.

"For Chrissake, Mary, the place is immaculate. Why don't you do what I tell you to do, just clean the rooms I use?"

"Please, Mr. Tom, the language."

Mary was straight from Ireland and still wholeheartedly embraced the Church.

"Sorry, but I want to sleep. Do me this one favor, will you?"

Bowing her head, she bit her lip as she painstakingly turned for the door, a brilliant evocation of dejection.

"You could sleep in your own bedroom, you know," she said. "It's clean, and I could get the rest of my work done properly."

Tom shook his head. "Too big. The guest room's cozier. And I like the door open on the yard and the garden. I like to listen to the bees buzzing before I nod off. If I had it all to do over again, I'd have the master bedroom put here instead."

"Well, why not?" she said. "You could have had it done whilst you were away on holiday."

"I don't know," he said, "it's going to an awful lot of trouble when I'm not even sure I'm keeping the place. I'm thinking of moving to Vegas. There are a lot of opportunities out there, you know."

She frowned in irritation, and he hurried to say, "Oh, don't worry Mary, I wouldn't leave without you."

"Right. Harry would love Las Vegas."

"Well, you go often enough."

"He goes, I follow to pick up the pieces of our ruined finances. And I can just imagine you working in a lounge there."

"Please," he said in mock annoyance, "my old fans are in the middle of their peak earning years. I'm sure I'd get a full-fledged stage show."

She rolled her eyes as she turned to leave, "Your heart's desire."

He grinned ruefully. They'd been having variations on the same conversation for eight years, each one tickling him. Only ten years older than himself, Mary had assumed the role of an older sister raising her young brother after their mother had passed away, a concept that peeved Tom's real mother to no end, she being alive and kicking in Arizona. Mary hadn't known when she'd started working for him that he'd been a successful pop star, as she would put it. But, when strange men and women kept showing up at the place, she'd made it her business to find out. Since then, she'd become proprietorial about his interests.

As she reached the door, he called to her, "Before you leave, Mary, could you call the market, have them send over a couple of platters and some drinks? You know, the flavored seltzer and a case of beer?"

"I have already," she said. "You always rehearse after a trip."

"Oh," he said. "Okay, thanks, and give Felix a buzz, will you, ask him to call it a day?"

"Can't. He doesn't have the phone with him."

"Damn, I told him to take it with him wherever."

"You did. He doesn't."

"Well, damn it," he said.

"Do you want me to go out there and tell him?"

"No, of course not, I will. You go home and have a nice day. What is it, *General Hospital*?"

"This early, Regis and Kathy. Grotesquely fascinating but keeps my mind off my ironing."

"Oh. Okay, take care."

She left and he looked back out on the yard. Felix broke from his circles and drove the mower on a diagonal across Tom's line of sight toward the garage at the end of the house. Was he finished with the grass? Tom wondered. It didn't look like it from here.

He started out the bedroom patio door, then thought better. Instead, he plopped splay-legged on the bed, his arms behind his head and waited. A few minutes later, soft knocking on the poolside door.

"Come in," he said, and Felix stuck his head around the side.

"You want me to go home now, Boss?"

"How did you know that?"

"Usually, you do when you get back."

Another traveler, from Chile, Felix had started the same time as Mary. His attitude was different, though; he styled himself as one who would slide by whenever he could. Except, the image interfered with his natural tendency to do a good job perfectly. Tom's brother Joe, also his financier, would complain about how much he paid Felix for the work he did, but Tom didn't care. Felix did more than just the grounds, and Tom was too smart to chance losing him over doing boring stuff all day long. So, he overpaid him outrageously and allowed him a huge amount of slack. Felix pretended to take advantage of the situation, but he never could, really. He did, however, do tiny things to drive Tom nuts, maybe his manifestation of the natural adversarial worker-management relationship. Like not taking the cell phone with him when Tom was at the other end of their world.

"Felix, how come you don't take the cell with you like I ask when you're out working on the lawn?"

Felix said in an exaggerated Latino accent, which was normally heavy despite living in the States for fifteen years, "Oh, I don't think I should do that, you know? Those things give you cancer in the head, you know? Look at all those executives who die from brain cancer; they have everything, and they let a little phone kill them. Not for me."

"Oh, bullshit, Felix, there's never been any proof of that. And even if there was, those guys were on the phone all the time. I hardly ever need to call you."

"Then, we don't need it Boss. I don't want to take any chances, you know? I got kids to take care of. You should watch out, too, Boss, you use it more than me."

"Sure, you don't use it at all," Tom muttered quietly, then more loudly, "I'm telling you, there's no scientific proof the damn things give anyone cancer."

"That's what all those researchers said about aluminum pots, too, you know? They don't give you Alzheimer's, right? But all those guys, they get rid of all their aluminum pots and pans anyway. I got rid of mine, too. From now on, I say to Miriam, iron sartenés!"

Tom stared at the small man in the doorway, his Dali mustache and his little goatee. A caricature, he thought, except for how edgy his raps could make people feel.

"Felix, if you're so health conscious, how come you don't quit smoking?"

Plaintively, Felix said, "I try, man, but it's hard!"

Tom nodded. "All right, take off. See you tomorrow."

"Thanks, Boss."

Boss. Christ, he hated that. He closed his eyes, ready to try to sleep.

"Boss?" He opened his eyes. "You need anything before I go? I could get you some coffee, a sandwich. A beer?"

Ovaltine, he thought idly. "Thanks, Felix, I'm cool. Take care of yourself, okay?"

"Sure, man."

He closed his eyes and listened to the sounds of Felix leaving, subsiding as the distance grew, and he wondered what was it when you had an extended family without an immediate one? A family that was gaining ground, closing in.

He slept, then was awake. Maybe he should have had that beer after all. He looked at the clock. Not even noon. The guys wouldn't be here until seven. What could he do?

Call Joe; nope. Nothing like a harangue early in the morning. Christine would be at work. He could call her, but that wasn't what he wanted, to talk.

He grabbed the remote control from the nightstand and flicked on the TV. Jenny. Jerry Springer. Flex Appeal with Kiana – boob job? Charlton Heston, *Omega Man*, an American Movie Classic. Bert and Ernie with Mary Steenburgen. Barney. "He…could…go …all…the…way!"

"Please, go all the way," he hummed, another oldie by Tommy … something—and the Shondells. Don would know.

Shit.

He got up and wandered into the kitchen. He pulled open one of the stainless-steel doors on the commercial-size refrigerator, one of his favorite first toys. He took out a can of beer, Old Milwaukee, and an elephant ear. He took a bite. Tucking the beer in his armpit, he secured the truncated elephant in his mouth. With both hands free, he reached for another can and another pastry, thinking he might as well make a day of it.

He parked the remaining beer and elephant ear on the nightstand and flipped through the stations until he found Jerry Springer again, "My Girlfriend Doesn't Know that I'm a Girl." Activating the corner screen, he picked up Kiana on the bench press. Stretching out on the bed with the beer and the cruller, he settled in to wait. Drowsing, he half-consciously channeled Felix in his head, don't need to, Boss. I know what you want, what you like.

Four

The two beers had put him to sleep, and he woke up when the bell rang, signaling that someone was out front. He waited until he heard the gate rumble once, and again seconds later. Tom knew then that Don had used the gate gizmo to get in, and they would be at the studio in a few minutes.

Tom jumped out of bed and started pulling himself together in a hurry. He gathered the beer cans to his chest, wiped the crumbs off the nightstand into his free hand to dump in the wastebasket, then started for the kitchen door. But the TV was still going, a rerun of *Bay Watch*. He put the cans under his chin, leaned over the table and hit the power button on the remote. He walked briskly to the kitchen, rinsed the cans out and dumped them in the recycling bin. He wiped out the sink, washed his hands, and headed out the back French doors to the studio on the other side of the pool.

Don was already there, hooking up his guitar.

"Hey," Tom said.

"Hey," Don replied flatly. Tall and lanky with an anime crop of black hair, he dressed in subtle rocker outfits in tribute to his only god, Eric Clapton. Today, he wore a black silk short-sleeve shirt with an array of almost microcosmic stars punctuating its dark shine. Black denim slacks completed his looks; that and a pair of rundown low-cut Converse Chucks. And, of course, Ann Taylor shades. Tom marveled that the man's eyesight was still intact after so many years wearing sunglasses inside.

Don played bass, and sometimes lead guitar, and also ran the rehearsals. The other three men sat near him, tuning their instruments, getting the feel. George, a roundish Black man, played keyboard. Originally from St. Lucia, he occasionally wore headgear from different places in Africa. Frank, a shy-smiling guy out of Whippany, New Jersey, about the same height as Tom, which Tom liked, played rhythm. And Billy, a ripped-muscled, bicep-tattooed, five-foot-eleven Marine wannabe from Queens, was on drums. Billy had to be talked off the ledge all the time. That or watch him destroy his kit with his enthusiasm, not to mention how he'd have everyone else panting at the tempo.

Tom checked them all out again skeptically, noting their contrasting personalities, their idiosyncratic character traits, their respective musical strengths and weaknesses, all the things that were different about them, but with one huge thing in common: except for Don and himself, they all were really, really young.

When he'd first hooked up with them six months ago, they had been extremely deferential to someone who had made it big- time while they were still in diapers, or almost anyway. He and Don tried the last few guys out at the house, which impressed them, but nothing compared to the equipment and niceties in the studio itself. Many of those cut last wilted amid the state-of-the-art sound and recording facilities. More impressive was an array of every kind of instrument under the sun: sitars next to Dobros, kettle drums opposite a baby grand, some exotic items hanging for show only, others there for occasional use to lay down a particular sound. Plush leather couches and easy chairs flanked a separate kitchenette outfitted with two commercial refrigerators. One was stocked with food and soft drinks, while the other was reserved exclusively for beer quaffed during weekend-long sessions. The newbies definitely felt measly amid all this offhand, casual wealth.

Their respect lasted for a month or so. After that, they began to relax, maybe due to their expectations that this new manifestation of the Experience would immediately take the music scene by storm. Eventually, though, when month followed month without a gig or a genuine recording session, Billy, Frank, and George began to let their hair down. Tom felt that was good for the band's chemistry, but Don never allowed them to forget who was in charge.

"You ready?" Don asked.

"Yeah, just a minute." Tom sat on the short stool in front of the microphone, lifted his Strat out of its stand and plugged in. He tried a couple of rough warm-up riffs and kicked himself for being so out of practice.

"You're out of practice," Don said.

"Yes I am."

"Well, do you want to do this or what? Or are we just wasting time, here?"

"Ooh, Papa Bear!" Billy said, followed by a Dragnet "Dum da dum-dum."

Don glared at him, which didn't faze Billy in the least. He beat out a brutal rap on the drums, finishing with a fading bass thump.

"Okay," Tom said, "I've been on the road and busy with some other things, too. I promise to get in some practice, okay? But, right now, let's just get on with it, and I'll try to play myself back into shape."

Don drew his head back. He paused for effect, then said, "All right. What's it going to be, new or old?"

"Hell, I don't know. New—?" Tom said, thinking that his mistakes on new material could be checked off as unfamiliarity, not laziness. But the promoters wanted the old stuff. "I don't know, what do you think?" he said, peering up at Don.

Don huffed, and said, "All right, 'Root It Out,' from the top."

They played, with Don motioning between notes to Billy to slow it down, nodding at George, ignoring Frank, and glaring at Tom every time he screwed up. Occasionally, he would stop them, make some comments, then have them run through it again. Other times, he would stop them, not say a word, and then say, "From the top again."

At one point, Don said, "Hold it," and leaned over to whisper to Tom. "What about laying one down, then run it back track by track so that they can listen for once to just what the fuck they're doing wrong?"

"I don't know, Don, you think we're ready for that?"

"You mean, are you ready? No, but we don't have to grade you right now."

"Yeah, but that'll just piss them off, won't it?"

"What do you care, it's your show. Besides, each of them has so much to fix, it'll take all night. We won't have time to get to you."

Tom nodded slowly, "Yeah, okay, I guess."

Don straightened up to find that Billy had wandered over to the refrigerator, where he was tossing beers to the others.

"Is it break time?" Don said.

"Yeah, thanks man, you want a beer?" Don shook his head, and Billy said, "You, Tom?"

They all sat, Don on a stool next to Tom's, George in an easy chair opposite the leather couch against the wall where Billy had thrown himself down, and Frank on another stool.

Billy took a long swig of his beer, then put it down on an end table. He picked up a telephone book and began to look through it, slowly, reading carefully before turning the page. He did this silently for a time, seemingly totally absorbed.

George watched Billy for a while, then asked, "What are you doing, man?" he said. "Why you reading the phone book, the white pages of all things?"

"I'm looking up Hitler, Mussolini, Stalin, like that."

"Why in the fuck?"

"You know, I wonder what they do, what their lives are like with names like that. What I really started doing was to see if I could find an Adolf."

"What, Mussolini?"

"No, man, Adolf Hitler. Did someone have the gonzos to name their kid after the world's greatest monster? Is there like an out-front fascist or antisemite out there that's willing to name his kid that? You know, to hell with the high water, fuck the torpedoes, shit like that?"

"'Boy Named Sue,'" said Frank. "Ima Hogg, Ura Hogg."

"Shit, those girls must a had great lives," George said.

"Sure," said Billy, "that's the idea, give them a call, see what it's like."

Frank said, "So, did you find any?"

"No, not yet."

"Well, then, what the fuck?" said George, exasperated.

"Yeah, but now I'm looking for Hitlermans, Mussolinos, and Stalinskis, like that. You know, they change their names to avoid the heat."

"Well, Jesus Christ," said George, "if they were going to change them, don't you think they'd pick names like Smith, or Jones, or something?"

"Sure," said Billy, "the smart ones. I'm tracking down the dumbfucks."

"Aw for shit's sake," George said, throwing up his hands. "And I take it you haven't found any, right?"

Billy shook his head, but then said in a sly voice, "No, but they're out there and I'm still looking."

"Aw, Jesus!" George expelled.

"Okay, okay, let's get back to it," Don said.

They played again for the tape, then Don played it back, explaining to each one where they'd gone wrong. To Tom's dismay, it didn't take all night, which allowed Don to thoroughly dissect Tom's sad, shoddy play.

Billy tapped a muted version of 'Wipeout' on the rubber while he waited, until Don turned to him and said, "Billy, in your head, man, will you?"

Sullenly, Billy pulled himself up and plodded to the refrigerator.

"Hey, I thought you were gonna leave me alone," Tom said under his breath.

"If you practice, I will," said Don.

"Okay, all right, I will," Tom said. He stood up briskly and joined Billy, who handed him a beer.

"Guys, put them down, now, and let's run through it again, for the tape, okay?"

They took their places and played. Afterward, Don again ran the tape back. As they listened, each of them began to nod, then move to the sound, except for Tom. Instead, he lowered his head onto his folded arms and winced.

"All right," said Billy when it finished, "now we go. How about 'Malachite Eyes'? That's what they all want to hear anyway."

Don gave Tom a glance, then cued them up.

Between bites of his sandwich, Billy said, "You know that traffic woman on WKNY?"

"Tracy Corcoran? Yeah, sure" Frank said.

"Well," Billy said, "I drew an inference about her today."

"Inference, wow," said George, "What dictionary have you been sleeping with?"

"Oh, I remember my tenth-grade English teacher making a big deal about the difference between infer and imply. 'You imply, I infer.' Anyway, about Tracy, I inferred today after listening to something she said, that she does not smoke."

"Oh, really?" said George.

"Yes. She has that whiskey voice, right?"

"Yeah, I remember Richard Lewis on the air one time saying that he was hot for her just from her voice," Frank said.

"Right, okay, well the rap today was about that food thing that the body can't absorb, it passes right through you. It gives you the shits."

"Olestra," said George said. "Procter and Gamble owns it. They're going to put it in Pringles to start."

"Yeah, you don't gain any weight, but it gives you the shits. So, they're talking about this, about how this attitude runs counter to the past years' efforts to eat right, shit like that. The D.J. says the government has made them put a warning label on it about the shits, and Tracy comes in and says, 'Yeah, and look how well that works with cigarettes.' So, I'm listening, and from this remark, I infer that she is not a smoker. My thought is that smokers wouldn't think of the label or how it doesn't work. They try to block that shit out. But she said it, which makes me think that she doesn't smoke."

"So, she doesn't smoke, you think?" Tom said.

"Oh, she still could," Billy hurried to say "and say the stuff about the label out of guilt about not quitting but wanting to. See, that's what I mean, I inferred that she doesn't smoke, but I didn't really find out for sure."

"Okay," said Tom, waiting.

"Okay, so she has this whiskey voice, and some people swear that the only way you get a voice like that is from smoking."

"But you think she doesn't smoke," Tom asked.

"Right."

"So, she's a boozer," George said.

"That would be my conclusion," said Billy.

"Your inference," said Don.

"Well, right."

"I thought one goes with the other," said George.

"Not me, man," said Billy, "I'm a boozer and I would never smoke. Count on it."

"Yeah, but you used to," said George.

"Yeah, but I quit. I'm never going to quit boozing, but I'll never start smoking again, either."

"I see. But you and Tracy have something in common."

"Exactly my point. I'm going to call her up, ask her out for a drink."

"Jesus Christ, man, what makes you think she'll go out with you?" grumbled George. "And you can't tell how she looks over the fucking radio, what if she's a total mutt?"

"Hey, after a few drinks, how bad can she look?"

"Oh God," George moaned.

"Okay, time to work," said Tom.

George leaned over to him, blocking the others' view, and whispered in his ear, "He's driving me nuts, Tom, he's just killing me with his simple shit."

"Yeah, yeah, I know, just ignore it, or laugh. Come on, let's play."

They played through a rough set and broke again. Leaning into the refrigerator, Billy turned and said, "You know you're running out of beer, Tom?"

"There's more in the house."

"Cool."

Billy popped the top and sat splay legged on the couch. He lifted up one buttock and broke wind.

"Sorry," he said.

"Inconsiderate bastard," mumbled George.

"Yeah, just be grateful it isn't one of those silent but deadlies, man."

"Silent, noisy, what's the difference, man? It's still a stink bomb."

"Stink bomb to you, man. To me it's a kind of a perfume."

"What? Get the fuck outta here, man, what kind of deviant are you?"

"Don't give me that bullshit, George, you like to smell your own. Everyone does, like dogs."

"Get the fuck—."

"Sure, man, and they all have like their own flavor."

"Sanding block," said Frank, "My dad would use this basalt sanding blocks, and phew, did they ever smell like farts."

Billy nodded his head sharply and held his hand palm up toward Frank, "There you are."

"Why is that?" said Frank. "Why do people like smelling their own farts, but not other people's?"

"Some kind of biological thing, maybe—territorial imperative or something."

"Oh, more high school bullshit vocabulary," said George.

"Nope. Discovery channel. Could be, though. Biology II: State of the Fart."

The others laughed, and Don said, "There was this guy in France in the 1800s who used to be able to control passing gas so well that he could fart songs."

"No fucking way!" Billy said.

"Oh, yeah," Don said, "He was so good, he became a stage performer, Le Pétomane. Headlined at Le Moulin Rouge."

"You're completely pulling my leg."

"No, he was a big success. Wore a tux with a split in his pants for better acoustics."

By this time everyone was laughing, Billy with his legs up around his head and both hands across his stomach.

"So, what are you saying, his name was Pétomane?"

"That was his stage name. Translated from French, the Fart Maniac."

Everyone cracked up again as Don went on, "His real name was Pujol."

"You mean like the car? So, what he did was called the Great Backfire?"

"Patron of the Farts," Frank said, causing them to roar again, redoubled as Tom suggested "Enfragrante Delecto?"

Helpless, Billy couldn't make a noise, the others laughing harder watching him.

Exhausted, they all sat quietly, trying to regain their strength.

"I guess the smell didn't bother the audience," George said.

"Maybe they gave out gas masks at the door, you know, like glasses at a 3-D movie."

They all chuckled again.

Don said, "What time?"

Tom looked at his watch, "Two-thirty."

"Shit, let's wrap it up. Workday tomorrow." He meant for the others. Even though they were paid standard equity while they rehearsed, they all had day jobs to pay the rent. None of them seemed to resent the disparity between them and Tom and Don, thinking of second comings such as Stevie Winwood, David Bowie, and Tony Bennett. The big money would come to them once they got on the road.

As they put their gear away, Don asked Tom, "When again?"

"I don't know. Not tomorrow," Tom said, thinking that he wanted to be sure to get in some practice before risking the humiliation he'd endured that night. "How about Wednesday?"

"Fine."

Tom moved closer and said quietly, "You taking these guys to the train station? You want to come back here and stay? It's late to drive all the way back into the City."

"You coming on to me again?" Don said.

"You wish," said Tom.

"Yeah, well, thanks, but nah."

"Sure, you like waking up in your own bed."

"Listen, if we were practicing tomorrow, I'd consider it."

"No, no, not tomorrow. Wednesday."

"Okay, then." He saw the troubled look on Tom's face, and said, "Man, it's only a couple days. You'll survive."

"I know I will."

"Okay, then."

Five

After the band left, Tom straightened up the studio, doing his best to leave Mary only some crumbs to sweep up. He headed toward the house straight to the patio doors for the guest bedroom, where after practices he slept more often than in the master bedroom. He dropped onto the bed and flicked the TV on with the remote, muting the sound.

He knew he wouldn't sleep. Even if he hadn't gone to Toronto, it wouldn't be any different. He could watch TV.

Tom rolled over to turn on the sound lowering it to a simple murmur. He jammed another pillow under his head and looked at a Craig Clayborne five-questioning Jeffrey Wright.

He pressed the up arrow and watched Connie Stevens peddling her jewelry line designed especially by herself. Fifty-two zircon-encrusted cricket pendants left, $49.99.

He turned on his other side, then back.

He muted the sound and switched the remote with the cell phone on the night table.

"Hello?"

"Christine. Did I wake you?"

"Jesus, it's three in the morning, what do you think?"

"Oh. I'm sorry."

"Tom, you do this to me all the time, and you're always sorry. Don't be sorry, just don't call."

"Okay, but, uh . . . .."

"You're alone, right?" she asked.

"Yes, well, yeah, sure," he said defensively.

"No, I mean you're lonely, right?"

"Well, yeah, but no, that's not it, that's not why I called."

"Then why?"

Tom hesitated. "Well, you know, I just got back from Toronto, and it didn't go all that well, and we rehearsed, and I sucked, and the band sucked, and . . . you know. The outlook isn't making me run right out to buy another pair of Ray-Bans."

"Oh." The groggy sound to her voice was gone when she said, "Well, I'm sorry to hear that."

"Yeah," Tom agreed mournfully.

"But what can I do? Why did you call me?"

"Well, to talk, I guess," he trailed off.

"And?"

"And" he said, "maybe you could come out?"

"Tom, it's three o'clock in the fucking morning. I've got to work tomorrow."

"I know, I just thought—"

She cut him off, "When did that happen?"

"—you could take the day."

"Tom, this is no good."

"Or the morning, even. I'll drive you in, you can sleep in the car on the way."

"Like last time?"

"I said I'd drive, personally."

Her silence on the line scared him. He almost coughed his breath loose when she finally spoke.

"Tom," she said, "This is no good, for me or for you. You can't keep calling me every time you're alone. You need to do something to take care of this, for yourself and for me."

"Chris, you're my best friend!"

"Don is your best friend." She waited, then said, "Did you ask him to stay over tonight? Did you?"

Reluctantly, he said, "Yes."

He could feel her rolling her eyes. "Go see a therapist, Tom."

"I'd rather see you."

"You need a trained professional. Who knows? If you're lucky, you might find one that will sleep with you, too."

"Chris! That's not why I want to see you."

"Oh, no? It used to be high on the list."

"Not lately," he said, "and not my choice."

She was quiet again. He hit his forehead with the heel of his hand.

"Tom, I'm going back to sleep. If you really want to talk, call me tomorrow at work."

She hung up.

Tomorrow, he thought. He flicked on the TV.

Christine wore a knee-length black dress belted at the waist, its sleeves short to mid-arm, and the neckline high, close around her throat. Except for a simple gold chain and a pair of gold earrings, she was unadorned. She wore a blood-red ribbon in her black hair, framing her face in a simple pageboy cut. Her makeup was minimal except for some dark eyeliner and crimson lipstick matching the color of her hair ribbon. She sat at the outdoor table with one leg crossed over the other and her arms folded in front of her.

Tom stared at her crossed legs, her knee like a delicate saucer of bone China stretching the white hosiery over dimpled hollows on each side. Amazing, he thought, that such a fragile structure could bear any relationship to the workman-like frames of men. He raised his eyes slowly over her slight body to her exquisite features and her deep, dark, pissed-off eyes.

"You didn't have to come all the way in, you know," she said in a moderately petulant tone. "We could have talked on the phone."

He took a sip of his Evian. She didn't like to see him drinking anything else this early.

"I don't like the phone. I can't see your face then."

"But that doesn't much matter, now, does it?"

He lowered his head, "It does to me."

She huffed in exasperation, "Oh, come on Tom, don't try to get over on me, pushing out baby's big lower lip again. How many times have I gone for that in the past, do you think, that it's so obvious to me now?"

He straightened up and leaned forward, clasping his hands between his knees. "Christine, I'm sorry for the asshole I've been, I really am. I miss you, a lot. And even if you don't want to be together anymore, I thought that we could," he hesitated, then shrugged his shoulders, "we might stay friends; you know, see each other sometimes."

"Oh, sure, Tom, we could get together once in a while, go out for a meal, go to a movie, maybe for a drink afterwards. Or maybe we could order in, have a glass of wine while we watch a video, and before you know it, who knows? Or you could call me up at three in the morning, ask me to come out, and we can dispense with all that movie-dinner-video-wine shit and get right down to it because you hate to be alone when you don't have anything to do!"

He recoiled inside, but only evidenced it to her with a quick wince. "I'm sorry about that. You're right, I shouldn't have called then. That's why I'm here now, to apologize. I'm really, really sorry, Christine. Really, I am."

She seemed to relent a little, accepting for a moment. She was tiny, too small to be a model, but so beautiful. He'd known her for so long, he knew he loved her, but not in the final way, he understood. There was always something between them, something that halted him at the brink. She'd finally had enough, a few months ago telling him that they just shouldn't see each other at all anymore. It broke his heart to hear her say it, but he really didn't believe it. They had seen each other a couple of times since, but something had changed, even when they spent the night together, something was missing.

She sighed, relaxed, and said, "You look bad. You haven't been sleeping."

Tom flipped his hand outward loosely, "I took that trip to Toronto. And, as soon as I got back, we had a long practice."

"So, you haven't slept. How was the rehearsal?"

He grimaced, slouching in his chair. "I sucked. Don was pissed, and the rest of them were all over the place. I don't see much light at the end of this tunnel right now. For a while."

"How was Toronto?"

"Aw, they want the same old same-old." He frowned, "So do the new guys in the band for that matter. Am I missing a train here somewhere?"

Christine leaned her forearms on the table. "A lot of bands are coming back with their old material, Tommy, using the dates as a chance to do new things."

"Shit, I don't know, Christine. I don't want to be Ricky Nelson, you know? His last tune a nasty little number about how they booed him off the stage because he wouldn't do 'Roses Are Red'?"

"'Poor Little Fool.' Ricky Nelson did 'Poor Little Fool.'"

He screwed his eyes up to hers, "How the hell do you know that? You weren't even born ten years when those songs came out."

She shrugged her shoulders, "I'm an oldies fan. Why do you think I went out with you?"

He pouted and she laughed.

"I'm sorry," she said, "but you're so easy."

"Very funny," he said, "Next thing you'll be the groupie IDing me in *People* magazine's list of old fart rockers."

"Oh, did that happen to you?" she asked.

"Yeah," he grumbled, then wished he'd kept his mouth shut.

"When?" Christine asked.

"Never mind," he mumbled.

She drew her head back slowly in thought.

"It happened in Toronto. Didn't it?"

When he didn't answer, she said, "You met a groupie in Toronto, and you went to bed with her. For Christ's sake, Tommy!"

She half rose from her seat, and he reached over grasping her by her arm and hand.

"Christine—"

"You screw this little bimbette, then come home to get me into the sack, and all because you're bored?"

"That's not it, Christine. I just wanted to see you, that's all. Really, I had no thought about that with you."

"Oh, bullshit, Tommy! You have no other thoughts than that if you can call it thought. That and your music, and maybe your clothes. I can't believe this!"

"Please, it's not what you're thinking. Sit down, please, I hate seeing you so pissed off. Don't leave like this, please. Take a minute to let me explain, then you can go if you need to, okay?"

"Why? Why should I let you explain anything?"

"Because we're friends, right? No matter what, right?" She hesitated, then seemed to grow angrier until he said quickly, "Because you're the only one who calls me Tommy except for my mom."

A flurry of emotions rippled across her face, a struggle that distorted her usually placid, cool features. Finally, she sat down again, forcefully.

"I'm not your mom away from mom, you asshole," she said, spitting out each word.

"I know, I know," he said, lowering his head, completely chastised.

"Oh, Tom, why do you do stupid stuff like this? I mean, things that are easy not to mess up, you mess up."

"I don't know. I mean it, I have no idea. Up in Toronto, she came on to me. I felt lousy after the meeting, and she pumped me up."

"I can picture it now," Christine said wryly.

"Yeah, well, it didn't last, believe me. The part about me in *People* magazine's oldies vault, that's where she spied me."

"I'm sure her lush young limbs made up for it. Well, I hope you took the proper precautions."

He shrugged.

"What? Tom, tell me you used a condom."

He sighed, "I didn't think to. You see there, it happened pretty spontaneously, like I said it did."

"But, Tommy, you always use condoms. For God's sake, what's going on in your head? Where have you been for the past twenty years?"

He was contrite again, then wondered to himself if he liked Christine so much because she made him feel guilty, or maybe that was the reason that they had never stayed together for good.

"God, Tom. And you wanted me to come over to your place for the night. Excuse me, I mean the rest of the morning. Didn't you have a single thought about me, Tommy. Don't you care if I'm safe even if you don't care about yourself?"

He shook his head, "You're right, Christine, you're totally right. I wasn't thinking."

"Again."

"Yeah. But I'll make you a promise." He placed his hand over his heart and said, "I swear, I will always wear a condom from here on in," and she sat back, nodding her satisfaction," whenever I try to get you to do the nasty, so help me God."

She whacked him with her gloves across the back of his head, "You schmuck, this is serious."

"Yeah, I know, too serious," he said, ducking from her follow-up shot.

"That's it, I'm out of here," she said.

"Hold, on, hold on," he raised his hands in defense, "no harm, no foul. Come on, you already made up your mind to kick me curbside, so what did I have to lose? It was worth a giggle, right? All right, a smile?"

She smiled despite herself.

"Good," he said, "progress. Very good."

"But you are screwed up, Tom. You know this, right?"

"Yeah, I suppose so."

"Why? You're doing what you want to do, you don't have to worry about money, so why?"

"I don't know, Christine. I don't know if I'm doing what I want. And if I don't have to worry about making a living, what's left?"

She sat back, making a face. "You know, Tom, you're one of those rarities, a spoiled brat who happens to still be a nice guy. People who know you like you so much that they don't think you're spoiled, but you are."

He nodded, "I suppose so. You know, I never did a hard thing in my life, not ever."

"Maybe you should think about doing something different."

"Like what?"

"I don't know, like maybe do something for the needy."

"What, you mean a benefit concert. I did Band Aid back then, and I wasn't too crazy about the way that turned out."

"That's because they scheduled you at five in the morning."

"Yeah, that's right. It aired here at one. The fucking Brits."

"When are you going to get over that?" Christine laughed, "Look on the bright side. At least you stayed cool. As I remember it was hotter than hell that day."

"It wasn't any better at night."

"Anyway, that's not what I mean, not some distant group activity. Something more direct might be good, something that gives you more control."

"I don't know about this, Christine," he said, scratching behind his ear, "I'm not too sure I want to get all that involved personally."

"Okay, it doesn't have to be that."

"Then, what?"

She pursed her lips in thought, "I know this guy who comes to the gallery who's in this weird charity group. It's kind of informal, but they give a lot of money away. The members are all really unusual, rich in different ways than you'd expect. He was telling me about it, Jerry is his name, Jerry Smith. He says they got the idea from The Grateful Dead, who have this strange charity named after one of their roadies who died, something like Yellow Dog, or Running Dog, something like that. Jerry says they just give money to people and outfits who need it, no questions asked, no overhead. He says they call themselves The Good Old Boys Club, sort of a joke."

"Uh huh," Tom said dully.

"I think it might be something you'd like, really."

"Uh," he said, "I don't know if it sounds right for me."

"And how the hell would you know without talking to them?" she snapped.

"I don't know. I just think I know."

"You're spoiled rotten."

"Yeah, sure I am. Now, can we leave it?"

She didn't answer but looked peeved. He spread his legs, leaning forward to rest his elbows on his knees and said, "So, how's the gallery going?"

"Good. Fine. We're making some money, seeing some good things. The web has really picked up business. People from Fort Worth are calling about works they saw online."

"That's great."

"Yeah, but we still could do better. Like if some major loaded musician types would take the rubber bands off their bankrolls, think about replacing the Ramada paintings in their living room, we might be able to pay some bills."

"Damn, Christine, I'm just getting used to that deconstruction shit you sold me the last time. You want me to buy new?"

Her expression turned serious, "What, you have two Grandy's, and that Sally Eve installation? They're nice, they're good pieces, they'll always hold their value. But you could stand to expand your perspective. I have this artist, Camilla Orosco who has murals that will take your breath."

"I don't know, Christine," Tom said, "how friendly is it? I'm not really that sold on sharp-edged stuff, you know? I like things that make me feel good to be around, to have them around. You follow me?"

She rested back in her seat, "Fuzzy art."

"Yes. Well, no, not like that, no big-eyed sorry children. But, prettier."

"Velvet."

"No! No Elvis bullshit."

"No," she said, "I mean it. There's been a retro revival of sorts of modern imagery on velvet canvas. I know one guy who's doing it here in New York, although the major school is in L.A."

He shook his head, "It doesn't really sound all that appealing."

She held up her hand, "All right. Let's go back to the Orosco murals. They're fabulous and they are elementally gorgeous."

He pursed his mouth, squinting, "You sure?"

"Absolutely," she said.

He rubbed the back of his head, "I don't know, Christine. I'm pretty happy with the pictures I have. Why should I change?"

"You'll like them, trust me. Look, I could send some pieces over and we could try them out."

"Oh really," he said, "you'd come out to my place? You would trust me? Me, to look at art, that's all? What could you be thinking?"

She laughed, then said with firm resolve, "I'll do anything for art."

"And a buck."

"That doesn't hurt, either."

"I'll bet."

"So, you want me to bring some stuff out?"

"I guess," he said, sitting back and stretching his legs.

"And you'll talk to Jerry Smith."

"Damn, Christine!"

She laughed, "I'm joking. But we could try some pieces."

"Oh, really? How so?"

She smiled slightly, "I can make it worth your while."

Surprised, he said, "Christine, you're coming on a little coquettish, aren't you?"

"I'll do anything for art," she said, firmly resolved.

"And a buck."

Six

Tom felt uncomfortable, out of context even in the familiarly impersonal environs of a chain hotel, this one a Suisse Chalet. When he called Jerry Smith to find out about the group, he'd been surprised to learn that they usually met in hotel suites.

"Yeah, why not?" Jerry had said, "None of us could ever afford the damn places before, so we spoil ourselves now. It's like leaving the lights on or a faucet running, big time. Big spenders, huh?" he laughed.

The memory reminded Tom of how he liked the guy right off, sight unseen. Just the same, he was pretty small-town himself, he thought. He didn't much like new situations of any kind, and he especially hated leaving water running and lights on.

"If only I'd finished school," he said, smiling ruefully to himself. The pretty blond woman passing by smiled back.

The desk clerk gave him the room number, and he took the elevator up to the 17th floor, rooms 1705-09. A member of the hotel staff greeted him at the door and ushered him inside. Exuberant riffs by Stevie Ray Vaughn filled the large sitting room replete with elegant yet uninspired furniture. Expensive reproductions of Manet and Monet decorated the walls, with a few Picassos thrown in. Two well-dressed women perched on the edges of facing French love seats talked earnestly. In her late twenties – early thirties, one wore her blond hair cut evenly at her neck culminating in two, sharp points at either cheek, a style he always liked. The other appeared to be in her fifties, her brown hair coiffed high, attractive all the same. Both wore precise makeup that complemented their handsome suits beautifully.

A third woman walked over to him and introduced herself.

"Hi, I'm Trish Smith, Jerry's wife. You must be Tom Weatherly."

"Yes," he said. She seemed about forty or so, a dark-haired, pleasant-looking woman made enormously more appealing by the well-defined laugh lines around her eyes. As though the world was an ongoing, warm joke to her, he thought.

"Jerry's with the others in the inner sanctum—we girls aren't allowed in there," she said with heavy irony. "I'll go get him, but do you want a drink first?"

"You know, I could use one, maybe a beer."

"Just a beer? We have everything. The boys love to play Nero at the banquet when we get together for these things."

He was tempted, but said finally, "I think a beer will do me just fine."

"Sure," she said, and turned to the bartender who stood waiting. She said, "Andre, what beers do we have?" She faced Tom again, reciting, "Bud, Michelob, Heineken, Miller, Miller Lite—all the domestic wonder beers you could imagine. A St. Pauli's Girl? Yeah, Andre, the St. Pauli's Girl."

She handed the bottle to Tom, saying, "Glass? No? Okay then, follow me."

She headed toward a doorway, knocked, and walked in without waiting for an answer.

"Jesus Christopher, Trish, what'd I tell you? This room is off limits."
A guy with a luxuriant head of black hair framing a pasty white face walked over and grabbed her around the waist. He was not tall, but lanky looking, and his skin was as pale as frozen milk, a sharp contrast to his yellow chipped teeth. He had a big nose and soulful eyes. The nose had been laid over on one side of his face at least once. He pulled Trish close to him and whispered in her ear, which made her laugh as she pulled away, saying, "Well, what did you want me to do, send him in with a note?"

"Dammit, Trish, I'm not kidding about that wet noodle."

"Yeah, your noodle is always wet," she said as she left.

Jerry glanced more soulfully than ever at Tom, "She never complained before."

He held out his hand, "Jerry Smith, Tom, a real pleasure. When Christine gives somebody a clean bill of goods, it counts heavy around here. And to think that you're the Tom Weatherly. A genuine pleasure, man, you really knocked out some great tunes."

Tom dropped his eyes, surprised by his own embarrassing pleasure.

"Thanks, Jerry, I really appreciate getting to meet you and your friends."

"Right," said Jerry, stepping sideways. Two other men sat at the table holding cards, with an empty chair drawn back, Jerry's obviously. Another guy lay full out on a couch watching a basketball game on a large projection screen television. Stevie Ray was just a murmur in here because of the din of the game.

"Over here at the table is Reese Wilcox from West Virginia, Virginia's biggest lottery winner back in 1986."

Tom leaned over and shook hands with a slight man who had sandy brown hair and thin features. Reese smiled sincerely, revealing the biggest robin-blue eyes Tom had ever seen.

"Reese sold shares in his ticket early on and used the cash to by lots of stock in latex condom and glove companies. Reese's hell on wheels when it comes to numbers, does it all in his head without error. That's Freddy Ruth next to him. Freddy built a lot of townhouses in Charlottesville, though he's originally from East Greenburg, Pennsylvania."

Another bony guy in plaid and denim, Freddy half stood up and gripped Tom's hand in a fierce vise that he quickly released before doing any damage. He sat back down and studied his cards through thick eyeglasses in round tortoiseshell frames.

"Over there is Ed Novicky, the inventor of 900-SPORTS. You know about that? You can dial 900-PRO-SPORT if you want to talk to a fellow fan of the team that you're watching, or 900-CON-SPORT if you want some guy rooting for the other team. If you just want to talk to someone who knows something about the game, you ring up 900-REF-SPORT."

"Really?" Tom said, gazing at the big square-framed man stretched full length on the sofa, which he filled end to end.

Jerry smirked, "You'd be amazed at how many guys want to talk during a game, any game. Ed says that his SPORTS lines out pull phone sex lines 10 to 1 in every major metropolitan market. Except New York, of course. And I guess I round out the portfolio. Aside from shooting stick for profit, which is why my teeth are chipped and I got a funny profile, I've been a car nut all my life. Goes with the white trash territory, I guess. So does rock and roll, and I couldn't stand riding around in my wheels listening to nothing while I was rewinding a tape. So, I messed around with it for a while, and came up with a set that let me play the radio at the same time I was rewinding. Chrysler tried to screw me out of it, but Toyota stepped in, and the rest is history. Of course, now it's all CDs, but it's too late, I'm keeping the money. And Reese has helped me grow it a lot since. Thank you so much again, Reese."

Reese glanced up, smiling, "You all are so very welcome," then turned back to the game, "Hit me." Freddy feinted a lunge at him across the table and Reese said, "Very funny. Now, hit me!"

Jerry grinned that winning smile, and Tom relaxed.

"So, you? You made yours rocking out, huh? Very cool!"

"Yeah, well, I've got a Reese, too. My brother Joe."

Jerry nodded, "Always good to have the family involved. Okay, let's quit bullshitting around. Take a seat."

They both sat at the card table, Jerry straddling his chair to face Tom. Freddy and Reese continued playing cards quietly next to them.

"This is how it works, the Rich Guys Club, the Good Old Boys Club, or whatever the hell we're calling it this week. We meet whenever we want to, but no less than four times a year. Usually, it's more often than that because we like to hang out together. No overhead except for an expense pool to take care of the hotel and the accounting bullshit. Reese is treasurer and he's bonded—his wife says he's kinky that way, but that's personal, we don't get into that sort of thing. No advertising, nothing like that. We just give away money to people who need it, you know, groups doing good work. No strings."

Tom said, "How do you decide who gets what?"

"We listen, we go out and take a look sometimes, and we vote. If one guy wants to pop, and the rest don't, he can do it on his own. Usually, there isn't any disagreement. We all have our personal favorites that we give to, so the American Heart Association kind of thing doesn't enter into it. Mostly, we're helping small outfits that never see the light of day when they're in the shadow of the big boys."

Tom nodded his head thoughtfully. "If you don't advertise, how do they find you?"

"They find us. We keep a low profile, but some people know about us. They know that sometimes we can help out, but their chances are better if they're discreet. We got a call from Brooke Astor the other day about a little thing that she couldn't do much with. Crazy old lady loves to party. She's the original like us, a new poor little rich kid.

"So, you interested? Cost you a million up front if you want in, and you can expect to pony up more later when you find your niche."

Tom swallowed. A million? He'd thought it would cost him that much eventually, but not right off. For that kind of money, he would have to go to Joe, who was a bit ticklish about unusual outlays of cash. Ticklish, hell, thought Tom, he acted as though it was his money. Of which half was, thank you Colonel Parker, truly yours, Elvis. Tom could care; he'd told Joe plenty of times to keep it all, his rocker brother only needed a playtime allowance.

"Hey, you're dry. Let me get you another beer."

"That's okay, Jerry, I need to hit the head myself. I'll filch one on the way back."

"That'll work, the bathroom's across the room behind the bar. Very efficient planning, I think."

Tom was on his way out of the game room before Jerry finished his sentence. A million bucks, he thought, relieving himself. Washing his hands glumly wondering what Christine had done to him. Snatching a beer from the bar on his way thinking about getting shitfaced.

He returned to the room to see everyone not playing standing behind the table. Reese flipped cards toward Freddy as he said without looking up, "Tom, you want to play? Plenty of cards here for everyone."

"Yeah, all bad," Freddy muttered. "Reese, you are a cheating mother-effer, man."

"Sure, but look at it this way. It's only possible to cheat smart folk."

"Oh, yeah?"

"Absolutely. Dumb clucks don't go for the bluffs." He winked broadly at Tom while Freddy dropped his head to study his cards. "Now, what you want to do?"

"Just wait a minute now, I'm thinking." He sat gazing at a seven of hearts.

"You go ahead and think with my bullet staring up at you. You know I got a face to go with it underneath. Your only chance is to go for it, slim."

"Yeah, yeah, hit me." Reese flipped the card, a nine of spades. "Damn! Busted!"

"You dumb cluck," Reese laughed, turning over his hole card, a five of clubs. "I'm the enemy. What're you listening to the enemy for?"

"Shit! I am a dumb cluck."

"Yeah, but there are those of us who love you, or at least your money. So, as I was saying, you want in the game, Tom?"

"Nah, I better hold on to my cash. I don't need anyone else to know how dumb I am, and I may need it to get home."

"Well, don't worry about that, Tom. You can stay here, or Freddy can get you to where you want to go."

"Sure," said Freddy, "I can do that."

"Well, thanks, fellows," Tom said, unsure of their ingenuousness.

Jerry returned with the beer and said, "Look, uh, Trish told me not to be such a jerk, that you shouldn't make any decisions now, but go home and think about it. She's right, of course. I just thought it'd be fun to hang out with you. Anyway, let's all order something to eat, and you can think about it when you get home."

"Steak and frites," called out Ed.

"Yeah, like always. Have you checked in with your cardiologist today?"

"Fine, order some health crap," Ed said, never once removing his gaze from the screen, "just make sure it's smothered in butter."

"Anyway, how's that sound?" Jerry asked. "Not Ed's heart-attack specials, just thinking it over when you get back home."

"Fine," Tom said, holding back from spitting up beer. He felt heat suddenly rising up his neck to is face. He gave his head a quick shake. "But I uh, pretty much made up my mind. I'd like to join in with you guys if you want me to."

"No shit?" Jerry yelped. "Hey, that's great!" He turned to howl, "Hey, fellas, you hear that? Tom Weatherly wants to come in with us!"

"That's good news, boyo!" Reese roared, rising to shake Tom's hand.

Freddy clapped him on the back, shouting "Rock and roll!" Ed stood up smiling, waiting his turn. Tom couldn't believe how good he felt about it all.

"Oh, and, uh, Tom," Jerry said closing in on Tom's ear while loudly faux whispering, "I fibbed about the million bucks—"

"It's ten million," barked Ed, causing everyone to shout laugh and shout at once.

"Nah, not at all," Jerry said, "it's ten grand in escrow 'til you get going. It's there for you to get a good start."

"Yeah," Ed joined in, "the million-dollar-ask helps discourage any romantics fancying rubbing elbows with us space cadets. Most come back to Earth quick when they first hear the ante is a mil'. But you seemed like the real deal right off, Jerry—like I said, especially when Christine vouches for you. We're real glad to have you with us. Here, let me get you a beer this time."

Seven

"Marbury House receives a quarter of its funding from the Feds, half from the great state of New York, and a pittance from the municipality itself. It means we need to raise the rest which, as you can divine, is an ongoing headache of major proportions."

Gertrude recited the figures as she took Norah on a tour of the physical plant, a huge rambling Victorian house with four complete floors and two stairways. The broad-stepped set in the front of the house had served the 19th-century family members. The narrow spiral staircase off the kitchen led to the landing where the servants' tiny rooms had been situated.

Most of the children had left for school already, starting a week ago on August 10th. The youngest children attended day-care in the refurbished basement rooms. Gertrude saw this as an opportune time for Norah to learn her way around the house layout.

"This way," Gertrude explained, "you'll know all the hiding places for kids ducking their social worker check-up—or a visit by a parent they don't particularly want to see.

"In any given week, we might have as many as twenty to twenty-five children passing through, some for no longer than a day or so, until their families can straighten out the legal paperwork. Others can be here for two to three weeks, and a few might stay for several months. They're usually the ones who are called 'potential wards of the state,' coming from the saddest of circumstances. Though they all are pretty sad here, when you think of what a normal childhood is supposed to be."

She led Norah in and out of different rooms, some with two beds in them, and up on the top floor, a refurbished attic housed eight single beds and two bunkbeds at the far ends. Between them, they looked in on a small room furnished with a desk and stool, flanked by an easy chair and a cot.

"This is the station for the overnight counselor. When we first got the house, we debated having it on the first floor to intercept any possible unwanted visitors versus putting it up here in case of fire. Since Buddy started, it hasn't been an issue."

"Buddy?" Norah said.

"Buddy Rosen. You didn't meet him with the other counselors because he works nights mostly, which means that with the usual rotation, we can have someone in the office downstairs, too. It's quite a luxury for an operation of our size."

"Yeah, it is," Norah said, biting her tongue as she thought about the one-weeknight, every-other-weekend schedule they all were required to keep.

"Of course, an average night for Buddy is a long night."

"Oh, really?" Norah asked, but before Gertrude could answer, a high tenor voice said, "Someone taking my name in vain here?"

Norah turned to find a large, white, completely bald man occupying the doorway. He wore work pants held up by suspenders over a big stomach, and he impressed her overall as being soft—soft skin, soft hands, round face with not a trace of a whisker.

"Oh, here you are, Buddy," Gertrude said cheerfully, "I thought I'd have to wake you up."

"No," he said in a wry voice, "God's gift of children woke me this morning. All of them, I think."

"Oh, I'm sorry to hear that," Gertrude chuckled. "Did you sleep well otherwise?"

"As though I kneeled to say my prayers," he said, "which I never, ever fail to do." They laughed again while he slipped past them into the small room without touching anything. He lowered himself into the swivel chair in front of the desk, sighing "Ah," as he sat. "I might take a nappy later, though."

"Good idea. Listen, this is the new counselor Norah Kealy from San Francisco. Teddy Flores recommended Norah, so I just couldn't let her get away."

Norah blushed, "Oh, yeah, right," she said as Buddy stood up to shake her hand. Towering over her, he dipped his head toward Gertrude while saying, "Pay no mind to the blandishments, she is the officer of morale, you know. So, you hale from San Fran. I went to school there. From L.A. Ran the streets until I came of age, then got the hell out of there straight to Haight Ashbury and Flower Power. The rest is history."

Norah opened her mouth to get out a "Huh." Just then, they heard a chorus of high-pitched voices swelling through the house in an approaching wave up the stairs.

"Oh-oh," Buddy said, cocking his head and cupping his ear, "school's out."

They all laughed and left to meet the children at the stairs.

In San Francisco, Norah had worked with women who had their children with them, almost like refugee families fleeing their country from the advance of a cruel conqueror. That the countries they fled were their homes and their enemies were their husbands and their children's fathers embittered her as much as them. Maybe even more so, she admitted to herself. But in such encounters, the frightened children still had their mothers to look to for some support, some kind of love. True, too, partial victories had been won just by the mothers taking their children out of the hell of their homes, even if more often than not they were sweet-talked by their men into returning. Later, they might come back, or they might be dead.

The children Norah saw at Marbury House moved her and distressed her in a new way. Most of them had been taken from or abandoned by both parents, which left not even the drag anchor of one ship-wrecked survivor to save them from the current.

After school, they spread through the house like beads of mercury, the older ones cranking up cassette decks or cd players if they had them, the younger ones heading toward the general play area to fondle or smash toys they'd only seen on TV before. Norah tried to meet each one, but it seemed like half of them were gone before the first week was out. Still, she determined to work hard to get to know every child that passed through the doors as well as she could for as long as they were there.

Most of them were black, though a few were Latino; not one was white. Girls outnumbered boys, except for a few very young toddlers. Buddy told her that the older boys usually ended up in juvie homes, advanced as they were. Many of the older girls, too, he said. The younger children usually came and went fast, Social Services quick to find them transient foster homes.

"It makes sense when you think about it," Buddy said, standing at one of the bunk beds folding freshly laundered clothes. He was tall enough so that he could fold them on the top bunk, saving his back from bending over. "The social workers and foster parents think the little ones have the best chance, unless they're crack babies, or their mommas were boozers. You know," he said, delicately folding the little arms of a Knicks t-shirt with his bratwurst shaped fingers, "prenatal alcohol syndrome. Those babies are impossible.

"Still and all," he said, "it's one thing to be fucked up by chemicals, and a totally different thing to be fucked over by your parents. The older kids can be bitter and mean."

He seemed prophetic. On her third day, Norah was rounding up the kids in the afternoon to do their homework. Rashan Lewis, age ten, who had been brought to Marbury that day, marched in front of her silently, his books tucked under his left arm. He pivoted 180 degrees, throwing a roundhouse without warning. Quick, Norah ducked, but not quick enough, and the punch caught her at the top of her right eye as she was stepping back. She tripped backwards over one of Rashan's tossed textbooks and banged the back of her head hard on the wooden sill of an old, out of use dumb waiter. Through the almost blinding light of her pain, she could see Rashan draw back his foot for the coup de gras, when a white cloud enveloped him and carried him away.

Her eyesight cleared, and she saw Rashan struggling in Buddy's arms like he was fighting his pillow during a bad dream. Buddy cooed to him, hugging him tight enough to keep him from inflicting any damage while allowing him to move toward exhaustion. Eventually, Rashan stopped twisting.

"All right, that's better. Now we all can rest. Excellent hook, though, right, Norah?"

"Oh, yeah," she said, gingerly patting her eye while rubbing the back of her head, "Mike Tyson."

"You hear that, Rashan? Mike Tyson has nothing on you." He glanced quickly at Norah. "Are you all right?"

"Yeah," she said, sitting up, then shifting to one knee.

"Yeah, you can deliver the knock-down, no question," Buddy said as he gently turned the boy around to face him. He knelt as he talked, "but it's not right to hit people out of the ring, Rashan, you see? Especially a new friend like Norah, that's not a good thing to do. You know it's time to do your homework, right? Right?"

Rashan slowly nodded his head, his mouth tight with resistance starting to relax. Norah stood up and began picking up the youth's books.

"Can you tell Norah you're sorry, Rashan?" Buddy asked him.

"No," he barked.

"Come on, Rashan, she didn't mean you any harm. And she's got a good right hook, too. So, what do you say, man?"

"Sorry."

"Okay, let's get your books and get to it. Do you want me to help you with your homework?"

Rashan nodded and took the books from Norah. As he headed to the dining room where homework was done, Buddy trailed him with his hands lightly resting on each of his shoulders. He looked back to Norah and, wide-eyed, he mouthed broadly, Fucked Up!

Norah nodded, laughing to herself woefully. They all were fucked up, of course. How could they not be? The next day, Rashan was gone, placed in a foster home somewhere.

On the weekend, after they had locked up, and checked that the kids were all in bed, they headed up to the fourth-floor office, and sat, talking.

"My marriage was lousy," said Norah. "My ex, Dennis, was so needy, he could suck you dry with his whining. Yet, when he was feeling good, I could do nothing right. And he had a wickedly accurate tongue, he could really zoom in on the things that I really hated about myself."

"Like what?"

"Oh, the usual girl stuff, my weight, my intelligence."

Buddy shook his head, "Very taboo."

"Yeah, well, he wouldn't come right out and say I was fat. He had this incredibly expressive face, like Marcel Marceau or somebody. He could scrunch it up, then drop it quickly and say, 'Bally's running a special, no initiation fee.'"

"Tacky, very tacky," Buddy said, "and obviously predicated upon a total fabrication. You are a beautiful, shapely woman."

She blushed. "You're making me blush."

"Well, it's true. It does amaze me how some truly stunning women have no idea of how fantastic they really are. You're in that category."

"Oh, yeah, right," Norah said, "just look at me." She pulled up a corner of her flannel shirt.

"No, a fashion plate you are not," Buddy said, "but it's appropriate to your occupation and your holdover student socialist politics."

She laughed and he said, "So, how did you split with the charming Dennis?"

"I finally smartened up. After he was all over me one evening, with how stupid I was—he had this way of being impatient, then exploding—I told him he either had to get professional help or get his ass out."

"Oh, my. And Dennis did what?" Buddy looked worried about the answer, almost cringing.

"Oh, no, don't think that. Dennis was never physical. He wasn't violent, merely ruthlessly belittling. He left. I found out later that he moved in with his girlfriend, can you believe it? He had a girlfriend!

"You know, as an Irish Catholic girl, I thought I was stuck with the jerk until Judgement Day. And I really felt bad about it until I learned he was screwing this little chippy. I saw her one night and I couldn't believe it. She looked just like me! He traded me in on a new model! Oh, she was shorter, but the same color hair, the same skin, you know, Black Irish – her name was Macdonald. Except, she was Episcopalian. You know, the 'let's pretend' Catholic church."

"Hey! My mother died of Episcopalianism."

"Oops, sorry. I don't know why I said that, I haven't been to church myself for a hundred years. But anyway, that was it for Dennis. I went back to school for my master's and ended up in San Francisco at the Ruth Washington Home for Battered Women."

"Ah, San Francisco, loved it." Buddy ran past the words. "And no romances since Dennis?"

"Eh, you know, the usual. Nothing that lasted more than a year or so. Most of them seemed okay, but none of them ever really understood how important my job was to me. Sooner or later, all of them demanded a change in my priorities, which was not going to happen."

"All of them? So many?" Buddy asked, his eyebrow raised in a burlesque.

Norah blushed, "Well, yes and no. Enough."

"Indeed," said Buddy.

"And what about you, Romeo? What's the story of your love life?"

"Oh," Buddy dragged out the word, "I determined that being in and out of love was too complicated. Like you, given what I do. So, I've pretty much decided to go celibate full time."

"Really?" Norah said, almost coquettishly, though she wondered why. She found that she liked Buddy enormously, but she wasn't a bit attracted to him.

"Yes," he said.

"No longing in your heart for some lost lover?"

"Oh, well, we all do that, don't we? But, no, I just want to do my work, go out to eat at good restaurants now and then, maybe see a decent foreign film. Makes life simple, which keeps me happy."

She studied the large man sitting across from her, his reddish-blond hair now closely trimmed, grown back after a buzz cut, his round face with the beginning of jowls, centered by a round bulbous nose, and his utter lack of any body tone. She wondered if his decision might have something to do with his physical presence, the fact that he was not a Hollywood leading man. She felt some shame in the assessment, and guilt that it might matter to her still.

"Oh," she said brusquely, "someone will come along who'll ring your chimes. You'll be back out there pitching woo."

"I sincerely hope not," Buddy said, "dating can be so expensive. You might have noticed that we don't make a lot of money on this job."

"Oh, I noticed," she laughed.

"And I guess we ought to do our jobs. I'll go check on the kids, then go downstairs. You can nap first if you like."

"Yeah, sure Buddy, but wake me up this time, will you? Don't stay up the whole night yourself. You need to sleep, too."

"Oh, absolutely," said Buddy.

But she woke up the next morning to the sound of the kids getting ready to go to breakfast.

Eight

"What we do," said Ed, "is observe for a couple of days, to make sure that everything is, you know, kosher. Of course, they know we're coming, so they're on their best behavior, hiding all evidence if any of abuse, embezzlement, and the like. But they get to know who we are, that we're not bullshitting around, we want some return on our investment. That's what they're supposed to get from our visit. That's the logic, anyway, which Jerry says is why we check 'em out before we hand over the check. That's what we do," he said, trailing off with, "as if we know what the fuck we're doing."

Tom laughed. He looked at Ed Novicky, six-foot three, Nordic blond-haired, big and utterly serious. Or straight-faced, anyway, seeing through tortoise-shell glasses his catastrophic view of the world. When he smiled, which was rare, a slight gap between his teeth heightened his affectation, deadpan comedy deliberately out of place.

They strolled up the sidewalk to an old Victorian flanked by two giant elm trees with leaves just turning orange-gold, Fall on its way. The stately manor seemed a bit shaggy, now home to the charity spun off to Ed by Brooke Astor. The great house still displayed old world splendor scaled down compared to some of the mini-Versailles towering above the coast. He recalled as a kid walking by fenced-off private beaches in front of the big summertime shore manors. Rumors ran around that some of the mansions boasted fifty rooms on four floors, able to sleep every member of the family, extended included. At least so said wagging tongues. Despite his newfound prosperity, Tom had never seen inside of any seaside palace of the rich and famous.

Not nearly as grand, the hoary mansion before him featured a wrap-around porch running off to the right side around a large corner tower. Faded yellow shingles covered the house framed by white cottage trim. What they could see of the roof looked bad, too, missing several shingles next to others curled up weathered through the years.

"I can see where half our dough is going right away," Ed said, stopping to pull a small notebook from his back pocket. He removed a golf pencil from behind his ear, wet the tip with his tongue, and scribbled. Advancing a few steps, he stopped again to jot down another note. "This place needs a lot of work—caulk, paint, gutters."

They reached the front stairway, and Ed loped up the steps, landing hard on the porch floor. He proceeded to jump up and down at different places, stopping at one point to make another note in his book, then jumping up and down again.

"These floorboards aren't all that bad, except for the one."

He jumped around more, hopping to different spots at random. Tom stood on the second step from the top, half-moving his hands to cover his ears, flinching at the thumping noise created by Ed's landings. The front door of the house opened, and two women leaned out looking, their expressions a mixture of puzzlement and alarm. One was tiny, gentle-featured with graying hair and glasses. The other woman was black, round, and much taller than the small woman, easily able to look above from behind without stretching.

"Hello?" said the small woman, "Can I help you?"

Ed stopped jumping and spread his gap-tooth smile, which Tom just then realized could be enormously warm and charming, a real icebreaker.

"I'm very sorry to disturb you, ma'am, I was just testing the flooring on the porch. I'm Ed Novicky, from the GOBC? Mrs. Astor's people put us in touch."

The small woman beamed a remarkable smile, "Oh my God, yes. Amelia, these are the men I was telling you about. Mr. No–?"

"—Vicky, Ed Novicky. And this here is Tom Weatherly. He's in a rock band."

Shit, thought Tom, grimacing and ready to go red-faced, but no one seemed to make the connection.

"Hello, Mr. Weatherly, I'm very happy to meet you and Mr. Novicky. I'm Gertrude Weintraub, the director of Marbury House, and this is Amelia Evans, our associate director and financial officer."

"How do you do," the black woman said as she shook Ed and Tom's hands. She was round in that middle-age way, showing, too, a few gray strands of hair in elaborate corn-row tresses. In her case, though, the old adage seemed to play true, thought Tom, "black don't crack." Her complexion displayed not a line, not even a laugh wrinkle, although her dancing eyes told him she laughed plenty.

Gertrude Weintraub's features, on the other hand, looked every bit her sixty or so years, fully lined and generously cross-hatched as evidence of a thousand emotions. Not hard to envision, given her line of work. She smiled beautifully, her eyes sparkling through the thick glasses she wore.

They heard a tumult of voices behind the doorway, and Tom noticed a number of little heads peeking out. Black and brown, of all different ages, they gazed up with wide eyes at the mysterious goings-on of grown-ups.

"It's okay, kids, nothing to worry about," Gertrude said, "We have some important visitors here to meet you all. Please, go back inside. We'll be there in a minute."

Amelia herded them inside, "Back to your chores, to your homework."

Gertrude turned to the two men and said, "Well, welcome. We truly are glad to see you. Please make yourselves at home. We'll be serving lunch in a little while. Right now, do you have any questions, or maybe you would like to see the house?"

"A tour would be good," Ed said.

"Fine, then. Let's begin."

They stepped into the vestibule, and Tom was relieved to see that the interior of the house seemed in much better shape than the outside. The walls and floors were surprisingly clean, considering the house's clientele, although papers and toys cluttered the playrooms, and crumpled clothes bordered the beds. As they walked, little girls and boys stared up at them with big eyes, brown or black floating in glycerin-covered pools of pure white. Seeing so many dark-skinned children startled Tom, who had assumed that he would be seeing white kids, too. Maybe a mix at least, with blacks in the minority consistent to the lay of the land. The realization embarrassed him now, and he stared back at them, uneasy with what they might be thinking, of how their lives might compare to his.

"These are two of our counselors, Buddy Rosen, who has been carrying Marbury on his shoulders day and night for years. And this is Norah Kealy, our newest counselor who came here from San Francisco with a ton of experience."

They shook hands with a behemoth of a man, who Tom barely saw as the other counselor stepped forward. She shook his hand hard and fast, then released it. "Norah Kealy, hello," she said, smiling just as quickly.

She looked pretty good to him. Dark-haired, not too tall, wearing a silk shirt covered by a vest and a short jacket, jeans, and a pair of penny loafers over white cotton socks. She was narrow and round in the right places, though more round, making him think she wasn't hitting the aerobics classes too much.

"Tom Weatherly," he said.

"I know," she said before moving away to shake Ed's hand.

Tom gazed at her, wondering, as the four of them chatted for a time. Then Gertrude invited them down to have lunch before they talked to Amelia about the books.

As they walked downstairs, Ed leaned in to whisper, "Did you get a load of that big guy? Wasn't he the giant Pillsbury Doughboy in *Ghostbusters*?"

Tom laughed, shrugging at the same time as he thought that the new woman must have meant that she'd known the Good Old Boys were coming, not anything about him personally.

The dining room of the old house had been cleared of every stick of furniture except for tables and chairs. Plastic tablecloths had been draped across a large dining room table, which was flanked by card tables and chairs forming a riot of different sizes. The counselors supervised the children as they lined up at the doorway to the kitchen. One by one, they marched in and out with a plate of food, lasagna, Tom thought.

He looked at Ed, who lifted his shoulders and dropped them, and they both stepped over to the end of the line.

"Oh, no, no," Amelia said, as she grabbed one of their elbows each and steered them to the end of the long table. "Guests of honor don't wait online," she said, placing them opposite each other at one end.

Tom was about to sit when she looked directly at him, sternly, "And what's up with this 'Good Old Boys Club' BS? I've never known nothin' good about any 'good old boys.'"

Stopped in midair, Tom said, "Why it's, you know, a joke. Uh, I think it is," he stammered, "I hope it is. I mean, it ought to be. A joke."

He looked plaintively at Ed, who broke a broad grin. Amelia and Ed both laughed loudly as, sheepishly, Tom slowly descended in his chair. Amelia patted him on the shoulder, saying, "You boys can call yourselves the sons of the south for all I care, as long as you come with the cash."

They all laughed out loud again, Tom joining in, but he still felt embarrassed and uncomfortable.

Except for the very youngest, the children sat at the smaller tables. Buddy and Norah circled, pouring juice into paper cups at each place setting. Tom gazed around at the room while he waited, which was bright from the white fall sunlight pouring through the high sash windows in the old house. The walls were decorated with a flower-patterned wallpaper faded a dull beige. Decades old, he guessed. At child-eye level, unframed pictures hung from the chair rails, rendered in every possible medium available to kids—watercolor, marker, crayon, pastel, even an occasional oil. Primitive American, Christine might call them, worth a bundle in Old Greenwich.

Gertrude took the seat at their end of the table, and Amelia sat next to Ed. Buddy sat at the far end, and Norah sat next to Tom.

"Okay, William," Gertrude said to a young boy. He and four other children went into the kitchen and returned with steaming plates that they placed in front of the adults. They then each sat at a smaller table where they ate, at the same time trying to keep the other children eating as well.

"With this many kids, we need to press some of the older ones into service, or we could never do it. Most of them like it, though, having a little job that's theirs to do. Anyway, please start. Enjoy."

"No grace?" Ed asked, which startled Tom.

"No, we don't have any formal prayer here. Gets too complicated, if we try to be sensitive to the various faiths that come through—Baptist, Catholic, Methodist, Muslim, even a Bahai once. We just tell the children to take a moment to themselves, if they want to, before they begin. If some tragedy occurs, of course, a death in the family, or some other event that would affect one of the children directly, as a group we will have a few minutes of silence to think of those who we have lost."

Ed pressed his lips together and said, "Good. I gotta tell you, I'm not crazy about a whole lot of old-time religion creeping into my good deeds. It's kinda hypocritical somehow."

"Well, we keep it in the background," said Gertrude.

"So, you're Tom Weatherly," Norah said to him.

Surprised, Tom turned to her to answer, but stopped. Closer, he could see that her dark brown hair framed an oval face with a sharp chin. Intense blue-gray eyes under sharp, full eyebrows dispelled any illusion of softness created by her smooth features or the roundness of her body.

"Yeah. I'm surprised that you know me."

"Sure. I love your music. I thought you were great when you did Band Aid."

"At five in the morning? You were up pretty late for your age then."

"No," she said, "I was up early. When I heard where you were playing, I asked my mom to set the alarm."

Asked her mom, Tom thought.

"So," he said, "how long have you been working here?"

"A little more than a month. I'm new at this myself."

"Yeah? What did you do before?" He mentally smacked his hand to his forehead, clearly remembering Gertrude introducing her and what she did before moving from Frisco to come here. And here he was, vintage rocker looking, not listening.

"I worked at a shelter for battered women," Norah said plainly, without any attitude that he could detect.

"—in San Francisco. In fact, my stuff's still out there. I don't know how I'm going to get it here. Ten years of junk. I'll probably have to rent a giant U-Haul," she laughed.

"So, you like working here?" he said.

"Yeah," she said, head bobbing, "I do. I like the kids."

Tom slowly nodded his head, his mouth pursed in approval. "That's good. They look like a good bunch of kids, "he said, gazing around.

"Oh, they are," she said. "How long are you staying in Marbury?" she asked.

"Oh, I don't know. It's up to Ed, really, he's the one who's actually running the show. I'm pretty new to this."

"I see. Because, I thought, maybe," Norah said, inspecting her empty plate," that if you were staying the night, maybe we could go get dinner together."

Surprised, Tom quickly looked at her again, closely, then said, "Well, sure. I mean, I'll check with Ed, but even if he needs to take off, I could stay for dinner."

"Great," Norah smiled, "my treat."

Nine

In retrospect, Norah couldn't believe how giddy she acted. It wasn't like he was the first celebrity she'd ever met. He wasn't even quite a celebrity anymore; it had been years since he'd had a big song on the radio. But she'd never talked to any kind of famous person this closely, or for this long before, she thought. And he had been an idol to her, one of her first. This close, she could see that he had the most amazing gray-blue eyes, like ice crystal, even though he otherwise looked just a bit tired. His hair was still beautiful black liquorish, except for the feathered silver sideburns at his temples. Or were they white? He was not as tall as she'd thought he was when she'd seen him in magazines and on television. Maybe five-nine and change. He was slightly built, too, despite the oversize sweater he often wore. Up close, he was a delicate-looking man, a lovely man.

"I'm sorry," she said nervously. "I don't really know what's available in Marbury. I knew this place was here because it's near where I live, but I don't know how it is, I've never really eaten here."

She had taken them to the Marbury Steakhouse, a close cousin to chains like Denny's, Tom thought. Though darker, with a bar out front and exposed, black-stained beams looming above for atmosphere. She surprised him the way she looked at him now, nervously, different from the frank way she'd acted in Marbury House.

"This is fine," he assured her, "I've eaten in tons of places like this. Like an old home to me."

A young woman sat them down just past the bar in a booth that was also made of dark wood, without cushions. As they slid in, she asked for their drink order. Tom ordered a beer.

"Could I have a vodka tonic?" Norah asked. Even as she said it, she regretted it, since she wasn't a big drinker. But suddenly, going out with this guy didn't seem such as great an idea as it had when she'd fantasized about it back in the house. Now he was a real person, a man showing a bit of stubble on his face at this hour and some tired lines around his eyes. She wasn't sure how to deal with this, or what she really wanted.

Their drinks arrived, and Tom thanked the waitress politely, telling her they would need a few more minutes.

As he scanned his menu, Norah peeked over hers and admitted to herself that he was still gorgeous.

She dipped her head down, and Tom watched her as she read. She was younger, but not too much for once, and he realized that she was really very good-looking.

Norah raised her eyes. "Are you ready already?"

"Yeah. I don't have much imagination about food, but then, I'm not hard to please, either."

"Oh." She quickly took a long sip of her drink. The waitress returned, and Norah ordered a salad and grilled monk fish. Tom asked for steak and eggs, and seeing Norah's surprise, he said, "It's habit. A mix of breakfast and dinner at the same time."

"Don't you worry about your cholesterol?" she asked, then wished she could kick her own butt, nothing like hinting that he was older.

"Cholesterol? What's that?" he said, and they both laughed guardedly.

They talked.

"My ex-husband Dennis was a jerk, a real Reaganite in sheep's clothing. He used to give lip service to social issues, but all he really wanted were some Gucci loafers."

"I never married."

"Too busy living the rock star life, huh?" She grinned, somewhat luridly.

"Sure," he said, straight into her eyes. Lowering them, she smiled again, this time self-consciously.

Then she said, "So, how does it feel to be rich?"

"No different," he said, surprised again by her candor.

"Oh, come on. You don't have to worry about paying the rent anymore."

"Nope. Now I just worry about dying."

They laughed together, fully, their heads leaning toward each other.

Standing at the foot of the concrete stairs that lead up the rise to her house, Norah said, "Well, that was nice."

"Yeah, it was."

"I was nervous at first, but you're easy to relax with."

"Yeah, well, I'm an expert at relaxing people, I do a lot of relaxing myself."

She laughed. Then, she said, "But, I'm nervous again."

"That's okay. I could be nervous, too."

"Uh huh."

"Well," he said, starting to turn away.

"You want to come upstairs for a while? Have a beer or something?"

This time she surprised him less unexpectedly.

"I only have a small room, but I have refrigerator rights."

"You sure it's okay? I don't want to get you in Dutch with your landlord."

"No, it'll be all right. Come on."

The house was a tall, white-shingled, three-story structure with a broad dormer at the top. It probably had been built in the early fifties, Tom thought. From experience, he knew that the rooms weren't very big, unless they'd knocked some walls down.

They went in the back way, stopping in the kitchen for two long-neck beers, Norah saying to herself out loud, "I'll replace them tomorrow." She led him up a set of cramped stairs in the rear of the house that switched back to the second floor, and again to the third where she roomed. On this floor, two low ceiling cubby holes were slightly expanded by broad dormers, their sash windows offering views of the yard in the back and the street out front. Norah's overlooked the front of the house.

Her room was furnished with a rocking chair, a bookcase, a bed, and a night table, all joined by a blue and gray braided rug. The minimum amenities required of boarding house landlords, Tom thought. Though, he noticed a vase on the bookcase with a few linen violets sprightly sticking out.

"Here," she said, as she reached for his beer and placed it on the nightstand. Without a word, she grabbed him by the biceps and pressed her lips to his. Almost passively, he allowed his hands to rest on her hips, then move around to the small of her back as she forced his mouth open with her tongue.

"Mmm," she hummed, "mmm," as she kissed him, then hugged him, almost too tight, he thought. He kissed her back, and she began to move her hands up and down his spine, kneading him under his shoulder blades, and down.

Tom felt himself stirring, and he began to squeeze her with his own hands, sliding them up around her shoulders, then down below her waist. He stepped forward so that his leg came between hers and started to lean her gently toward the bed.

"No," she said.

"No?" he copied, confused, almost shocked.

Norah dropped to her knees and quickly undid his belt, unbuttoned his jeans, and pulled down his zipper. She searched until she found him, then closed on him with her mouth, voraciously.

"Holy hell," he said.

She stopped, lingering a little bit before rising.

"Uh-oh," Tom said, but Norah began to unbutton his shirt, kissing his chest as she slowly revealed each bare space.

"Good God," he said as she peeled his shirt and jacket off as one, "where have you been keeping yourself, in a fucking nunnery?"

"Close enough," she said as she twisted him around and onto the bed so that she could work on his shoes and pants.

When he was completely naked, she gave him an affectionate kiss below, then stood and began undressing herself.

Tom watched, feeling somewhat stunned. Norah threw her jacket at the rocking chair, and nearly tore off her denim shirt. She wore a camisole trimmed with lace beneath, which she quickly pulled over her head, uncovering her breasts. They were full, with dark areoles and nipples already buttressed. She tossed the shirt toward the rocker, opened her belt, and unbuttoned her jeans, pushing them and her underwear down in one motion.

She stepped out of them to kneel on the bed, straddling him, her socks still on.

Tom tried to rise, but she pushed him down with the palm of one hand in the middle of his chest. With her other hand, she grabbed hold of him and guided him inside, lowering herself gingerly. She was already slick, he thought, amazed.

Norah raised and lowered herself slowly, several times, moaning softly. He tried to say something, but she covered his mouth with one hand, and moved up and down again, back and forth.

Too fast, he thought. As if she knew, she slipped off and caressed him with her mouth while running her hands around his back, squeezing and pushing him toward her.

Tom felt as though he was slipping away, turning into liquid. He tried to move but couldn't. Norah released him and nudged him over onto his belly and began to massage the small of his back with one hand while she held and stroked him with the other. When she felt him begin to pulse, she stopped, gripping him tightly, until he subsided. Then, she began again, this time running a finger down his spine between his cheeks as she fondled once more. The opposing pressure was killing him, he thought, but once more, she eased off. Then, she started licking.

"Oh, man," he groaned, "what are you doing?"

"Enjoying myself," she said between licks.

"Yeah, well, I'm not used to this."

"That's a surprise," she said. Resuming, she murmured, "You are a delicious man."

He started to feel it all coming to an end, and she seemed to sense it.

"Is something about to happen?" she said as she turned him upright and moved on top of him again.

Getting ready to explode, he thought of how different this was from the others—the latest, the girl in Toronto, Christine—suddenly, he stopped.

Norah continued rolling her hips for a moment, then slowed down until she was still.

"What?"

He grimaced, then said, "Uh, before we do this, maybe we should consider," he paused, not believing he was saying this, "uh, you know, protection?"

"Oh," she said. She sat looking down on him, almost expressionless, and he could feel himself getting smaller.

"I didn't think of it," Norah said. "I supposed it really didn't matter, I guess. I'm pretty regular, and I just finished my period a day ago. So, we should be okay."

"Yeah, but you know. Just to be safe?"

Norah slowly nodded her head, "Okay. But I don't have anything. I'm not sure my diaphragm would even fit me, even if I had some gel. Tell you the truth, I'm not sure I could even find it."

"I have some condoms in my wallet," he said, wondering how old they were.

"Oh yeah?" Norah laughed, "how old?"

"Well, I've had them well past high school," he said, and they both laughed. Norah rolled off and lay next to him. "Let's take a look," he said, clambering off the bed over to his jeans. He brought the wallet over and sat cross-legged as he searched.

Norah rested her head on his thigh. Seeing him limp, she flicked her tongue, saying, "We could do other things, you know. I don't mind," she said, "I kind of like it, sometimes, you know?"

"Yeah, well," he said, not wanting to tell her the real reason why he stopped, "I'd like to be with you, though, you know?"

"Oh, you," she said, giving him a hug.

"Yeah, let me open this and . . ." he said, tearing the foil, "we'll just see."

Tom held the rolled-out condom up to the lamp light.

"Looks okay, I think."

"Yes," said Norah, "this is so romantic."

They both laughed.

"It does kind of take the edge off," Tom admitted.

She sat up and reached for the beers. "Here," she said, "let's get back in the mood."

They giggled, knocking their heads together.

"Ouch, dammit," she said.

"Jesus I'm sorry," Tom said. He kissed her on the forehead. Then he kissed her lower, on the eyebrows, first one, then the other. He kissed her closed eyes until she turned her face to his, and they kissed, long.

Tom found his arms around her, tight, but not too tight. She had embraced him, too, a perfect fit. She seemed surreally soft, as though an extra layer of gentleness encased her skin. He felt different somehow, comforted.

Norah moved her arms around him and down again. Silently, she felt about the bed, knocking her beer bottle on to the floor, still groping until she found the condom. As he watched, she carefully unrolled it over him, then reclined, pulling him with her.

"So," she said, wedged close to him afterward, her head resting on his shoulder, "were you ever married?"

"Me?" he said, screwing up his mouth in a pained smirk.

As soon as she saw his expression, she could kick herself, remembering she'd already asked him before.

"No," he muttered.

The deal was done, she thought, so she might as well forge ahead.

"Not even close?" she asked.

"I was engaged once, I think."

"You don't remember? Who was she?"

"A long-time friend back in New Jersey. In the old days, when we just started playing out, mostly in dives."

"How close were you?"

"I used to live with her, if you can call that living." Norah laughed, and he went on, "Man, she just hated the rock and roll band scene. She was jealous of it, the time I spent with the other guys rehearsing, the fact that the bar crowds liked us. Of course, we had alcohol on our side. But she didn't like it, she didn't like me talking to any other girl, ever. Even though we were right there in front of everyone, hundreds of people, she'd be suspicious—'What did she want?' she'd ask, time after time, 'til I started answering with stuff like 'She said if I played "Cocaine" she'd give me a blow job in the parking lot.'"

Norah snickered, "Oh, geez."

"Yeah," Tom said, gazing at the ceiling. "Actually, that really happened."

Norah lifted herself up and looked at him. "You're kidding! What did you do?"

"Well, I'm never one to turn down a blow job," he said, and they both started laughing, she punching his shoulder as she lay back down. "To tell you the truth, though, I couldn't play it, I didn't know it."

He licked her hand resting on his chest, then bit it. As she yelped, he began to lick and nip at her wrist, her arm, up and down her clavicle, between her breasts, licking and biting, pulling gently on her nipples in turn. He worked his way down her rib cage to her navel, discovering a soft, almost transparent line of hair leading below, which he traced and swirled with his tongue. He licked her inner thighs lightly, caressing her breasts and her hips at the same time. He parted her with his tongue and lips as he moved his hands beneath her to massage and knead her cheeks. As he licked and sucked, he could hear her breathing turn heavier, almost labored. Her body tensed, stiffened, relaxed, then tensed again. He continued deliberately, exploring, probing, then concentrating upon a constant movement, pressing her steadily, evenly, relentlessly. She tried to shift without leaving, holding herself as still as she could, caught between an irresistible need to squirm and a desire to stay centered. He felt her undulate tensely, then sigh luxuriously.

Tom remained where he was, pausing, then beginning again. He went on until she almost pushed his head away, "Enough."

He crawled up and put his head on her shoulder.

"That was wonderful," she said, "I think. Maybe too wonderful."

"Impossible," he said.

Ten

"People can say they've learned how to do their jobs when they realize that's what their work will always be like. You know, when they see that there won't be any more surprises. This came to me years ago in my first job as a juvenile probation officer," Norah said.

On his side, his head in his hand propped up on an elbow, Tom listened to her talk face up to the ceiling during the night.

"It was when I figured out that for as long as I worked there, I'd be trying to reason with the unreasonable, or unreasoning, trying to produce logic acceptable to the illogical. And key to the whole thing was my own imperative not to lie, not to manipulate them. Dangling the carrot wouldn't work. These kids needed to learn the ways of life, and they could learn them only through the truth. If I persuaded them in any other way, I would just be using another type of illogic. That might make things easier in the short run, but in the long term, they'd have gotten to me. They would have made me as unreasoning as they were."

He was surprised to find himself listening to her talk so long about these things, but it was interesting.

"The only way to avoid this was to deal in the harsh truth, which meant that I couldn't allow my own emotions to sway me. I couldn't try to be nice. So, I faced it. The fundamental knowledge was that I was parenting 28 children in place of their own illogical, absent parents, both literally and virtually. Immediate satisfaction came to me when I effected this kind of . . . when I reasoned with my charges honestly. And after learning this, knowing this unfeeling nature of my work, I understood that the next stage was the absolute potential of it, career potential. Beyond the little victories of being able to do the job, I had to ask myself, was the job worth doing, say, forever?"

Just a while ago they'd been wrapped around each other wrestling in the old way, their limbs hard to tell apart. A funny kind of thing, he thought, when they were closest that way, he looked past her, over her shoulder. Now, in the dim moonlight coming through the sash window, he watched her while she talked, her arms at rest overhead, her breasts flattened out, nipples at ease. She had her ankles crossed and the dark puff of her bush was the only contour left. Like women at the ocean, he thought, curvy and provocative standing and walking, or even lying sideways on one hip. But lying flat, ass up or down, they spread, looking beached. It was the fluid make-up of them, he supposed, a human waterbed. If the human body was ninety percent water on the average, women must be at the ninety-ninth end of the liquid spectrum.

"Well, this sort of thinking bothered me, to say the least," she continued. "I recognized then that I had to pit the day-to-day achievements of my work against the overall accomplishments. The trouble was that I doubted that any lasting good came from probation work. For one thing, the laws of society and therefore the premises of my logic were hardly perfect. In reasoning logically with the kids, I knew that the truths of the rules I tried to impress upon them were absurd."

She was different, that was for sure. He slowly shook his head, "Sheesh."

Norah raised her head, "What?"

"Oh, nothing," he said. "But tell me, do you ever read *People* magazine?"

"No," she said. "Well, maybe in the doctor's office now and then. Why are you asking?"

"I didn't think so. Oh, no reason. You don't strike me as the *People* magazine type of person. I was just confirming it."

"Oh," she said, appearing slightly wary. "I'm talking too much."

She thought he wasn't listening. "No, no, go on," he hurriedly said, "I mean it. You were saying how stupid the rules are."

"Oh, yeah. Anyway, I had to convince these kids that they had to obey them. There was this one boy named Glenn who had been sent to a vocational training school way the heck up state. He'd never been away from home before, and the judge sent him there. So, he ran away, and where did he go? Home, the first place they checked, of course. They picked him up and I talked with him.

"'Glenn,' I started, 'you know you have to go back to the training school.'

"'I'm not going back,' he said. 'Un-un, not me. If anybody tries to make me, I'll beat the shit out of 'em.'

"'Oh, sure, Glenn. You'll just beat them up, and they'll leave you alone. Look, the judge said you have to go to Allied for six months. You only have two weeks left to go. If you go back and finish up, you can do what you want.'

"'I ain't going back. I'm eighteen, I don't have to do nothing anybody else tells me.'

"'Yes, Glenn, you're eighteen now, but you weren't when you stole the bicycles. When you're finished at Allied, then you can be your own boss, but you have to finish up what the judge ordered, because you were seventeen then, still a juvenile subject to the judge's ruling.'

"'I don't care,' he said, 'I ain't going back. Nobody can make me. That dumb-ass place, who wants to go back there?'

"He went on, and I knew that he was right. No one was going to force him to finish out the two weeks at Allied, unless I did. I could have the police pick him up, but then the judge would place him in a juvenile detention home, which was as good as nothing. Or the judge would dismiss him because he was eighteen. The two weeks weren't worth the trouble. I kept thinking, what good would it do him, anyway, he really couldn't learn much of use if he wasn't willing. Allied probably wouldn't have wanted him back. Yet, if I could've just convinced him how much easier it would be for him to just finish out the two weeks, he might be okay."

This was painfully too long, Tom thought. He wondered how she could keep on doing this for a living.

"So, I decided to try another tact, go after him with the positive elements at Allied, the spending money he was making, his girlfriend there. I knew that he'd left on a whim, just like he made all his decisions; what he felt like doing right at that instant, he did. I felt that if I could persuade him to think beyond how he felt, he'd be better off for that.

"I geared up, and started in on him, and after a long, long argument, going over it again and again, old Glenn finally said he'd go back."

She sighed, and Tom draped an arm over her shoulder and gave her a squeeze.

"Yeah, I know. I have no idea whether he really saw the light, but at least I felt that I'd gotten him to see an easier way this one time. I mean, I was fully cognizant that this was all I'd gotten, but it was enough then. Then I remember projecting myself in a future scenario in the same work but in a different capacity. But at the time, that was where I wanted to be, where I felt both myself and my work to be essential together. Pragmatically speaking, the big picture was for other people, I thought; regardless of the cosmic impact, that little win made me feel good. Cosmically speaking, I felt extremely satisfied being convincing, arguing logic successfully one on one, the absolute pleasure of persuasion at its simplest and therefore its best."

"Man," Tom said.

"Yeah," she said, "pretty pathetic in a way. But that's it, that's what you get in this line of work, tiny little positives that don't last a day."

"But you're still doing it."

She shifted her gaze to him.

"I mean, in a way it's the same."

"Yup," Norah said, turning back to the ceiling, "Sure is. I went into family therapy for a while, then battered women, and now this. But I really learned just how much I could expect from that first job."

He shook his head, "Seems less rewarding when you look at it like that."

She looked back at him, "It can be a challenge to keep going. I tell you, they were dumb, too. I had these two guys who stole a bunch of lawn mowers in their neighborhood. So, the cops went around asking if anybody knew anything about it. The guys said, 'Oh, no, we don't know anything.' A week later they're going around door-to-door, asking if anybody wanted their lawns mowed."

They both laughed, their eyes smiling into each other's.

"Did you ever hear of anything so dumb?"

"Oh, I've known some light bulbs short a few watts," he said. "One guy in a band I was in way back, he played bass, a real short, stocky dude, with teeth big like Chiclets. He had short, fuzzy hair, and he wore a Navy watch cap. So, at first we called him Sluggo, you know, like in the old Nancy comics? His real name was Eddie. One day someone noticed that he had this tattoo on his arm, really strange looking, not like a professional job at all. These thin-lined letters that spelled out 'The Drieter.'"

He shifted onto his side, resting his head on his forearm. "So, we're at this, all of us thinking what the hell is a drieter, trying to figure it out. 'Til finally, I ask him; 'Eddie, what does that mean, 'The Drieter?' And he looks at me kind of like he doesn't want to answer, but he says in this gravelly voice of his, 'Awe, it was a tattoo I gave myself one night, but I was fucked up drinking, and I fucked it up. It's supposed to say, 'The Drifter,' but I fucked up the '*f*,' and put in an '*e*.'"

Norah burst out laughing and Tom grinned, inspired. "And so, the rest of us are turning away from him, mouthing to each other, 'gave himself a tattoo?' 'He fucked up the '*f*,' and now he's 'The Drieter?'"

By this time, Norah was falling apart, rolling and laughing watching Tom's silent bug-eyed burlesque, then even more when he started laughing with her. They roared together, tears squeezing from the corners of Norah's eyes.

"He was giving himself a tattoo?" she asked, disbelieving between her cries of laughter.

"I know," laughed Tom. "From then on, to us he was Eddie the Drieter."

"My God," she said, "he could have been one of my kids!"

"Yeah, well, he probably was, or some other probation officer's kid. Oh yeah, Eddie was a trip, but he could be scary, too. He had this other tattoo on one knuckle, a diamond, and when I asked him about that, he said I didn't want to know about it. When I bugged him, he said it was a gang thing and it was bad news. It was like he was trying to put it behind him. I know he spent time inside. When I asked him what for, he said rape. But he said it was a put-up job, that he was framed."

Suddenly serious, Norah said, "Do you think it was?"

"I don't know. He was such a nice guy. I think he drank. I think when he drank too much, he didn't know what he was doing, like fucking up the '*f*.' He was a pretty good bass player except for when he drank. Then, he'd take over with this frenetic metal tempo. We were ready to fire him over that, but then he started missing practices, then gigs. We threatened to fire him, but before we could, he just sort of disappeared."

"That's sad," she said.

"Yeah, I really liked Eddie, he was always a sweet guy to me, and he never drank around us. But sometimes shit happens," Tom said.

He slid over on his back again, and they drifted silently for a time.

Norah pulled herself over close to him, her arms wrapped around his chest. "So, that's what it's like to be a rock star, huh?"

Tom rolled his eyes at her, "More than you can imagine. It's amazing that any bands work out. Mostly, it's just dumb luck." He glanced at her and said, "I think you know now, what happened to all those juvies of yours when they grew up. They didn't."

She chuckled, "But you weren't a bad boy, were you? You don't act like a reformed criminal."

"Oh, no, I was an altar boy, just like every other Irish Catholic kid dominated by his mother."

"You're Irish? Weatherly doesn't sound Irish."

"What, you think that's my real name? This is showbiz, lady."

"No lie. So, what's your real name that you had to change it to Weatherly?"

"I'm not sure I should tell you."

"Oh, come on, after all we've been through? Look, I let you have your way with me."

"Yeah, but you might not have if you'd known my real name."

"Well, of course not. I wouldn't have known you were famous."

"Hey! I thought you recognized me!"

"Oh, please, I was fifteen."

"Man," he said indignantly, "You're really persuading me to share, you know?"

"Oh, come on," she said, cozying up to him, "you can tell me. We're old friends, now, aren't we?"

"According to you, I'm the old friend." He hesitated, "It's Collins."

"Collins? That's it? Certainly Irish. Collins," she said, then smiled. "Tom Collins. I get it."

"Right. Who wants to be a rock star named after a drink your parents used to imbibe?"

"That is funny."

"Not hilarious, just not worth the risk." He paused for a moment. "My dad's dead. Mom is in Tucson, now."

"I'm sorry about your dad."

"Yeah, well, don't worry about it, it was a long time ago, twenty years. It was quick, a heart attack."

"Uh huh. Any sibs?"

"One sister married and teaching school in Illinois. A brother in Florida who also punishes me as my financial advisor."

"And you all get along okay."

"Mary's eight years younger, a surprise child. We don't have much in common. But I like her a lot, and she has a boy and a girl of her own who are great. I just don't see them too often. Joe, I hear from way too much."

"What about your mom?"

"Holidays, when I'm around. I call her every blue moon. But I'm forever missing her birthday. I suck."

"Oh, please. So, you had an ordinary childhood. Why'd you go into rock and roll?"

Tom shrugged, "I love music, and playing out. I wasn't any good at sports or anything, so I started playing a guitar. The alternate way to meet girls."

"And I suppose you met plenty of them."

"Not in those days. And never any as lovely as you, my dear," he said in a syrupy voice.

"Oh my," she said, touching her fingertips to her sternum.

He covered her hand, and they lay quiet for a while, fingers intertwined.

After a while, Norah said, "When you were playing with guys like Eddie, did you ever think you were going to be a big success?"   "Hell no!" he said. "Well, I mean, not with Eddie or that band. But I was young and didn't think that I would be playing with that band forever—The Jet Mobiles," he chuckled, and she laughed, too.

"You know, I just knew someday I would have my own band and write my own stuff. But then, I didn't care. I just loved playing out, playing music, any kind. Guys in bands are like that, they always think that they could hit it big at any time. The music business is so crazy, look at how old Huey Lewis was when he got hot. But they all really love to play. You'll see any number of guys my age still playing in wedding bands, or lounges, and they're willing to play just about any kind of music. Though, I did have one old buddy of mine from those days who once swore to me that he would never play Mustang Sally again. He said he was out of wedding bands forever. But, what the hell, he was my age now, he was entitled. And he was the greatest musician."

He drifted for a moment, and she could see that he was revisiting those times.

"Then there was this friend Diggs who could really play keyboard, classically trained. He got into a Reggae band called Third World, and they told him that the band dressed in matching dashikis to play. So, after the audition, they gave him a dashiki and told him to show up in some neighborhood in South Boston. That's where this all took place. Anyway, the day of the gig arrives, and Diggs doesn't have a car, so he's going to take the T like he always does. About two hours before the show, he packs up his electric board and puts on his dashiki. And there he is, this white guy wearing this traditional African garb, riding on the Boston subway to South Boston among all these black people. And they're staring at him, and he's trying to push the train faster along in his mind. So, he finally gets there and walks up to where the other guys are setting up on stage. And the lead singer in the band, a guy from Jamaica takes one look at him and says, "Hey, Mon, what are you doing wearing your dashiki? We just bring them with us on a hanger and change here.""

Tom and Norah laughed together, and he continued, "All the other guys in the band started kidding him about it, and Diggs thought it was pretty funny, too, until he realized he still had to wear it home on the T after the show."

Norah laughed again, and Tom finished, "One of the other guys in the band gave him a ride home, so it wasn't all that bad."

"And is Diggs still playing?" she asked.

"Oh, yes," Tom said. "He plays a lot in Boston, he's so good. But he married and they had kids, so he didn't really want to travel. That limited his options."

"Kids will do that," Norah said. After a pause, she asked, "'Do you have any kids?"

"Nope. Like I said, never married. Another trait of Irish men, they marry late. At least, that's what my mother says. But I didn't marry at all."

"And none out of wedlock," she said.

"Hell no! Too paranoid to take a chance. You saw that."

"Right. So, lucky you," Norah said. Seeing him start to frown, she said, "I mean never getting married."

Tom looked at her, "Oh, come on. You're all right now, right?"

"Sure," she said, "no worse for the wear."

"Right," he said, "none of us are."

They lapsed into silence, which turned into sleep.

Eleven

Tom was dozing when she said, "It's late. Or early."

He opened his eyes to see the gray glow of early sunlight slipping beneath the window shade.

"Morning," he noted.

"And good morning to you, too," Norah said.

"Oh, yeah," Tom said, smiling. He rolled over to look at her. She had the sheet pulled up over her shoulders.

"I'm going to have to get up, soon, to get ready for work."

"Yeah," he said. "I guess I should pull myself together, too."

"You don't have to get up. You can leave when you like."

Tom felt uncomfortable. He'd heard this kind of talk hundreds of times before, it seemed. Hell, he thought, he'd used it himself hundreds of times.

"No, listen," he said, "if you're getting up, I'm getting up too."

Norah arose from the bed without ceremony and headed for the bathroom door. Tom found himself watching her leave.

She raised her arms above her head to stretch, pulling on one elbow with her other hand, accenting the S-curve of her back and hips. Some people just have it, he thought, natural grace and beauty. He felt that familiar hollowness in his stomach, even though they just finished rocking the bed, rocking the world. Amazing, he thought.

"Gosh," she said, smiling ironically, "taking me to work in a limo the morning after the prom."

"Oh, yeah," Tom said, slightly abashed, "I have a car back at the ranch, but it's a real gas guzzler. When I'm out seeing people, like a record company—or Marbury, for instance—I often take a limousine so I can make phone calls. I guess I forget how spoiled I am, I guess."

"Come on, I was only teasing," Norah said, pulling on a piece of his shirt to lean into him.

She sprang from the car and headed up the walk. He jumped out after, saying, "Hey, wait. When will I see you again?"

She reached the first step of the stairway and turned around, her cheeks flushing slightly. "Oh gee," she said. Gesturing breezily with her hand, she said, "Whenever."

She was in control. He knew it, she knew it, and both were enjoying it immensely.

"How about next weekend?"

"Yeah, sure."

"Great. I'll call you here because I don't have your home phone number."

"Here is where I'll be," she said. She leaned over from the first step and grabbed him by the nape of his neck to kiss him, more affectionately than passionately. She pranced up the steps, throwing a "bye" over her shoulder as she entered Marbury House.

Tom stuck his hands in the rear pockets of his jeans. Magic, he thought, wonderful magic. What had started out like so many nights before had turned into something completely different from anything he could remember ever happening before, rock star and otherwise.

Norah.

He walked back to the limousine.

"The Northern Parkway," he said to the driver, "I'll give you the directions when we get near the exit."

"Yes sir."

Tom settled back in the middle of the seat, ready to drift off into dreamland.

He bolted upright abruptly.

"Hey, buddy, I hate to ask you, but could you put the window up?"

"Absolutely, sir."

"I'm sorry, I don't usually like to do this, but I have to make an important phone call," Tom murmured as the window slid up. When the blade of the glass nestled firmly into place, he grabbed the car phone and dialed quickly.

"Yes," Mary said. When she had started with him, she used to say, "Weatherly residence," but he soon persuaded her that anonymity was better.

"Mary, it's me," he said.

"Mr. Weatherly, it's good to hear from you. We miss you here, especially Felix."

"Yeah, I'm sure Felix misses me. Listen, I'm on my way home, but I need a favor. I want you to call Dr. Fields and make an appointment, it's something of an emergency."

"Oh, Tommy, are you sick?" she said.

"No, no, I'm fine, it's just a sort of precautionary thing. I stepped on a rusty nail, and I want to get it checked out."

"Well, that's what you get running around all over everywhere. I'll call Dr. Fields right away."

"Great. Here's a number you can call to reach me to confirm." He rattled off the car phone number.

"I'll call you right back."

"Great, thanks, Mary."

He cradled the phone and leaned back. Then, he tapped on the window glass.

"Hi, uh, I'm sorry, but there's been a change of plans. We'll be going into Syosset first, 350 Undervelde Street."

"That's fine, sir."

"Good, thanks."

Tom leaned back in the seat again, then shifted forward and pulled the empty cellophane condoms package from his back pocket. He looked at it ruefully, then stuffed it into his jacket pocket.

He was tired, maybe too tired to sleep. He reached into the minibar and pulled out a beer. He nodded off soon after, the half-empty bottle tucked between his legs.

In the studio, Tom determined to bull his way to playing well despite his lack of practice. After he'd postponed rehearsals for the past three weeks, he knew that Don would go ballistic if he played poorly. He worked over his unplugged guitar in furious fashion for a half-hour before the others arrived. He hoped hopelessly that he could get some kind of rhythm going that would carry him through, promising to himself that if he could slide through today, he would dedicate himself for the next three weeks getting into shape.

He whipped through a riff, and felt his fingers tie up at the end, already tired from the effort. He broke it off and heard a van approaching on the driveway. Oh, man.

He stepped to the French doors facing the pool to look down the long, winding gravel road, and breathed relief. The wrong van, a different van, Christine's from her gallery bringing the new artwork that he'd bought in that moment of weakness. Except, he wasn't sure if he could tell one moment of weakness from another. He unslung his guitar and propped it against the wall, then headed to intercept her at the main entrance of the house.

The van pulled to a stop, and Christine hopped out to walk toward him. She wore a silver-beaded black denim jacket over a short black knit dress, mid-thigh, no hose, and black leather, clunky clogs on her feet. A dark, blood-red band holding her hair tight to her head served as her sole concession to color. Looking at her as she drew closer, Tom marveled at how petite she really was, and slender. Nary a spare calorie care in the world, she exuded complete self-assurance and power in the old-world way of women.

"Hi," she said, reaching up to give him a peck on the cheek. "How you doing?"

"Good, good," he said, nodding, shifting his eyes down, confirming his riff on women's wiles. "How about you?"

"Great. How was Marbury House?"

He hesitated, then said, "Pretty damn interesting, really. I liked it."

She smiled, surprised, "That's good."

"Yeah. I think I'm going to go back soon."

She twisted her head up, angling her gaze at him. "Really?"

"Yeah, I think there's more that can be done there."

"Well, I am surprised," she said.

You look fucking amazed thought Tom. He saw her eyebrows draw together, and knowing what was coming next, he moved quickly to head it off.

"So, this is the art?" he said, walking to the van. He peered in the sliding side door, which had been opened by one of the two men here to help Christine hang the pieces.

"Yes," she said, "it's all there, and I think you're going to dig it a lot." She put her arm through his and pivoted them toward the front door of the house, "I'll show you where I think they would go great."

Tom turned back to the sound of another van speeding up the driveway. Shit, he thought. He disengaged her arm and said, "Yeah, okay, but I have to go rehearse. Listen, your judgment is light years better than mine. Why don't you hang the stuff where you think it ought to go. If I don't like where something is, we can talk about it later."

As he strode off toward the studio, she carped, "But Tom, we should do this together. It's your space." When he didn't answer, she called out sharply to his dwindling figure, "What shall I do with the old pieces?"

"I don't know," he yelled back over his shoulder. "Put them in the attic or sell them. I gotta go now."

Christine placed her fists on her hips and sniffed. He should be invested in his environment, she thought, how exquisite art could create a new ambience for him. A profound change in his sense of self. But he couldn't be bothered, which made her wonder if he bought it just to please her, the tired old game of their tired old time together.

"Where to, Ms. Dvorak?" Duke the driver asked over the corner of a large, oblong packing crate.

"Oh, we're not ready for that, yet. We must make room for it, first."

She led them into the grand foyer where de Soto's *Oceania* dominated the front wall. When she'd brought over the de Sotos and the Myrcks, Tom had followed her everywhere around the house, hanging on every word she'd said. How the works of the two artists complemented each other so well, a miracle given their different origins, showing that the experience was the same, the same artistic vision as proof of a revolution. Now he wanted her to sell it, or worse, stick it in an attic somewhere. True, the revolution never materialized; de Soto and Myrcks were pretty much passé now. And that was the problem with Tom. He should know that they were over by being current, he should pay attention to what she had to teach him, not do things just to please her. That was the endemic condition with Tom, always trying to please everyone without ever connecting with anyone. It was as much that which broke them up as the fact that he couldn't keep his mutton in his pita.

Hah; she laughed at her own joke, another instance in which he was trying to please everyone.

"Okay," she said, "take everything off the walls and put them in the attic."

"Everything?" Duke said, a dark man almost as short as she was, but looking like he weighed as much as a piano.

"Well, all right, maybe not everything. Where I point, take those down."

"And the attic, where would that be?"

Shit, she thought. "Mary!" she yelled, "can you show these men where the attic is?"

Twelve

Billy, George, and Frank all greeted Tom warmly, which made him feel better about what was coming. Don nodded his head at him as he passed by, which withered him, chasing away the warmth he'd just felt.

"Okay, tune it up for a couple of minutes, then we'll go." Don leaned over to Tom, "Well?"

"Well, I didn't get much time to practice. I was in Marbury all week, you know?"

"Marbury? Oh, that charity thing you're doing. Man, you have too much money."

"Not to hear my brother tell it. He was pissed when I told him how much I needed for their house."

"Yeah, I'll bet. Upended his carefully planned embezzling, I'll warrant."

"Hey, if you can't trust your brother to rob you blind, who can you?"

"Maybe a wife?"

"Sure, but you got to be married first. Anyway, that's not out of the question, either."

Don jerked his head back and laughed, "What? You?"

Tom turned his head coyly to the strings of his guitar. "It's possible."

"You're kidding me. Who?"

"Well, I don't know yet, it's like way early. But there is someone I met. She seems pretty special."

"Holy shit," Don said in a staccato laugh, "God help her. And she's at Marbury? Man, now you'll really be putting in the string time." He turned and said loudly, "Boys, we'd might as well pack it up and go home. Tom, here, he has feline business that is going to keep him in Long Island from now on."

"Hey, don't be a jackass," Tom snorted. He looked at the blank faces staring at him, and said, "Let's go. "Little Bitty Things" from the top."

They played well, and he played well, half pissed and half inspired by airy thoughts of Norah. Lord, Norah. He couldn't get her out of his mind. Norah, man.

"That wasn't half bad," Don said. "You sure you haven't been practicing?"

"Check out the blood where my blisters used to be."

"Huh. Quite amazing."

They played the set almost flawlessly. Don could do nothing but tell them to take five. Billy immediately headed to the refrigerator and began tossing beers at everyone.

"So, what're you doing for turkey day?"

"What, Thanksgiving?" George asked. "Shit, man, that's two months out." He paused. "I don't know, my sister's, I guess."

"You ain't going down to the island?" Billy said.

"Naw, man, that's too expensive. Maybe for Christmas."

"Yeah, I guess. That would be better. When it's colder."

"Not these days," said Frank. "Could be sixty degrees Christmas day. I read it in the *National Enquirer*. Says the world's going to melt according to some meteorologists. They call it 'global warming,' from too much pollution in the air."

"Yeah, global warming, I love it," said Billy. "But it's not going to be sixty where I'm going. It's never sixty there, even in the summer."

"Where's that, Alaska?"

"Close enough. Somerville, Massachusetts, where I grew up."

"Massachusetts. You tellin' me it's never sixty degrees in the entire year in the whole state of Massachusetts?"

"Never. It'll probably be ten degrees below this Christmas."

"What about the summer? It's never sixty in the summer there?"

"Nope. Shoots straight to ninety; do not pass 'Go,' just sixty. Ten below or ninety above, that's what you get in dear old Somerville."

"Oh, for the love of fuck," George said.

"Yeah, it's an amazing place. Right where I live, there's a funeral home on the corner, Bleitz Funeral Home."

"Yeah, so what?"

"Bleitz Funeral Home. It's spelled b-l-e-i-t-z, but it just as easily could be spelt b-l-i-g-h-t-s, like locust swarms blotting out sunlight when they ravish entire crops. Or grasshoppers!" he said, eyes as wide as saucers. "Get too many grasshoppers, they turn into locusts, horrible clouds of them devouring everything in their path. B-l-i-g-h-t-s Funeral, get it? Might as well call it the Plague Funeral Home."

"The Cholera Funeral Home,'" Frank said, "just down the street."

"Right. Our designer society has reached the point of offering death-specific funeral homes. Next thing you know we'll have Car-Wreck Funeral Home, maybe Gas-Leak Funeral Home—beware of runaway crematoriums!"

"You know what man?" George said. "I think you spend too much time by yourself."

"So you think I'm nuts. Think about this; Tom Wolfe said we're the richest society in the world, enough gazillionaire to make the Sun King envy us. Shit, man, we even have designer water! The bane of our existence, that's what Tom Wolfe says."

"And who the fuck is Tom Wolfe?" George snapped.

"He's just one of the leading writers and arbiters on conservative style in our nation, is all," Billy said with a sniff.

"What, you a personal friend of his?"

"No, I don't know him, I just read some stuff about him."

"Yeah, Tom Wolfe Toilet Paper in the Tune Inn," George said.

"Hey, man! Don't you get that our entire culture is being Balkanized? Everything is going to be customized, it's just a matter of time. Every person's going to be able to create their own exclusive little world. You can write it down; you heard it here first."

"Oh, yeah, as if any customized world of mine would include you?" George said, grinning at the others.

Billy's face tightened, reddening as he started toward George.

"All right, all right," Don said, moving between them. "Enough bullshit. We've got work to do." He turned to Tom, "What's it going to be?"

Tom shrugged, "How about 'Don't Get Me Started?'"

"From the top, 'Don't Get Me Started.'"

Christine had worked her way through the house with the two delivery men, removing the old pieces first, then telling them where to hang the new ones. "Up a little, over to the left, no, now to the right. Down a smidgen, no, a hair up . . . good."

After a few hours of this, the men looked more and more exasperated, understanding at the outset that they were only supposed to drop off the art. Christine knew that their willingness to help out a cute little brunette would go only so far, so at the end of the third hour, she threw in an extra hundred bucks if they agreed to stay for the whole job.

"A hundred each?" Duke said.

Christine hesitated, then said, "Okay, sure." Why the hell not? She thought. Tom was good for it.

At the end of hour four, they'd reached the last room, Tom's guest bedroom where he actually slept. Christine knew that it was deceivingly neat; Mary had hung up all his clothes, straightened the night table and his desk, put all the CDs, DVDs, and tapes back on the shelves as she did at the end of every day. She was gone now, Felix, too.

Christine looked at her watch: six-thirty. She had to let these guys go soon, extra money or not. She surveyed the room and as she looked remembered what a kid Tom still was, "too immature to be my age," he'd always say. Situated across from the king-size bed was the de rigueur entertainment center. His desk fronted two French doors, and on the opposite wall he had a bulletin board above a small table, both full of memorabilia, some dating back to his childhood.

She stopped to gaze at a white index card attached to a red ribbon, "Third Place" written on the card, for his brindle Boxer at a little dog show, she recalled, when Tom was nine years old. She shook her head.

The only painting in the entire room hung over his bed, a beautiful Hoyer landscape of the Shetland Island Unst. Gorgeous, she thought, never out of style even in this day and age. Shame to take it down, but where could it go? The new work had to go up.

Reluctantly, she told Duke to put it with the rest in the attic and hang the new one in its place, a stunning Marroquin celestial abstract. Gazing up at the brilliant shafts of color spangling across the canvass, she distractedly told the men they could go home.

After they left, she stepped back without looking to sit on the easy chair opposite the bed. Stunning work, acute, likely to go out of style quickly. She slowly moved her head back and forth. Never less than genius, though, no matter what. Regardless, wasted on Tom, she sighed to herself. Then she shrugged her shoulders, knowing he'd buy new whenever she said so. Not to get into her pants, though. Those days were over.

She cupped her chin in her hands wondering why. The thrill was gone? Too easy? Too old?

Christine shuddered, not yet. All sorts of guys still gave her the look, and plenty tried their luck. But Tom . . . she shook her head.

Staring unfocused, she sat for a while. Then she stood up, pressing her skirt down to her knees.

Slowly, she strolled around the room touching a few things. An old silver tray with a glass bottom etched with his grandfather's initials on the edge of a chest of drawers. An array of coins, nail clippers, tweezers, pen knives, and a Seiko watch hid the tray's monogram; Tom had shown it to her once before. Next to it stood an old holy water sconce turned upside down and a small bank in the shape of a globe. She lifted it, surprised by its heft, at least five dollars of pennies pinning it to the chest.

She wandered past a night table on his side of the bed, piled high with books, each containing a bookmark except for one on top spread open upside down. She read the title; *Winter*, Len Deighton, easily 800 pages, one hell of a read if Tom got that far. Maybe split in the middle just to keep it from falling over. She moved on.

Over at the old walnut vanity that served as a desk, she poked at the layered mounds of paper mixed with catalogs and newspapers. She ignored the days-old copies of the *Daily News*, *Post* and *Times* in favor of glancing at a *Village Voice* headline:

The Godfather, Part III: Like Godfather
"Coppola and copilot Mario Puzo blast off for some cosmic Shakespearean netherworld of tearful soliloquies and dynastic tragedy."

Huh, she thought. If they say so. She laid the paper down as she sat on the dull gray industrial swivel chair Tom used at his makeshift desk. She pushed piles of papers around, nothing else catching her attention. Then she saw what looked like a medical form appear on her right.

Christine grabbed it and glanced at the sender's heading: Long Island Diagnostics. She flipped the triptych open and scanned down past the company heading again to the patient's name and address—Thomas Collins—to the middle of the page:

> Procedure No. 654839-78
> Date: 01/14/1995
> Blood Type A+
> Panel Results:
> Anemia – negative
> Diabetes – negative
> Hepatitis A, B – negative
> HIV- negative
> TB – negative

She stopped reading with a jerk. HIV? What the fuck is he doing getting tested for AIDs? She felt her stomach drop to the floor, knowing without seeing she had blanched dead white.

Christine pushed the paper back onto the desk. She arose and took a slow, deep breath.

At least he was negative, she thought. And they hadn't been to bed together for months. It seemed like months, anyway. Weeks. So, who is he screwing lately?

He'd just returned from Toronto hoping to jumpstart some engagements. Not much luck with that. Which didn't rule out him jumping the bones of some throwback groupie. A retro-groupie, she decided, more likely for a one-night stand.

She swung her head back and forth, features drum tight. Then she sighed. Incorrigible. Why did she bother?

Christine walked over to the phone near the bed and called a cab, too tired to deal with any more of it right now.

Thirteen

Tom woke up close to noon the next day, groggy from the beer, pizza, and never-ending mindless bullshitting. He wondered if any of them really listened to the others. Except, he could remember most of the arguments, like which cats had the advantage, lions or tigers. Tigers were bigger, but they go it alone. Lions rolled in gangs, the chicks being the baddest badasses of the lions. Only hunting, though. Sir fully maned daddy lion moves them out of the way with one roar, always eats first. Only the younger dudes might have his number—sometimes the juniors double up on the old. So, what about hyenas? They kicked lion ass on a regular basis. Not so; they ambushed better, but lion prides chased them one on one. And tigers? They're top honcho, no question. Why you say that? You just said lions can gang up on loner tigers. Possible, but look at where tigers live, Asia right? So, how many Asian lions are left there? Not too fucking many. That's just bullshit, humans put down most of the lions. Oh really? Then how come they're so many tigers still left there? Well, maybe they're hard to catch—you just said they run alone. Harder to find. A pause: Okay, so maybe Asian lions decided to run alone? Why are they gone? Because each of 'em ran into a tiger.

They all nodded their heads in unison. Then one of them said, you know, anthropoids operate pretty much the same way. And another one immediately asked what the fuck is an anthropoid?

Tom squeezed his temples trying to relieve the memory in his headache. A soft knock on the door. "Mr. Weatherly? Are you up? I have coffee."

"I'm not Mr. Weatherly! That was my old man. And, yes, Mary, I would love some coffee. You have a bucket, right?"

She entered tsk-tsking, "Yes, if you want to spend the rest of the day in the loo. Drink this for now, I'll bring some more. Breakfast?"

He grinned in pain, "Not quite yet. Lemme think it over."

She smirked and left.

Tough night, he thought, or morning, really. One beer led to another, a shot, one more, relax with a bit of a spliff. Oy.

Don joined them for a beer, a gesture of satisfaction with their rehearsal. But then he left, which left the youngsters pressing their immunity to the aftermath of late-in-life substance abuse. Of course he wasn't that old, Tom reckoned. Except for the mileage.

He shook his head bullishly and downed a healthy slurp of coffee. Sitting in bed felt good. Then the phone rang.

Shit. So far to stretch, he mourned, reaching across to the Princess phone on the night table.

"Yeah."

"Tom? Is that you?"

Tom scrunched his eyebrows. The voice sounded vaguely familiar. "Whom may I say is calling?"

"It's Mel."

Silence.

"From Murray's Classics?"

Oh. Fuck.

"Yeah, Murray's, how you doing? What's up?"

"It's Mel, Tom."

"Yeah, sure, sorry about that, I just woke up. Had a night session last night."

"Of course. Rocking it out, huh? Well, I'm really sorry to wake you this early."

Tom glanced at the clock on the nightstand; 11:30 a.m.

"I thought you'd want to know as soon as it got here." Before Tom could answer, Mel at Murray's spilled. "Your car, 1975 Chevy Nova two-door coupe, right out front like new."

Tom sat back. The car, his car, the first he'd ever owned.

"No kidding," he said.

"Yup, pretty as a picture. Silver-gray paint job, blue interior, front bench seat, as ordered."

"Really?"

"Uh huh, straight six, automatic trans, a.m. radio, full spare tire. Even a '75 manual still in its plastic wrapper, never opened."

"Wow, that's great. And the mileage?"

"714 miles. Granny back in Wescosville must've taken it to Sears a few times for maintenance."

"Damn. Amazing."

"Yeah. Harder to find than the SS model, believe me. I'm still surprised you didn't go for one of those. Those 350 LTIs do kick ass."

"I know. You called me every time you found one. But this one, this is special."

"I get it," Mel said, "high school memories."

"Well, like that." Tom said. Mel didn't need to know he'd bought it when he was 25.

"Right. So, uh, when do you want to come get it?"

Shit, Tom mouthed.

"Or do you want me to drop it off? I can do that, no problem. I could be out there in say, an hour."

Tom screwed up his mouth, rubbing his stubble. Mel had delivered one of his cars once before, which morphed into an all-day visit by the loquacious salesman.

"No, no, Mel, I'll come get it. I can't wait to get behind the wheel."

"Oh, okay," Mel said, somewhat more quietly. "Well, then, it'll be right here waiting for you. It's not going anywhere!"

"Excellent, Mel," Tom said, "that's great. Can't wait, I'm excited."

"Okay, I'll be waiting right here."

"Good. Oh, uh, how much's the damage?"

"Sixteen."

"Sixteen, huh? Fine, I'll bring a check."

Sixteen grand, Tom thought, sudsing his hair in the shower. A rock star tariff? He shook his head, can't be helped. Joe won't be happy, though. He shrugged and rinsed.

After a quick bite served up by Mary, he stepped outside to wait in the driveway circle for the taxi. Montrose wasn't too far from the house, so no need to pop for a limo.

The yellow cab arrived, and Tom tossed himself through the doorway sprawling on the seat in the back. Straightening his legs in front of himself, he called to the driver "Murray's Classic Cars in Montrose."

The cabbie flipped his flag down and shifted into drive. As they pulled out of the driveway, he said, "Disco? New Wave?"

Confused at first, Tom answered, "No, give me that old time rock and roll."

The driver grunted, turning right onto Pearce Street. After a mile, he came to the parkway exit and headed south. He maneuvered off onto Montrose Avenue, drove another two miles, and stopped at the curb in front of Murray's.

Tom hopped out, a ten-spot ready in his hand. "Thanks, pal, keep it," he said not looking back as he marched toward the show room stopping halfway there in front of the sparkling, shiny-gray Nova.

"Damn," he breathed.

"Beautiful, huh?" Mel said, gently slapping him on the back. Tom turned to him, a round man half a foot shorter, grinning up. Maybe five years younger, Mel looked older, probably from his girth and hair loss, highlighted by a few coal-black strands crossing his bare pate. His broad, open smile saved him though, beaming genuine warmth and anticipation. Tom really liked the guy.

"It is beautiful," he said, looking Mel in the eyes. "You outdid yourself, buddy."

Mel almost melted in pleasure. "Thanks, Tom, that means the world to me." He reddened a little, then pushed out a hand, "The keys—go have yourself a ball."

"Thanks, Mel, and here's the check, well deserved," Tom said, handing it over.

"Aw," mumbled Mel, now blushing. "Go on, now, get outta here," waving his hand, fingers flicking.

"Yup," said Tom, stepping over to the sedan. He opened the door and slid in behind the wheel, larger than he remembered. Everything else looked the same—semi-shiny vinyl, matching blue plastic foot mats, seat belt for waists only. And the smell, old world new car smell. Tom recalled reading how car manufacturers actually sprayed the scent into the car to reassure new owners of its newness. He didn't care, to him it smelled just right. His new first car again after all these years.

He slipped the key into the ignition slot, turning it over as he deftly pressed the gas pedal. It came to life richly, better than the Monte Carlo SS parked in his garage. Though he did love that car, too. He pulled the lever down to "D" and turned the Nova toward the entrance, thinking back to his first ride out of the Chevy dealership, carefully looking right, left, right then easing out onto the vacant street. He drove carefully all the way home to his dad's apartment, twice as long as it usually took.

Smiling while remembering, he started the turn from Murray's onto Montrose, spontaneously leaning to reach the knob on the standard AM radio.

Wham!

Tom lurched hard back into the door, rebounding off the steering wheel back against the seat.

What the fuck?

He shook his head, felt around his arms and legs, then sat still.

Fuck!

The guy he hit showed up at his passenger side window, staring in like someone at the zoo. Big like a pro wrestler, he wore a wrinkled tan raincoat and dark trousers over heavy black brogans. His face reminded Tom of beefeaters he'd seen in England. Between the lapels of his coat, his maroon tie rested to one side of a wrinkled white dress shirt, the top button open. A traveling salesman? Tom wondered idly.

To add to his shame, Mel showed up fully sympathetic regarding his treasured customer's colossal world-class fuckup. When Mel suggested calling for a tow truck, Tom cut him short asking him if he had a crowbar.

Without a word, the big guy walked back to his pickup and returned with an industrial-size crowbar. In a matter of seconds, he wedged the crowbar between the two vehicles' conjoined fenders, popping them apart with a screech. "Excellent," he said, walking back to his truck. He returned with a huge set of pliers and quickly bent Tom's waffled fender clear of the wheel. "There, that's done," he said. Fender free, lucky me, Tom whispered beneath his breath.

He thanked the guy profusely, telling him that Mel would take care of his truck, no problem. Mel nodded head up and down almost enthusiastically as he handed him his card. The big fellow grinned, tapped the card against his forehead, climbed in his truck and left.

Tom waited until Mel disappeared into the building, then stepped to the front of the car and smacked his temples with his hands hard enough for both to rebound. Motherfucker! he shouted silently.

Outside of a slightly bruised shoulder, his only pain came from his crushed ego. On his way to meet with Norah, he felt himself spiraling lower and lower replaying the disaster in his head.

Shit, Tom muttered again. What did Jack Nicholson say in *The Shining*? A momentary loss of muscular something . . . per second per second? Now he was comparing himself to an axe murderer. Mother Mary of God.

And Mel pushing him to leave the Nova after waiting all this time. The poor car looked like shit, now, but the big guy did a good job with the fender. He could drive it until the new fender came in. Next Wednesday, Mel said. There are a lot of old Novas out there, he said, though matching the color might be a challenge. Then he goes again.

"You sure you want to drive it now?"

"Yeah. I've waited this long for it." Mel didn't need to know how many years he'd tooled around in his first Nova with a fender crumpled the same way from another mishap.

"Oh. Okay, then, I'll talk to you later." Mel pivoted toward the showroom, humming, "Take it easy."

Fourteen

Norah stepped out on the front porch of Marbury House and saw the gray Nova parked at the curb. She squinted to see if it was Tom sitting at the wheel when the driver's-side door opened. He emerged as if riding a wave.

"Nice car," she called out.

He nodded his head, wearing something of a forced smile. She trotted down the steps as he walked around to open the front passenger door. She flashed him a smile and slid in on the bench seat. She waited then for him to walk around and slide in beside her.

"So, vintage?"

"Yeah."

"What, a GTO or something?"

"Nope. 1975 Chevy Nova."

"Really? Souped up model?

"Un-un. Nothing fancy, just a straight six."

"Oh." Norah paused, then said, "Kind of a plain gray wrapper, isn't it?"

He glanced at her. "It had its moments," his eyes back on the road. "My very first car. Brand new at four grand."

"That so?" She looked down, rubbing the middle of the bench seat. "So," she said, in an exaggerated throaty voice, "what exactly did you do in it?"

"As much as I could get away with."

They both laughed, and she noticed him seeming to relax.

He flashed clenched teeth like Bogie in a gangster film.

"I fucked up. Smacked the shit out of a front fender pulling out of the dealership."

"What, back then?"

"No," he shook his head back and forth, "Just now before I came to pick you up."

"Really? I didn't see anything bad."

"It's on my side, away from you on the curb. It's bent to shit. The guy I hit pulled the fender loose from his pickup with a crowbar. Big as a bear he was. Nice enough dude, though."

She stared at him going over it again as he drove downtown completely distracted.

"Well," she said, "Put it out of your mind. It's done and you can get it fixed, right?"

"Sure. It's only money." He mumbled, "And time."

Norah sat back. She gazed straight ahead at the empty thoroughfare, wondering if he'd be brooding throughout lunch and the drive back.

"Listen," he said, "I'll be done with my self-scorning self-pity in a minute. You'll soon see the irrepressible, charming, bon vivant me again beloved by a multitude of people everywhere. Maybe even double figures."

She barked a laugh as they pulled up to Enrico's Italian Deli.

Inside, they split a Caesar salad and a small pizza with anchovies, delighted by a delectable amount of alicis sardines on top.

"This is great," he said, "a real game-changer."

"I know! I come here for lunch almost every day. Lots of times carryout for dinner."

"Whoa, that does sound like excellent double-dipping. And you know, if we both get the anchovies, we don't have to worry about a goodnight kiss."

She straightened up, "Cool your jets there, buddy boy. Just because you got over on me one time doesn't mean you're guaranteed a goodnight kiss."

He didn't remember it that way but quickly replied, "Right, which is why I'm playing the delicious fish card."

They both laughed and he waved his hand for the check.

Back at the house, Tom quickly hopped out and hurried around the car to open her door.

"How gallant!" Norah said, holding her fingertips gently on her chest.

"Not really," he said as she stepped out. "Just don't want you to see the damage."

"Oh. That bad, huh?"

"To my image," he nodded. They stood together quietly for a moment until he said, "If a goodnight kiss is off the table, how about a midday peck?"

She smiled, her eyes shining. "Suppose you come inside and say hello to some of the kids?"

"Really?" he said.

"Yeah. They're off today, teachers conference." She grabbed his hand. "C'mon, it'll be fun. Really."

"Okay," he said, still skeptical.

They entered the front hallway to a raucous din coming from the dining room. Norah led the way to a dozen children inside yelling and shouting over the remains of lunch. Some pushed each other back and forth, others sprayed fragments of food while talking. A few younger ones just gazed around wide-eyed. Boys outnumbered girls three to one. The kids ranged in age from five to thirteen, Tom guessed, though he was lousy he was at guessing. All of them ran the wonderous spectrum of brown complexions.

"Always happy at mealtime," Norah said, "even if just PB and J."

"No complaints, huh?"

She lowered her head sideways, "Eh, a few bitch about wanting Wonder bread." She turned to Tom, "Our chief cook and bottlewasher Louise won't have it— 'No white bread in my kitchen,' she says. I think she just means the bread."

He smiled watching the kids play with their crusts.

A little boy left his chair and started to circle the room, guiding himself with one hand lightly touching the chair rail. He traveled around close to Norah and Tom, squeezing behind them to maintain contact with the railing.

Tom craned to see him reach the door to the hallway. The boy raised his hand from the guard into the shape of an airplane climbing up through the air in the doorway. Reaching the other side, he glided his hand back down onto the railing to continue his tour.

When he reached the far corner past the table again, Tom murmured to Norah, "What's he doing?"

"I don't know," she whispered. She called out then. "Devon, what are you doing?"

"I'm just tracing circles around the room," he said, continuing to the next wall.

"Oh." She looked at Tom with a shrug.

"Huh," Tom mumbled. He watched the boy, Devon. Five? Six? Who knew? He was beautiful, with such a calm way about him, like a classic statue. What was the name of Venus's companion?

"Cupid," he uttered.

"Eros," Norah said. "The Greeks were first. The Romans renamed him Cupid, another nasty takeover." Gazing at Devon while he played, she murmured "Curly brown hair and copper complexion, I can see it, a modern little god flawless in the flesh."

Tom glanced at her. Greek? Rome? What else did she know out of the ordinary?

Just then Buddy walked in. As soon as the kids saw him, they yelled and charged, the first to arrive tackling him, one wrapped around each leg, sliding down to sit on his feet.

"Great," he said, "more avoirdupois."

He tried moving forward, looking like a truck mired in mud. "C'mon, you little savages, stand on your own four feet."

They persisted, and he started to peel one off at a time, leaving space for the next in line.

"All right, all right, go ahead, wait some more for dessert."

With that, they all abandoned his limbs and sat back on the floor.

"But first," said Buddy, "Ten to twelve-year olds, clear the dishes. Seven to nine, trash duty. Six and under, go pound sand. No, I mean go get your schoolbooks for homework time."

The children dispersed like dust devils crossing a desert.

"That's that," Buddy said. He glanced over to Norah and Tom. "Oh, hi. Nice seeing you again." He put out his hand, enveloping Tom's.

"Yes, yeah. Quite a show."

"Well, teacher conference days are big around here. Must keep the little darlings busy at all cost."

Tom gestured with his hand, "So, what's the story on the little kid doing laps?"

Buddy's expression tightened. "He arrived here a few days ago, ward of the state. His mother's a junkie, his father, a pimp who also deals, in the wind. The New York DHS picked Devon up after a neighbor's complaint. Apparently, his mom was stoned and bloody on the kitchen floor when they arrived. She said she'd fallen against the corner of the kitchen table, which has no corners. The table's round."

"Huh," Tom said. "So, is the poor kid screwed up?"

Buddy shook his head, "Doesn't seem so. He's very bright, a sweet kid."

"Yeah," said Tom, "he seems to be."

Tom cruised up Northern Boulevard in his '86 Monte Carlo SS, the engine's purr both comforting and frustrating. Comforting from the confident power the big engine exuded. Frustrating because the '75 Nova was back at Murray's Black Hole of Calcutta repair shop, its body repair men once again trying to match the fender's silver paint job. Only God knew when he'd get it back. You think they'd have a half-filled can of paint left over, he huffed to himself. Meantime, he was burning a hole in his pocket driving the gas-lapping super sport dragon. He just hated wasting money, he sighed, couldn't help it.

He passed the St. Herman Golf Club on his way to River Rock Road. Don was waiting for him in Steuben's Steak House to discuss the next move. Tom wasn't looking forward to the meeting or any next move.

They sat in a worn wooden booth, its high sides obstructing the view of the bar adjacent to a small bandstand on the right. Tom noted the faint waft of stale beer in the air and the crud embedded in the floor for all eternity.

"So, I was thinking," Don said, "it might be time to take the act out on the road."

"Really?"

"We aren't ever going to know until we get in front of a crowd." Don said. He paused a beat, then continued, "I talked to Bobby Dubois about playing a set or two." Seeing Tom's alarm, he said, "No publicity, just a pop-up. Said we would do it for lambchop dinners."

"Here, at Steuben's Steakhouse. In Syosset."

Don nodded, "A small venue for a tryout."

Tom vigorously shook his head, "No. Too close to home. No way am I going to take a chance of bombing in my own backyard. Remember the old saying, don't shit where you sleep."

"Unless you shit the bed," said Don. "We're dying, here, Tommy. If we don't get going soon, we will never get going."

Tom turned his mouth up in a forced smile. "Yeah, yeah, I know. I just don't know, though. You know?"

Don pushed back from the table. "It's simple. Do you want to do this or do you not?"

Tom let loose a long sigh. "I don't know. Honestly."

"Well, fuck." Don slid out of the booth and stood up. "Give me a shout when you know."

He turned to leave, and Tom said, "Wait a minute. Wait."

Don stopped.

"You think we're ready for this?"

Looking exasperated, Don said, "When do you think we'll be ready?"

"God, I don't know. I don't feel ready."

His lean wheelman sighed, "You're more ready than you were a month ago." We're heading into October."

"Yeah, well," Tom said, looking both contrite and resentful, "that's a far fucking cry from 'showtime,' ready," he said, framing his face with hands outspread.

"You could say that about your whole fucking career."

"Oh, very funny, wise guy."

"All right, all right, I'm sorry," Don said quickly, "it's just—you seem distracted . . . at practice. Not fully into it. We're heading into October."

"Oh." Tom hesitated, "Well, I'm sorry. Nerves, I guess."

"Sure," Don nodded, "We all get the yips. When we get up in front and start swinging it, good or bad, they go away."

"Not the bad," Tom mumbled. He gnawed his upper lip, thinking. "All right, I'm not saying we should fold altogether. Let's get through a few more rehearsals. At the same time, we'll look for a venue further out in the boonies. Reduce the risk of total flameout."

Don rolled his eyes to the ceiling. "You know, you're a fount of positivity."

"Yeah well, that's the way I roll. Anyway, you're no jolly Santa yourself."

"Don't I know it," Don said, sitting back down. "But please don't get distracted from the job at hand." Tom said nothing. "We'll aim for November, before Turkey Day. People visiting the old homestead might want to visit some old band. Yes?"

Tom lifted his shoulders, then let them drop.

"Okay, let's talk joints we could play."

Fifteen

After leaving Don at Steuben's to let Bobby down easy, Tom opened up the Monte Carlo on the boulevard, making it back home in record time. He pulled up fast in front of the house, stopping short of the closest of the three. He hit the remote to the automatic door, which ratcheted up at glacial speed. He estimated enough headroom above to guide the car inside. He eased in slowly, remembering the time after a night's liquid exploits entering too fast too soon, gouging the hell out of a vintage Bronco's top. He had Murray's fix it, then immediately traded it in plus another ten grand for the. The garage door Remembering the fiasco, he'd learned his lesson, at least this time.

He jumped out and zipped past Felix on the opposite side toying with riding tractor. Tom headed to the side door leading into the kitchen where Mary stood making something scrumptious for his lunch. Cold, of course, since she never knew when or even if he would be home at any regular human being's time.

Tom saw appetizing ingredients next to her on the counter, including fresh brown bread and some other healthy yet inviting condiments. He spotted chips, too, which made him happy, though he knew they also were low fat and saltless. Still, they tasted better than other healthy alternatives, like the great fake chocolate conspirator carob. It looked like yummy dark chocolate and tasted like shit. Yet, the health food nuts raved about it. Some people just had no taste, he concluded.

He started toward the counter and stopped. Over on the other side of the butcher block island sat Christine. Perched on a stool, she leaned both elbows on the wooden top, cradling a large mug of tea between her hands. Steam curled up from the rim, passing by her eyes gazing at him, dissipating in the overhead light above.

"Well, hello," she said.

"Yeah," Tom said. "Hello to you."

Silence reigned for a moment, broken by Mary's accelerated vegetable chopping.

Tom shifted his weight to lean against the counter. "I'm surprised to see you," he said. "You got some more art to show me?"

"No," she said, smiling broadly. "Just finishing the punch list for your new works. Also, to see if you wanted to go out to dinner."

He blinked. "I haven't had lunch yet."

Christine nodded, "I know. I just thought we might catch up."

"Oh."

"Yes. It's been a while."

"Right." He moved again. "But you know, I've been busy. Practicing and rehearsing. Doing other things," he trailed off.

"I understand." She lifted and dropped her shoulders, "Maybe you could take a break. You look tired."

"I always look tired." He paused. "It's my calling card these days."

"Sure," she said. "I get it."

"Yeah," he replied. "Listen, I've got to go, business stuff. But help yourself around the place."

"I always do," she said, smiling.

He turned on his heel and headed to his music room. He passed by the piano and drum set to a double-door closet. Leaning over a pile of boxes, he angled past the empty clothes bar to a back corner of the top shelf. Grunting, he poked around until he felt his fingers fold into the sound hole. Hooking the edge, he gingerly extracted an old acoustic guitar. Careful to clear it from other things stuffed in the closet, he out with the guitar and held it up for inspection.

All the parts seemed to be intact. He walked over to his writing desk and sat down. He gripped the stock and strummed once.

The noise made him cringe. Terribly out of tune. He quickly started strumming while plying the tuning pegs. Slowly, the guitar started to strike some sort of semblance to proper sound. He recognized the instrument's inherent limitations, clearly not a Martin or any make like one. He shrugged, good enough for busking.

He slipped the strap over his shoulder and quietly steered away from the kitchen to another side door. Once outside, he hot footed over to the garage and carefully propped the guitar in the back on the floor against the shotgun seat. He slipped in behind the wheel and plied the remote raising the door as he turned over the engine. With the door halfway up, he took his chances and gunned the Monte Carlo out of the garage down the driveway.

He arrived at Marbury House in just 20 minutes, noting that he would need gas to get back to the house. He popped out of the car, guitar in hand, and hopped up the front steps to the door. He rang the bell, clutching the guitar by its neck at his knee. The front door opened, followed by the screen door swinging outward, causing Tom to take a step back.

Buddy leaned out holding the door ajar. "Why, Mr. Weatherly, what a surprise."

"Tom," Tom said. "Please call me Tom."

"Of course. So, Tom, what brings you back to Marbury so soon?"

"Uh," he said, "I, uh—I brought my guitar."

"Oh," Buddy drawled, "Yes, I see that." He paused, then said, "Come in, come in, please."

Tom grinned gracelessly as he passed Buddy into the vestibule. He heard sounds from the sitting room off to the right, small, high voices in mild exchanges.

"The kids' playtime after lunch."

"Sure, I remember, recess at St. Margaret's."

Buddy blinked. "That's right. Back in the sixties. Parochial school monitored by class squealers and brass-knuckled nuns."

"You remember, too."

"At night, in a cold sweat."

Tom tried to stifle a laugh as Buddy continued cheerfully, "Anyway, you got your six-string with you, why not lay down some hot licks for the shorties in the breakroom?"

"Right, sure." He lifted the guitar up higher, then paused. "Is Norah around?"

"Norah? She'll be here later, sharing the night shift with me."

"Oh."

Seeing Tom deflate slightly, Buddy said, "She'll probably stop by early to help with supper. She usually does." Buddy turned to leave, "Doesn't have much else to do."

Tom perked up. He watched Buddy run up the stairs, then headed into the sitting room.

Inside, he found the boys playing football with paper triangles, opponents sitting across an old wooden coffee table. One player flicked a triangle up in field goal attempts through goal posts formed by the fingers and thumbs of his opponent. Each flick triggered an argument, "You missed!" "You moved your fingers!" "Did not!" "Did so, I get a do-over." "Go ahead, you'll miss again. You suck at football." "I do not!" "Do so!" "Not!" "So!" "Not—So!"

Tension stretched thread-bare thin between them, wad flicking in shaky balance versus straight up butt-kicking. Tom noted that the other kids watching urged them to keep playing in a futile effort to save their turns. One of the players was bound to jump the other, no question. There could be blood while upsetting the onlookers. Too, the pre-teen girls would screech and scratch at the ruinous interruption of their midday soap on TV across the room. Tom concluded that consternation would break out unless a diversion defused the situation.

He quickly plopped down on an empty couch perpendicular to the two occupied camps and began to strum.

"How can I miss you when you won't go away?" he sang, stopping at once at the zombie looks staring at him all around. No vintage Dan Hicks for them.

He switched chords and tried again.

"Your cheatin' heart . . . will tell on you," he trailed off. Going the wrong way. Something closer to contemporary.

"What's love got to do with it, do with it? What's love but a second-hand emotion?"

The young boy ready to kick a do-over wad slowly raised his hand.

"S'cuse me, sir."

"Yes?" Tom answered quickly.

The kid's larger, classical features, light tan in color caused him to look like a teenage David at the beach. Except for his raised flattop, its ragged fade overdue for a trim he probably couldn't afford.

"Somethin' the fuck wrong with you?"

Tom pulled back, speechless.

"I mean no disrespect, but we're tryin' to play a game here."

"Uh-huh."

"And the young babes there, they tryin' to watch *General Hospital*."

"Who you callin' young babes, Jerome?" one girl said, her pixie features framed by a haze of orange-red, cotton-candy hued hair. "You ain't but twelve you self." She turned to Tom and said, "But he's right. They don't repeat what they say on this show. So please, don't mess it up for us."

She looked bright and lively, and he felt like an ass. "I'm sorry, I just thought you might want to hear a few tunes."

She shook her head, "We like hip-hop, sir. I don't believe you know one thing about that, am I right?"

She was right, he did not know about that.

"If you still want to sing, which is very nice by you—am I right?" she said to the other kids, who all nodded up and down saying yes and mumbling over each other in nice tones of words he couldn't get. "So, maybe you could play and sing for the other kids here, the little ones in the back room behind the stairway?"

"You're right. That'd be better," he said as evenly as he could, hoping his face wasn't red from the embarrassment flushing through him. "I think I'll just head on over to the young kids."

"Thank you so much, sir, for understanding."

He nodded and waved, leaving silently, still wondering if they could see the tail stuck between his legs.

At first, he thought he'd pivot right out the front door. Guilt stopped him, dragging him instead inside the doorway opposite the stairs. He trudged over to a back door into another lounge where just a half dozen little kids lounged. A couple played Uno while one watched, waiting for his turn. Two others paged slowly through a beat-up Little Golden Book about Robin Hood. Devon sat on a beat-up easy chair, surveying the other kids. When Tom cleared his throat, all turned eyes upon him. He stepped over to the couch opposite and sat down, the guitar balanced on his legs.

"Hi, kids. Want to sing some songs?"

The music session was quite a success. After moving sleepy Devon to a good seat, Tom started them off with "Ninety-nine Bottles of Beer on the Wall"—subbing in "*Coke*" for "beer," to keep the Policia at bay. He figured, too, that the kids would think of the sugar-spiked soft drink rather than the magic white powder. He learned to stay away from both addictions, though the fizzy brown stuff was hard to quit. Guinness also was a fine feed in a bottle, especially when enhanced by carbonation. Which brought him full circle back to the beers on the wall.

He closed his session with Edwin Starr's classic, coaching the kids to sing the chorus together, followed by his refrain.

"War! Huh!" shouted the kids full-throated.

"Yeah!" Tom countered.

"What is it good for?"

"Absolutely–" pointing to the kids.

"Nothin!" they brayed.

"Say it again y'all!"

"War! Huh! What it is good for?"

 "Yeah!"

The tiny voices screeched, "Nothin!"

"Uh huh!" bellowed Tom, urging them to sing it again. They howled the refrain, cueing Tom to fly into Starr's rousing rap until Buddy filled the doorway with his door-filling form.

Tom slowed down to a mild peep.

"Wow," said Buddy evenly, "that's a marvelous rendition. So spirited."

"Uh," mumbled Tom, "uh, thank you?"

"Yes indeed. It's a shame you need to stop now so I can get the children their afternoon snacks. Then, homework time."

The kids outside in the hallway groaned, which brought Tom to realize that they'd been listening to him play and the little ones singing.

"Come boys and girls, ladies and monsters," Buddy said in a singsong rhythm of his own. "Time to refuel your wet little brains with Pringles and carrots. Another balanced snack from Mother Marbury."

He turned and ushered the youngsters out of the room with his hands spread. "Let's go little lightning bugs, come join the cicadas."

Peering past Buddy, Tom could see the young girl who had dressed him down and Jerome peeking in.

"You're crazy funny, man," said Jerome, "but you're pretty good layin' down licks."

"I ain't never heard them songs before," the girl said, "they got some life."

"Good beat, but you can't dance to them?" Tom said.

"Huh?"

"Never mind. Another allusion to my misspent youth."

She frowned and started to turn away.

He asked, "What's your name?"

She half-turned back, her hand on her hip. "Shirylee."

"Nice to meet you Shirylee. You, too, Jerome," he said, giving him a nod. "Next time I come around, why don't you join me. I have a few other tunes you might like even better."

They left without saying anything. But they didn't say no, either.

Tom sat down on the couch feeling pretty good about the whole shebang. While tuning up his guitar for another singsong, he heard a slight rustle. He glanced up to see Devon in the doorway.

"Hey, Devon, finish your snack so fast?"

Without answering, Devon walked over to Tom and presented his right foot, shoelace loose. A closer look revealed that the left foot lace was equally at large.

Tom leaned over for a closer inspection, saying quietly, "You want me to fix them?" Devon nodded. Tom straightened up and said, "Looks like you're stuck in a shoe-lace situation. Let me see what I can do."

Bent over tightening the laces on the first little shoe, Tom noticed the tongue sloping down one side. He tried to pull it up, recalling how much the feeling of it stuck down in his toe annoyed him. Maybe little kids didn't feel it or didn't care, but maybe, too, they felt it and didn't like it, but didn't know where it came from or how to fix it. Tom wasn't going to take any chances; he jerked the tongue up while quickly tying the left lace. He reached over and tied the other lace.

"There," he said, "that's done."

Devon didn't say anything. Instead, he crawled up onto Tom's lap to cuddle, laying his head on his chest. Surprised, Tom didn't quite know what to do. The little boy felt good in his arms, warm, not moving. Content, easy to hold. Slowly, Tom moved his arms up to wrap around the little boy's back and shoulders. He realized then that Devon had fallen asleep.

Tom started to stress, thinking maybe he should wake the little fellow so he wouldn't miss his snack or homework, heaven forbid. Tom didn't think Devon was skipping so much schoolwork that he couldn't make it up. Still, he could be hungry. God knows the little boy had been hungry before in his short life. The sweet lad had plenty of time to make up for it, especially here, Tom decided—or maybe rationalized. Maybe he should rouse the cute little mouse in his lap. But the kid felt so good and warm close, snoozing softly. There were worse things in life, Tom thought. Waking could wait.

Sixteen

For the first time in years, almost since her marriage had ended, Norah enjoyed being this close to a man. Embarrassing as it was for her—or him? And him. Unbelievable how good it felt, though.

Tom was a child, she realized, living in *Aladdin*'s world. Of his very own making, too, she admitted, rich by singing pop tunes, not gouging consumers or waging war. From modest means, so he said.

"Of all my parents' kids, sister and included," he crowed, preening with a sweep of his hair, "I'm the only one who was an only child."

She laughed again. He could be such a dufus—on purpose she hoped.

"Is cinnamon a homonym for synonym?" he asked innocently. "Or is it visa-versa?"

Norah exploded a burst of laughter. How could he say something so astonishingly stupid yet at the same time amazing?

"Cognitive reappraisal," he replied. "Noticing, then restructuring your thoughts as a homonym for an antonym." He must have seen her puzzled look. "You know, like in the movie *Auntie Mame*. She's poor, so she decides to determine that she's rich, and starts spending and buying as though she can afford it, which she cannot, of course."

"Auntie Mame? Who's that? What's that? How the hell do you remember such stuff? And why?"

He grimaced, "I read it in *Psychology* in an MDs waiting room. I can't remember everything, I don't have an eidetic memory, just an idiotic one."

"Oh really?"

"Yeah. Putting it plainly, some people call me an idiot savant, but really, I'm just an idiot."

No," she dragged out. "You're definitely idiotic some of the time."

She laughed then despite herself. "I don't think people call them that anymore. Savants maybe."

"Oh. So that leaves me out altogether. Well, that's just swell, then, isn't it."

Replaying it in her mind as she drove, she wondered if he even understood who he was quoting or what he was saying. He was like a sweet little boy. Endearing, not a big deal self-satisfied rockstar no matter how hard he tried.

"I reached success at a high level of mediocrity," he liked to say. "If I'd known I'd be locked into one thing, I'd say, 'no thanks,' and wait instead." He nodded, then frowned. "I could be fooling myself. Maybe I never had it to go any higher than the middling ground. I should be thankful for what I have maybe."

"Oh, I don't know. C'mon now, you were great. 'Malachite Eyes' was a great pop love song."

He eyed her skeptically, "What, you saw it on a 'Remember the '80s' show?"

"No! Hey, I'm not that young. I've clocked plenty of mileage my own self."

"Hah."

"Anyway, you must've been a teen heartthrob in those days."

"In those days I wanted to be Peter Frampton. He could really lay down some sweet licks."

She frowned, "Uh huh, but he was hard to dance to. Too many slow solos."

"Really?"

She shook her head up and down, reliving a memory pained. "After 20 minutes of 'Do You Feel Like We Do,' we'd all be moving back and forth like zombies. Eventually we'd signal to each other, time to take a break."

"Huh."

"Now, 'Malachite Eyes,' that's a great slow dance groove."

"If you say so."

"I do say so."

"And what of my other tunes did you like?"

She sat back.

"Right," he said. He stretched his arms up high, then folded them over his shoulders holding his neck. "No matter. 'Malachite Eyes' made me rich. I guess that's something."

"Maybe," Norah said. She saw him looking at her for an explanation. "You know, privileged and all."

"Privileged?"

She nodded, looking down at her hands. "Yes, the morals of privilege. The rich can afford privilege. The rich have access to privilege. The poor do not. The privileged resent those who don't have privilege for laying a guilt trip on them. Yet they shrug off their privilege fellowship with those others who do."

"Is that so?"

"Yes, for the most part."

"I never looked at it that way. It wasn't as though I was ungrateful, especially to my wicked-sma't financial brother. He's the wiz that made me not just rich, but filthy rich."

He suddenly went silent.

She waited, then couldn't help herself.

"Okay. Do you ever feel guilty about it?"

He turned his head to her. "Not much. Uncomfortable. I like my big freaking house, my nifty wheels, the clothes, all that. Mary taking care of me, even Felix jerking me around." She looked puzzled, so he said, "Mary's my cook and housekeeper and Felix takes care of the grounds and the cars. Except he doesn't whenever he can get away with it. Anyway, they're both great, but sometimes I feel I'm out of place there—shit, most of the time. I don't even sleep in the main bedroom. I prefer a guest room or a couch in the rec room near the fireplace and the big screen. I might as well be on the road in a hotel, you know?"

Norah seemed to gaze solicitously.

"Okay, enough about me, let's talk about you. So, what do you think of me?"

She giggled, still unsure that he was not particularly deep. "I heard that before. Bette Midler in *Beaches*."

"Okay, you got me," he said. "So, what about you? Gimme the lowdown."

"I've already told you my life story. My shitty marriage, how I ended up here, what I do to pay the rent."

"All right then," Tom said, "now me. Did you know I used to smoke Silva Thins? Back in those days stylin' was everything."

She of course laughed again.

Norah admitted to herself seeing him mostly as shallow at first. Colorless small talk could be understandable as a useful defense mechanism for self-centered rockstars, whether they were smart or not. Then he started talking in depth about obscure subjects she never expected.

"You know, I got into the Good Old Boys Club after first admitting I never did a hard thing in my life."

"Really?" She said, failing to hide her lack of surprise.

"Oh yeah. I've had it pretty good most of the time. There're a hell of a lot of people out there putting out amazing music I could never do. Yet, they're all damn near starving, working crappy jobs hand to mouth."

Norah tilted her head back, "So, did you try to get them noticed?"

He scrunched up his mouth up as though in pain. "I was too busy hustling myself. You know, even when you hit it, you're always scared somebody's gonna take it away." He leaned back, "By the time it occurred to me to help a brother out, I was passé." Eyeing her cooly, he went on, "Hence, the. Do something good for others for once."

"Yeah. I get it," she said. "Never too late. Good on you."

"Right. We good old boys, we band of brothers, brothers in bands . . .." he trailed off.

She shook her head, so weird, she thought. Why did she spend the time? Except he was strangely engaging and pretty good in bed, which hadn't happened again after that first crazy night. Another idiosyncrasy, he hadn't come on to her since. It had to because of her landlady.

Early that first morning, they came down the back stairs into the kitchen surprised to find Mrs. Landry scrambling eggs. Mrs. L turned to the noise they made and froze.

"Oh," she exclaimed softly. "You have company."

"Yeah," Norah said. "This is my friend Tom." She gestured to him standing above a step up. "He stopped by to give me a ride to work."

Mrs. Landry looked at him, saying nothing.

"Tom, this is Mrs. L—Mrs. Landry, my landlady."

"Hello, Mrs. Landry, very nice to meet you."

After another minute of silence, Norah said, "You might recognize him from MTV. He's a popular musician."

Mrs. Landry shook her head, "I don't watch that program."

"Oh, well it's short for Music TV," said Norah.

"Uh huh. So do you play an instrument Mr.—?"

"Collins."

"Collins. Like the drink."

Norah watched him wince almost imperceptibly, surely not noticed by Mrs. L. But he did, definitely.

"I do play an instrument."

"I see. What, the piano? Violin? Trumpet."

"No, I play guitar and sing."

"Is that so? Like in a Mariachi band?"

"No, more R and B—rhythm and blues."

"Oh, I see," she said. "Well, that's nice." She turned back to her stove. "Can I interest you in scrambled eggs and some toast?"

"No, no please," Norah said, holding up her hand.

"There's plenty to go around. Coffee, too."

Norah grabbed Tom's arm and started for the back door.

"Thanks, Mrs. L, but we were just on our way out. Tom's going to drop me off at work."

"Can't work on an empty stomach."

"That's true, but they'll have something at Marbury I can munch. A bagel or something. I'll be fine."

"You sure that's enough? I also have orange juice."

"No, no, thanks. I'll see you later tonight."

Inside his car, Tom said, "Man, that was awkward."

"Yeah, she's really nice. But you didn't want to stay, did you?"

He looked at her sideways, "Uh, not really." He turned his head to the highway while saying, "To think, you told me I could sleep in as long as I wanted. Imagine me walking in on your landlady alone in my skivvies."

"Oops," she said. "That would've been—"

"Awkward. Like I said." He glanced at her again, then back on the road.

"Oh, don't worry about it, she's cool." Seeing him skeptical, she quickly followed up, "Really."

No matter. The limo took them to Marbury where Tom walked her to the front door, where he looked like he would leave it. Nothing more, not even a polite peck on the cheek, which drove her up the wall. She ended up kissing him. This after he made a big deal asking her when he would see her again. So different, so charming, especially given the night before when he acted so cocksure. She started laughing, realizing her unintentional double entendre.

She decided then to find a new place. Whether he came around again or not, she needed the freedom to do whatever without adult supervision.

Days later Norah arrived at Marbury in the afternoon near the end of snack time. She felt worn out from looking for an affordable apartment. So far, no luck.

The kids were already at the dining room table, munching their Fritos while filling the air with a din of high-pitched, noisy conversation. After a quick peek, she wheeled about toward the front room searching for Tom. No one there. She went through the other rooms until she reached the back playroom and peered inside.

Tom lifted head up to see her. Devon was asleep on his lap, his head resting in Tom's lap.

"Where you been?" he whispered to her.

"Oh, you know. Around," she whispered back. A fat fib, she thought, though she wondered why. Better to tell him she was looking for new digs?

Despite their quiet exchange, Devon woke up yawning. He glanced over at Norah and peeped "Unh," and climbed down from Tom's lap.

"Norah," he moaned, hurrying over to hug her legs.

"What are you doing, Sleepyhead?" she asked softly, resting her hands on his shoulders. "Did you miss snacks with the other kids?"

He gazed up at her, nodding solemnly.

"Well, okay, we can go get you something in the kitchen."

As Norah turned to go to the kitchen, Devon stopped. Looking back, she saw him holding out one foot pointed at her.

Norah said, "But first we need to tie your shoelaces. Here, sit on the couch."

"Man, I just tied them," Tom said.

"Yeah, well," Norah said. Norah jerked the shoe tongue up and quickly double knotted its laces, thinking again for the nth time the kid needed to learn how to tie his shoes.

"There. Now you look like something, Mr. Falvey."

Devon smiled and pushed his other shoe up into her lap. "Oh. This one, too."

While she tied it, she called back to Tom still sitting on the couch behind her.

"I see you brought your guitar with you today."

Tom nodded. "Yeah, I figured I needed something to do. You know, get their attention and all."

"Sure," she said. "How'd it go?"

"Well, a hard sell at first," Tom replied, "until I switched playlists."

"Really?"

He nodded again, "Yeah, for little kids. The big ones kicked me out. The squirts liked the change—we did a little sing-along—until Buddy came to round them up for snack time."

"Oh. Nice," she said standing up. "You're all set, Devon. C'mon, I'll bet you're hungry. Let's see what we can find in the kitchen.'"

Norah turned to Tom. "You hungry?"

Tom shook his head, "Nah, I came from a late breakfast with Don."

"Don?"

"Bass. You remember, also our band manager. I'll introduce you sometime. Maybe at a gig we're planning."

"Oh, yeah? I thought you shelved all that in favor of sing-alongs with the Marbury House Chorale."

Tom smiled tightly. "That may pan out later. Right now, we're preparing to go out on tour again. You know, a mix of oldies and new tunes."

"Oh," she said, "Well, we'll miss you."

"You will?" Tom said.

"Sure. Who'll lead our repertory company?"

"Oh."

She saw his disappointment, which produced a knee-jerk reply. "I'll miss you. I've enjoyed our outings."

"Oh, all right, then. That's great!" he beamed. "And the band's not going anywhere anytime soon. Lot of work to be done before that happens."

Devon pulled at her pants leg.

"Okay, pardner, let's find you some grub." She flashed a smile at Tom as she turned and led Devon to the kitchen.

At the same time, Buddy ushered the other kids, both big and little, single file into the sitting room.

"These unruly charges," he said sonorously, "demand an encore before they dive into their homework."

"Really?" said Tom, astonished.

"Absolutely really," Buddy said. "They have exactly ten minutes before I wall them all in their study nooks."

The youngsters cried a cacophony of "no's" and "not fair."

"Well, okay." Tom turned to the mob of kids, big and little. "So, any requests?"

They all roared at once indecipherably.

Tom exaggerated a cringe, and said, "All right, all right, now, everyone wait. Wait." They all went quiet, and he said, "Repeat after me."

He strummed a note, then moaned, "Un-nahuh."

The kids remained silent.

"C'mon, now. 'Un-nahuh.'"

Some of the older kids led by Shirylee and Jerome tried it softly.

"Unnahuh."

"Louder—un-nahuh."

"Unahuh!"

"Huh!"

"Huh!"

"Huh!"

"Huh!"

"Tell me what I say!" he sang loudly, strumming his guitar fiercely, "Tell me what I say, now!" nodding at the kids.

Norah stood out of sight in the hall near the door, listening to him belt out Ray Charles like he was born to it, bringing the kids to life. The uproar overflowed through the entire house out into the street no doubt—anyone hearing him couldn't resist, she was sure of it. And he brought the Marbury kids along for the ride.

She slowly turned her head back and forth. He definitely was a rock star for sure, no cognitive reappraisal or whatever the hell going on here. Maybe more of an old-time rock n' roller. In hiding? If so, she wondered why. She wondered what else he was, too.

Seventeen

"So, what's the name of the band?"

They had just arrived at noon for their morning practice session, Billy sitting behind his kit when he posed the question.

Don stared at him. "What do you mean 'what's the name of the band?' The Weatherly Experience, like it's always been."

Billy said, "We should rename it. Something new to show it's new, we're breaking out a new sound."

"The old sound worked pretty well," said George. "Name recognition matters, too."

"Not if it's old. Mention some names and people think they're past it, old timey. Shit, some think most old rockers are all dead."

Tom and Don exchanged glances.

"All right," said Don, "What do you have in mind?"

"I dunno, I'm just the drummer. Something cool."

"Cool. Like what?"

"How 'bout Sound at the Speed of Light?" said George.

"Or Speed at the Sound of Light," said Billy.

"Light at the Speed of Sound," added Frank.

Tom's head lolled as Don barked, "No Speed, no Light, no Sound. You guys all have one track minds."

"I have a no-track mind," said Billy. "I've lost my long-term memory and my short memory's shot. It's all good."

"What's left?" said Don.

"I live for the moment."

"Yeah, well then, you can forget about changing the band's fucking name."

"At least for now," Tom offered.

They remained silent for a moment. Then Billy said, "Chaos Theory. How about that? Or The Chi-Light Zone? Only spell it C-h-i-l-i-t-e." He paused for an instant, then said "How about the Bleitz Funeral Band?"

Don started moving toward Billy, and Tom gently blocked his way. "Let's just play."

After laboring through the first set, Don called timeout for a water break. As usual, Billy headed directly to the refrigerator and filled both his hands with bottles of beer. He circled the band setup, handing out bottles to Frank and George, then to Tom and Don in turn. Both declined, so Billy shrugged and sat on his stool. He bent over to prop two bottles between his hi hats and his snare foot pedal. Then he lifted the remaining bottle back over his head and drained it like water coursing down a dam.

"Jesus Christ!" uttered Don.

"Hey! I was thirsty!" Billy bellowed.

"That's fine, but you better keep up," Don snapped.

Billy sneered, "Just watch me."

The practice ran long, though Tom felt pretty good again, showing life so far in his play. Maybe because he was thinking about Norah, how sweet she was beneath her business-as-usual front. He relished that moment the last time they went out when he dropped her off at her place. When he turned to leave, she cried out, "Aren't you even going to give me a goodnight kiss?" Red faced and smiling, he wheeled around and bounded up the steps to put her in a bear hug. She stretched up to kiss him hard, holding him tight, not letting go. In that instant everything changed again.

She still seemed cool to him though, after their one night together. Happy going out, pleasant and fun but not amorous. Maybe she decided to step back after the landlady incident. It certainly threw him off. Or maybe she saw it as just one crazy encounter with an old rockstar past his shelf life. Funny how he felt the opposite, growing a crush on her for real.

Billy broke in again. "Babes invented love, you know, the same way men invented jerking off."

Everyone stopped. Head listing sideways, Frank spoke. "Jerking off was invented?"

"Oh yeah," answered Billy coolly, "by some teenage knuckle-dragging bad boy back in the day." Seeing the blank expressions, he continued, "You don't think it was a fucking broad, do you?"

Frank said, "Apes do it. Bonobos spank the salami all the time at the zoo, right in front of everybody. Kids, too."

"So actually, monkeys were the first wankers," George said.

"Monkeys do jerk off," Billy nodded, "which proves the point. It's always male monkeys pounding their puds, never females."

"Not at the zoo, anyway," added Frank.

"Right. That's because chicks can get laid anytime they want. But girls would rather moon over pics of Brad Pitt and Tom Cruise in *People* magazine than do the nasty. That's why we have to shovel all that lovey-dovey shit at them to get it on. But babes are amazing because they invented falling in love and they love it."

"Amazing," George said.

"So, what're we supposed to do?" George asked.

Billy mouthed half a smile. "Fake it. Tell 'em what they want to hear." He started humming, "Ooh, baby, when's it gonna get easier?"

"And if that's a no-go?" Frank asked.

Billy shrugged. "Do guy stuff, something you like they don't."

"Like pool, or poker," Frank said.

"Yeah. Baseball, hoops, pool, poker. You know. Men invented most all the games, anyway," Billy said.

"All the fun games," said Frank.

"Sure," Billy said, nodding up and down.

"And when they aren't fun anymore," Don said, "you guys can always pound your puds. A million times."

They stopped dead.

He followed up with, "Or practice as if a gig is coming up in two weeks." Let's pick it up: 'Don't Know Why.'"

Silence again. Frank finally spoke out. "Are you saying we'll be playing out in two weeks? You booked a show?"

"What I'm saying is our best bet is to play every practice like we're two weeks out. When we are, we'll be sure to let you know." No one said a word.

"Okay, then," Don said, "from the top, 'Don't Know Why.'"

When they finished, Don surprisingly nodded without comment. They immediately followed up with the "Don't Know Why" companion piece "She's Back Again, Again."

Don gestured his approval once more, astonishing Tom since he knew his solo riff sounded ragged. He wondered if Don was getting fed up with the youngsters' antics and just wanted to quit.

"All right, we're getting somewhere." He glanced Tom's way as he said, "Need to clean up that solo, Superstar."

Tom allowed a slight frown to appear as he pretended to tune his strings.

They called it a day, and the three side men left.

After making sure they were gone, Tom stopped at the fridge and pulled out two bottles of beer. He meandered over to hand one to Don and sat down.

They sipped silently for a few moments. Then Don muttered, "Our drummer operates on a wide-open spectrum of unconsciousness."

Tom peered over at him. "Think so?"

Don said sourly, "He leads a life of loud-mouth desperation."

Tom laughed. "Billy can get to you, all right."

"Yeah."

Tom leaned back. "Hey, you're not thinking we should let him go? I mean, he definitely takes time to get used to. He's not the best at kicking it," he shook his head, "but not the worst either."

"Not much good at hitting the money beat."

"Right, but good enough." He noted Don's telltale expression, dour as if he had just tasted something off. "For now, anyway," Tom continued. "I mean, we're supposed to play in just a few weeks. Who we gonna get by then?"

He waited for Don to respond, then said, "I hear Animal's available. He's tired of the same old Muppet playlist."

Don slowly grew a wicked smile. "We could check out Animal," he said, "I think you mean he's done with Muppet gags."

"Gigs, gags," Tom said, relieved. "Either Billy or Animal, who the fuck can tell the difference?"

Don laughed. "Okay, let's see what happens after the show."

"All right," Tom answered, smiling.

"So, where you off to?" Don asked.

"To pick up Norah," Tom said, "she wants to look for some new digs. She feels pretty cramped in the loft she's in now."

"Oh yeah?"

"Yeah. It's more of an attic than a room, tea for two."

"That does sound tight," Don said.

"Well, there's also the matter of privacy if the landlady rents the other side."

Don smiled slightly, "I can imagine."

"Don't," Tom said. "You should talk, you and your honey in separate, neighboring accommodations."

"Hey! She lives in the house next door; I live in the house next door. You should think about it." Seeing the look in Tom's eyes, Don quickly followed up. "Okay, off limits," he said, hands raised open.

"Good. So, Thursday?"

"You can't tomorrow?"

"No, I volunteered for the overnight shift. Give Amelia a break."

"Man, you are after that merit badge."

"Got to," Tom said. "When my folks let me join, they only bought me the cap. Said they'd get me the full Scout uniform if I lasted a year."

"Smart parents."

"Yeah. But I do wear the cap on federal holidays."

"Where, inside your house?"

Tom smiled, "In the bathroom. Locked."

Don laughed as Tom went out the door.

Eighteen

He pulled up in front of Marbury, always amazed that a space awaited him every time every day despite the neighborhood parking crunch. And every time, every day, he searched around for a No Parking sign, or even one dictating One Hour Parking 7:00 am—10:00 pm. But nothing, even across the street, view obstructed by low hanging maple leaves.

"Did you ever notice in Hollywood thrillers, when DeNiro or Cruise drive up to a big place like the Staple Center?" his brother Joe once said. "There's always an empty parking space right on the curb smack in front of the doors. They get out and walk right in, no problem. Like they never have trouble parking while in our lives, real life, we always park a good mile away. If we're lucky."

Tom shook his head. He knew that some meter maid would tag him for ten bucks sooner or later. The ten bucks didn't bother him. It was the waiting.

He entered the house and immediately found himself enveloped in a swarm of kids, young and younger, yelling at him to sing, to be funny. Backing up against the closed front door, he raised his hands trying to deflect gently the mini madding crowd. Laughing nervously to himself, he wondered if this was it.

Suddenly, a voice behind him said, "Death by diminishment."

Buddy stood behind the pressing mob, arms akimbo. "All right, enough, you little hooligans."

He proceeded to wedge his body into the middle, gently moving one child after another in his wake. "C'mon, big kids back to the dining room, little monsters into your activity room. Big kids, homework; little pests, line up for your Almond Joy drinks."

Tom laughed as each of them left the hallway. "You're a tough operator," he said.

"Yeah, thank heaven my reputation exceeds me."

Tom smiled.

"If you're here looking for Norah, she's out seeking new quarters."

Tom replied, "Yeah, I know she won't be here until late. I'm here to give Amelia a break. Buddy, I'm your roomie tonight!"

"Yes," Buddy nodded, murmuring, "how special."

Tom said, "Right. Anyway, what's the agenda?"

"Big kids, homework, followed by '*The Fresh Prince of Bel-Air*.' After that, '*In Living Color*,' sometimes '*The Cosby Show*.'"

"I get it. Do the little ones ever get a turn?"

Buddy shrugged. "Early morning shows, cartoons. I think they like '*Doug*' on public TV. Mostly, though, they just talk to each other at the top of their voices. I usually wear earplugs when on cafeteria duty."

"A wise precaution."

"Indeed."

"Okay, then. Guess I'll saddle up and sing them young'uns a song."

"Go to it, Slim. Dinner's at six for the Bros and Sistahs."

Tom left the foyer for the sitting room, grinning all the way. Inside, he was surprised to see Shirylee perched on the couch against the wall opposite the doorway.

"Hey, Shirylee," he said, "what's up?"

"Gettin' out, Mr. BB'."

Tom winced a bit. After seeing him leading the little kids in rock and roll singalongs, one of the older kids called him a white rapper—a Beastie Boy. The other big kids exploded in laughter, confirming their new nickname for him, BB, or Mr. BB for respect. He did his best to grin and bear it.

"What do you mean?" he asked her.

"Goin' to live with my stepsister Myrtle. She goin' to watch out for me. I'm gonna' get my own room."

He saw her suitcase for the first time, a roughed-up polyurethane bag held together by a single leather belt.

"Well, that sounds great, Shirylee. Stepsister, huh? Will you still be able to go to your school?"

"Yeah, junior high at Lincoln."

"That's great."

"It's all right. I' be outta here anyway."

"You're not going to miss the other kids—not us?"

"I miss them some. I miss you, Mr. BB."

"Aw, thanks Shirylee. I'll miss you for sure."

They smiled together and he left to join the little ones.

After regaling them for two hours, Tom happily granted their release to head to the dining table. Most of them rushed through the hallway door as he allowed himself to plunk down on the sofa with a free-form twang on his six-string. He encored with a heavy sigh.

"You tired Mr. Tom?"

He glanced up over the wide slope of the guitar to see Devon standing in front of him. Tom pushed himself to sit upright.

"I'm not tired, Devon, just resting."

"Good!" said Devon.

"I think so."

"Then you be able to play again right away—right?"

"Uh," Tom swallowed, "not exactly right away, but soon."

"Good! I like your songs and the funny things you say. I like you a lot."

"Well, Devon," Tom said, "I like you a lot too."

Devon grabbed his left-hand fingers with his right, twisting them around, slowly rocking back and forth on his feet. He rushed over beneath the guitar as Tom lifted it up. Hugging both of Tom's legs, he mumbled, "I love you, man."

Tom laughed, "You're amazing, you know that?"

Buddy pushed the door open and said, "Well, well, well, what have we here?"

Grinning, Tom said, "This bright young lad says he loves me, man."

Nodding, Buddy said, "A common occurrence. Nothing that Mrs. Weintraub didn't expect."

After dinner and the last of their homework, the oldest kids started up the stairs to get ready for bed. The girls headed to their large lavatory centered amid the honeycomb of their bedrooms. The boys continued up the stairs to the attic, which had been modified into one long room with 10 beds on each side of the slanting mansard roof. Dormers made the space seem larger, though 20 beds and the extra bunkbeds at each end countered the illusion. The common bathroom stood near the stairway, and the night counselor's tiny office was at the far end.

Seeing all the beds lined up, Tom realized that the number of children at Marbury exceeded by at least a third the two dozen Gertrude had told him on his first visit. He had guessed as much watching the close order drills run to keep everyone on schedule. Still, he found sobering the sight of the boys climbing into bed. He wondered if Buddy kept a bottle of good cheer in his desk drawer. Probably not a good idea to ask.

Hunched over to keep from hitting his head, Buddy walked down the middle of the long attic toward his quarters. He unlocked the door and turned on the light as he disappeared inside.

Tom tried to hurry down, but the kids shouted out to him as he came by, asking for a goodnight kiss, or to tuck them in. Tom pinballed back and forth, covering the heads of some with their blankets, and ruthlessly tickling others laughing and cringing as best as they could. He told jokes, not hilarious jokes by any measure, but the kids still howled at every punchline until he finally made his way to the office door.

Buddy lay supine on his cot, the bottom forming an amazing trough almost touching the floor. Noticing Tom frozen in amazement, Buddy said, "I am a ponderous man who knows his limitations, or at least the bed's."

"I can see that," Tom said.

"There's another cot you can use propped in the corner next to the desk. I'd get up, but . . . what for?"

"Not to worry, Buddy, old buddy, I have you covered," Tom replied as he stepped over to the unassembled cot. He slipped it out of its canvas cover and laid it on the floor.

"By the way, you wouldn't have something wet in your desk to calm a fellow traveler through the night."

"Bottom drawer left."

Tom reached down to pull the drawer open. Inside, he saw a of pointed white paper cups nestled next to a pink bottle of Pepto Bismol.

"Hmm."

Buddy raised an arm to gesture loosely with one finger. "There's Milk of Magnesia in the opposite drawer, if that suits you better."

"Naw, that's okay, I'm good."

"Oh." He dropped his arm down, his hand hanging languidly in the air. "You meant something more substantial. Sorry, I quit that quite a few years ago."

"Yeah," Tom said, starting to put the cot together. "So did I."

Buddy raised his head. "Oh? Really?"

"Yeah, for the most part. I'll raise a glass occasionally for wedding toasts and the like."

"Me too," Buddy said, "with grape juice."

"Oh, you're serious. How come?"

The big man sighed as he dropped his head on his arm crooked back on the pillow. "Too many vices. I had to give up at least one. As you can see, diet was out of the question."

"Yeah, I get you." Tom cleared his throat.

"Oh, I know I'm attractive to select perusers," he drawled, "but I just can't be bothered with all that—the pursuit, the passion, the proprietary intoxication transformed into stifling mistrust, the anger and fury that accompanies the inevitable end." He rolled over to face the wall. "I'd just as soon do without from the start. Hence, for me, nothing but grape juice."

"I see," murmured Tom. "And Marbury House?"

Buddy rolled back to face Tom. "Oh, the children are sweet and honest, and so very, very vulnerable. They are easy to love even when they are mean. And they certainly can be mean. But who can hold that against them, given their circumstances?" He waited for an answer, then went on. "Anyway, it's easy here at Marbury. They come, you comfort them, and love them. And then they go. Simple."

He waited. Tom shifted around on his cot, where he had sat without thinking. He couldn't think of anything to say.

"How about you, Mr. Music Man. Your fondness for Norah, how far, how deep, how wide does it go?"

Tom felt taken aback though he wondered why. He spoke hesitantly, "I'm not used to feeling like this. We hit it off so fantastically in such a different way than I'm used to. It's so foreign to me, we're so honest with each other. I thought we were closer than close. Yet, she seems distracted sometimes. She's almost always busy after hours, even when we're together out looking for new digs. Then I start wondering if there's someone else for her. I mean, not specifically, like some other guy. Not someone, but anyone. I don't really know, you know?"

Buddy nodded up and down. "New to you, isn't it? Adults acting like adults."

Tom shrugged, "Maybe. One of us at least, and not me."

"And volunteering at Marbury? You know, you don't have to do this. Your money's plenty enough, let me tell you."

They both laughed. Tom said, "Yeah, I know but I thought it was a way to stay close to Norah."

"And how's that turning out? I mean, you could slow down, try to see her only in her free time."

Seeing Tom's face becoming even more solemn, Buddy hurriedly said, "Norah might be trying to slow things down with you. She did survive a crappy marriage, let's not forget. She just might want you to slow your roll, you understand?"

"Yeah. Maybe, I guess."

"All right," Buddy said, shifting to sit up on his cot. "How is she otherwise when you spend time together?"

"Great. She really seems warm, you know? After cracking wise on me, she comes over and gives me a nudge with her hip. I mean, I almost have to sit down to cover my, uh, involuntary reaction. Know what I mean?"

"Yes. More than I prefer." He lowered his body to rest his head on his hand propped up on his elbow. "No matter, that sounds good, very promising. Still, maybe you want to constrain your overtures to evenings when she's off."

"Well, she's never off. She always has someplace she's committed to. I'm here tonight, but she's still going out to look for a new place."

"Oh." Buddy puffed out some air, "It's hard to find a new place around here. Especially considering our paltry pay. God, it's so good being a social worker."

"Yeah. I'm seeing that."

"Well, you understand. We live in the shadow of the city that never sleeps, never mind trying to eat properly."

Buddy watched Tom's features slowly descend into a fixed sense of resentful anger.

"You know," Tom said, "I told her she didn't have to do it. Goddamn."

"All right. But how many times have you visited her at her place after the oh-so-awkward occasion when you ran into the landlady at breakfast time?"

Tom slowed down. "Well, uh, not so often."

"You mean, like never?"

Abashed, Tom dropped his head. "Man, she tells you everything."

"Yeah, I'm the closest she has to a best girlfriend right now. So, you take her out to dinner and a movie, drive her home, give her a peck on her cheek, then take off."

"Not always."

"Really? You lingered how many times?"

"Just the once. She called me back for a goodnight kiss."

"Oh, my Lord. You must be a rockstar if you never had to learn how to date."

"I did my share of dating in high school."

"Yeah, in the days when you dropped your dates off at their parents' before midnight. I imagine you did marvelously well, though, when you went parking on the blacktops bordering the lush fields of Pennsylvania. Walking all the way to first base."

"Hey, man, cut me some slack. I was trying to be a gentleman!"

Buddy waited until he saw Tom's breathing slow.

"All right. Let's move on. She still likes you. She told me so."

"That's a surprise to me."

"Yeah, yeah, wise guy. You need to get off the mark. Tell her that I spilled the beans. Don't worry, she'll forgive me. Then, drive her to the places she wants to check out, wherever she wants."

Tom cocked his head. "You know, she could stay at my house." Seeing Buddy ready to flash a look of horror, he added, "As a guest, in the guest room. We could carpool to Marbury, have dinner, then go look at other places."

"That's sweet, and I want a cut of the frozen wedding cake in the fridge on your first anniversary."

"I have plenty of room!" Tom barked.

"It isn't about room, my dear boy, it's about adulthood. She's her own woman—for the love of Jesus you should know that much by now. To win her over you need to set her free."

"Uh huh, the Sting playbook."

"Go ahead, don't trust me," Buddy said, dramatically throwing his hands up in the air. "Ruin your love affair with whom I warrant is the first grown-up woman you've ever known. Certainly in this capacity."

"Well, shit-fuck-howdy."

"Yeah, yeah, yeah, just do as I say. Squire her around to wherever she wants to go, and keep your mouth shut when she says she likes a place. Believe me, it's your key to emotional happiness."

Tom pouted silently, turning his sour face down.

"Do it."

Tom exhaled and said at the bottom of his range, "Okay."

"Thank the Lord for amazing miracles."

"So, I drive her around," Tom said, "wherever she wants to go. Smiling at whatever she sees. That's it."

"That is exactly it, my boy."

"Does this mean I have to give up playing for the kids?"

The question surprised Buddy. "Well, I don't know. How do you feel about playing for the kids?"

Tom hesitated, then blurted, "I love it. I love them. They're the best audience I ever had."

Buddy blinked. "I believe you answered your own question, Tom. They're your children as much as anyone's. Go to town."

The two men grinned at each other until Buddy reached over and turned out the light.

Nineteen

Reluctant to have Tom help her in any way, Norah found his plain logic hard to refute. Except, she never wanted anyone to help her ever. But he swore he wouldn't interfere. He would drive her whenever and wherever she found a place worth a look. He promised to stay in the car while she checked the premises alone. That's it.

She really couldn't argue about it. Having access to a car with a silent chauffeur improved her chances exponentially of finding decent living space. But the real reason she hesitated had her gnawing her lower lip. At the end of every argument with herself, she identified her desire to accept Tom's offer because of how sweet she was on him. Still . . .. "Okay," she sighed.

He drove in front of Marbury House in his gray Nova, back in his hands at last and looking as though not a scratch had occurred.

Norah stepped over to the open driver's window.

"No Monte Carlo?" she asked.

He shook his head, "Saving gas. The SS burns it like an F-16."
Seeing that she didn't know what he meant, he said, "F-16s are top-dog Air Force fighter jets. Substituting jet fuel to gasoline, an F-16 uses roughly the same as 800 to 1,000 gallons of gas per hour of flight."

She shrugged, "Maybe they ought to call the planes SS-16s."

She watched him gazing up at her silently, his expression exuding mild disdain at her irreverent joke.

She pursed her lips, not too happy seeing the Nova's blue bench seat. The Monte Carlo had separate seats up front, wide like first class on a commercial plane. She loved them for their flexibility. She could move her seat forward and prop her feet or even her knees on the dashboard. At the same time, Tom moved his seat as far back as he needed when driving.

The Nova bench did not provide such flexibility, which meant the driver dictated its distance from the steering wheel and brakes. This generally ruled

Norah out of any occasion to drive. If she did, Tom's knees would be up to his ears. Also, she viewed the bench leerily. He might be saving gas, but she wondered how long the distance between them would last on the bench.

They followed a basic plan. At day's end, he picked her up in front of Marbury House. In the car, she shared the list of possibilities and their addresses. Tom would sketch a route referencing a host of maps and occasionally an atlas to plot the quickest trip out and back. Depending on how much time Norah spent at each address, they might see as many as four flats. Not good news necessarily, since seeing that many places in a day usually meant she had ruled them out quickly. Then Tom would take them to a nearby restaurant for dinner before dropping her back at Mrs. Landry's.

Occasionally, she might see something worth considering. One place had a day bed for sitting and sleeping under an old-fashioned French window. But the oven and range combo were undersized for her taste, and there was no dishwasher. The cramped closet could never fit her current wardrobe, never mind the boxes still waiting in San Francisco.

She needed to get that stuff shipped here, she thought. But where would she put it? A storage space maybe, but that meant more rent, which she certainly did not need. Dump all of it, she thought, which sent a sharp pang through her. All those memories— trinkets, ticket stubs, and papers from when she was a kid. And all those worn, out-of-fashion clothes, which still fit, one point of pride.

Norah shook her head. Clearly too much to ask.

She tumbled back into the car.

"Well?" Tom said evenly.

"The landlord wants a quarter of what I make in a month for space the size of a little girl's playhouse."

"I get it. A Marx Christmas special."

"Yeah, except the entire crib's only one floor."

"Oy," he said pursing his lips. "Curtains? You still get nice curtains, yes?"

"None that I saw," she said, "or want."

"Right." He turned the key, and the Nova throbbed to life. He looked at her and said, "Dinner now?"

Norah twisted her face. "I'm not really very hungry."

"Oh, c'mon, you got to eat," Tom said, then mumbling, "I gotta eat."

"I know," she said. "I'm sorry, but . . . why don't you just drop me off at Mrs. Landry's. You can get something to eat right afterwards."

Suddenly appearing tired, Tom said flatly, "Look. Mrs. Landry's place is a good forty-five minutes from here. My house is fifteen. Let me take you there for dinner. I'm sure Mary left me something good to zap, or we can just raid the icebox. I'll take you home after that."

"That's asking a lot from you. Don't you have practice or something?"

He shook his head back and forth, "Yeah, but you'd be doing me a favor if I miss it. Anyway, we practice in the afternoon. Most of the new guys have other gigs in the evening. They get home at three or four and sleep 'til noon, maybe even later. So, I can drive you or call you a cab, anything you want. Here—" he said, reaching into the glove compartment. He sat back and handed her a portable phone.

"Hit 'directory: take-out food,' and order something. The delivery guy will be at the house same time as us."

She thumbed through the entries in the phone while saying "I've never done this before. Indian, Chinese, Greek—" throwing up her hands. "Which one? What do you want?"

"Chinese is always good. Order the Chef's Special."

She hit the button and placed the order. She pivoted to Tom. "Address?"

They arrived on the heels of the delivery car. Tom jumped out to fetch the goods. Norah watched him while also taking in the house. More like a Cali mansion, she thought, all white on one level seeming to stretch on forever. She'd seen a few on vacation from S.F. to L.A, rubbing shoulders with a couple of conscious-ridden film stars. Seeing such a spread here in suburban New York surprised her, though. She wondered if he bought it as-is from the previous owners.

She scoped out the white gravel loop leading to the double doors beneath a columned half-rotunda framing the main entrance. Before that, though, the gravel driveway veered left to a three-door garage.

She turned her sight back to Tom, peeling off a few bills from his clip and handing them to the driver. The driver smiled brilliantly and drove away down the loop. Tom slid behind the wheel of the Nova and jabbed at the remote stuck in the open ashtray. The garage door closest to the house slowly rose to the steady clink of the chain. Tom guided the car inside, killed the engine, and hopped out his door to open hers.

Norah looked around and saw the Monte Carlo in the middle space next to a garden truck at the far end. She turned around to see Tom on the top of a two-step, two-by-four stairway leading inside.

"C'mon, into the kitchen," Tom said. "Mary and the rest are long gone home."

Norah slipped beneath his outstretched hand into a small hall leading into the kitchen, a large space with every appliance necessary to fete any number of guests. When they entered, though, the house seemed eerily quiet to Norah.

He placed the bag on the wooden island, then collected plates and silverware. Norah pulled up a stool and began to empty the bag. Tom produced a bottle of white wine and two glasses. She filled their plates as he filled the glasses. He held up a pair of chopsticks, followed by a questioning look. She shook her head no.

"Hah. I thought you were from San Francisco."

"Try Cherry Hill, New Jersey. Doesn't matter, lots of people use chopsticks in Jersey, too. I just never could get the hang of them."

Tom smiled knowingly. "Neither could I," he said, tossing the sticks over his shoulder. They clattered on the floor as Norah laughed punching his arm. He winced theatrically, rubbing his arm hard.

They then dug into steaming plates of fried rice and General Tso's tofu chicken, spring rolls, and shrimp tempura on the side.

Afterward, they stretched out on loveseats perpendicular to each other in a small, adjacent sitting room. Both stuck thumbs into their trousers trying to make room for the excess of their grand bouffe.

"That's the best Chinese food I've ever had," Norah said. "Ever."

"Better than San Francisco? I am surprised. It is definitely one of the great perks living here. You know, on the East Coast among the old money gazillionaires. Best takeout in the world."

"I can see its worth as an irresistible mortal sin."

"Wait 'til you eat Greek or Indian. The tapas are to die for, too."

"You lucky stiff. How do you stay so skinny? Am I missing a vomitorium around here somewhere?"

"Just bathrooms."

"Well, maybe I should waddle over to one. To use in the usual way, that is. Then I better call a cab and pack it in."

"It's late," Tom said. "You'll get to your attic well after midnight. Stay here tonight; I'll drive you to Mrs. Landry's in the morning."

"Oh, Tom, come on. We're breaking protocol."

"Not really. Just fine tuning. It would be easier for both of us if you stayed here until you find a new place. That way, we could go together to Marbury in the morning, and afterwards check on new prospects. If we're rehearsing, you can take a cab to Marbury. I'll pick you up for supper."

"That's a great plan," she said, "except for me living here."

"It's the best way to work it," Tom said. "Listen, you can camp out in the master bedroom. I never sleep there anyway. I hang my hat in the guest room. You'll have complete autonomy."

She sighed, exactly what she had hoped to avoid. Except she wondered why, too, she wanted to keep him at arm's length. Especially considering the way he'd behaved during the last few weeks. They both seemed tired of doing the same thing every night. She started to wonder if she wanted another place at all. An isolated change of venue might help.

"I'll stay tonight. The rest remains TBD," she said.

"Great, because to tell you the truth, I'm bushed."

Twenty

Norah started to pick up the dishes from dinner when Tom stepped in. "I'll get them. First, let me show you the lay of the land."

He took her back to the kitchen to a hallway that led to a slate foyer and the front doors. On their left a large entranceway opened onto a spacious living room, carefully furnished with exquisite sofas paired with complementary easy chairs. The setting faced an enormous fireplace that harkened back to 18th-century hearths. French windows from floor to ceiling looked out on the white-stone driveway loop.

Tom stopped to say, "There's a bench in the foyer next to the front doors where you can wait for a cab. That is, if I can't take you to work."

He started to the left again when she stopped him.

"These paintings," she said, "they're amazing."

Tom looked around. "Yeah, they're nice. Literally state of art, so I'm told. I really don't understand them myself. The colors are pretty."

"You didn't pick them yourself?"

"Uh, no. I have an old friend who does it for a living."

"Wow. He must do well. He's really good."

"Yeah, he's a 'she.' I've known her since the good old stadium days. You should've seen the stuff she sold me then."

He gazed at one painting with slashes of vermillion, freesia, and cyan diving together horizontally left to right on a lemonade background.

"All the stuff you see here cost a small fortune. To be honest, I really don't get them. Most of them, anyway. But she comes around every now and then saying it's time for an update, to get real. Then I find myself with a whole new set in a whole new style, or 'genre' if you're 'hip.'" He craned his neck looking around, "Apparently, I am not 'hip.' Or 'with it' for that matter." He paused. "Still, you have to put something on the walls."

Norah nodded knowingly. "Do you get your money back?"

"Huh?"

"For the old stuff. Does its 'with-it' half-life pay back your investment?"

"Huh. Fuck if I know. The financial transactions go through my brother. I hope I make the money back."

Seeing her gaze around while hiding her skepticism, he said "I should call Joe and ask. That's a good idea," he murmured, glancing at her as he led the way.

"Here's the master," he said pointing to the left. "It has its own bathroom of course. In fact, all the bedrooms have private baths. 'En suite,' they call them. Means you can get to one only through the bedroom door. Once in, you can never get out," he said, "the only drawback."

Norah smiled, chuckling a bit, her attention slowed as she glanced into the room. Again, the space was enormous. A giant king-size bed framed by four exquisite walnut posts supported a bright patterned canopy gorgeously decorated with cherry blossoms. An antique desk occupied the opposite wall, with the rest of the spacious boudoir filled with French loveseats and chairs. A lovely vanity surrounded by a host of full-length mirrors stood to the remaining wall within easy reach of both the bed and bath.

"God," Norah breathed, "did your friend pick out these furnishings, too?"

"Oh," Tom said, stopping next to Norah in the doorway. "No, she's strictly an art broker. All this stuff conveyed with the house."

"Really? Who sold you the house?"

"I don't know, some banker. Joe handled it. He's the one who found it. I just live here."

"I can see that," she said.

He strolled a few steps further down the hall, stopped, and opened a door. "The guest room, where I am the permanent guest."

Inside, Norah saw another large room with a king-size bed in the middle. Placed on both sides of a polished cherry headboard, matching nightstands displayed stunning porcelain lamps delicately decorated with ancient Asian farmers tending blue fields amid dainty trees. She had to believe they were the real McCoy, though she had no idea where they came from or how long ago they were cast. Incongruously, a pile of half-crumpled tissues covered the base of one, while a contemporary radio alarm clock sat on the back edge of the other table.

The rest of the room displayed similar use; guitars propped against the wall hidden by shirts hanging from them. An upright piano with the keys cover closed served as a shelf for CDs, diskettes, and piles of magazines, newspapers, and other printed materials. She noticed a large closet half open, with clothes both hung on rods and piled haphazardly on the floor. She shuddered a bit inside, suddenly happy she would be bunking in the master bedroom.

"It's not usually this disorganized. Mary insists on coming in every few weeks or so to straighten up everything." He screwed up his face, "I usually mess it up again in a few days. You know, the circle of life. Anyway, the master's in pretty good shape."

Norah smiled, nodding up and down.

Norah could not sleep. And for no good reason, she thought. The bed felt great and the soft feather pillows—though there were too many, like in most hotels. The temperature was cool, but not cold, making the covers cozy. She couldn't blame noise, or quiet for that matter. She just couldn't transport into that loveliest of space, sleep.

She recalled having an MRI of her shoulder, how she freaked out when she slid down inside the tube, its top just inches above her face. Clearly the same as a coffin's lid. She bailed immediately, while the technician soothed her, calming her down, asking if she'd like a blindfold and some earplugs. Worried about failing to get the information needed by her doctor, she agreed to trying the blindfold.

Eyes covered, ears muffled, she slid back into the tube and waited. Music filled her dark universe, where she floated far and wide, slowly drawn into an extrasensory experience. Free of gravity, she drifted off in cozy comfort, unbelievably relaxed with no sense of time or space—until the technician said she was finished, she had done great. Norah felt great, though a bit blue too because it was over. She felt that way now swaddled in lux bedclothes in a perfect sleep environment. Only, amid such tranquility, she just couldn't sleep.

In the morning, she heard a soft knocking on the door. Ugh, she said to herself.

"Yeah?" she called out.

"Time to rise."

"Shit," she uttered, louder than she meant.

"I know, me too. Mary's put together a takeaway breakfast—lots of coffee—which we can dig into on the ride in."

"Can I take a shower?"

"Hell yeah. Take two."

"Thanks."

She showered longer than she should have, but it helped bring her around. Still, yesterday's clothes. She shook her head, no choice; she had to hurry back to her crib at Mrs. Landry's. But did Tom have that on his daily list? Well, if he didn't, she'd have to persuade him.

Mary greeted her warmly in the kitchen. Tom sat at the end of the butcher block table. He gulped a big swallow of coffee as he rose to leave.

"Let's roll," he said, grabbing a bag off the counter.

They jumped into the Monte Carlo. He backed out of the garage in one learned curve, shifted, and gunned down to the outer gate. After looking both ways, he shot out onto the two-lane road heading south.

"You brought out the heavy equipment this morning."

He lowered his head slightly sideways, "We're late, so we'll engage in some quantum physics and jump the shark."

She squinted, trying to reconcile the mixed similes.

"So," Tom said, eyes fixed on the road, "how'd you sleep?"

"Great," she lied flatly. "The Sandman was good to me."

"Well, that makes one of us."

"Really? You had trouble?"

"I always have trouble. Day and night. You know, when people ask me if my glass is half empty or half full, I tell them mine's busted."

"Wow," she muttered, "that's pretty dark."

"Sometimes I don't know whether I feel depressed about everything because I'm tired all the time or because I have so much information."

"Jesus," Norah said, "have you always been this way?"

"I had some good years until I was nine—nine, ten, eleven—they were okay."

She blurted out a laugh, immediately assuming a long face afterward. Tom shot a look her way, then back to the road.

"I'm sorry," she said, "I just find it hard to understand how you can be so miserable with all the things that've happened to you. Good things."

"Yeah," he said, "Well, like you said, that's the problem with privilege. I've gone around and see people who don't have it so good. To the point where I resented them, like you said. I've hung out with people who have it just as good as me or better doing the same, and never gave it a thought." He slowed at a traffic light and turned his left blinker on. "Now," he said as he made the turn, "I can't get it out of my head."

"Oof," she said. "Catch 22."

"Oh, don't worry, I'll get over it, back to normal insouciance." She laughed, and he continued, "I prefer deconstruction. You know, FDR announcing the surprise attack on Pearl Harbor, saying, 'today is a day which will live in infamy.' I see my luck as a day that will live in 'famy.'"

She screwed up her face again trying her best to hold back her laughter, covering her mouth with her hand.

He turned his head to face her. "It's a privilege being alive."

He killed the engine, and Norah jumped out of the car and hurried over into Mrs. Landry's back door.

Twenty-One

After dropping off Norah at Marbury, Tom turned the Monte Carlo around to head back to the house. The band planned to meet at noon, which might give him enough time to catch a couple of hours sleep and a quick shower.

He felt pretty good, then not so good. He never would have unloaded all that shit on her if he had caught a full night's sleep. Then again, she seemed interested, genuinely engaged in his deep morose secret self. Not so secret now, he realized. At least she laughed in the right places.

Tom gunned it back to the spread, pulling up fast and stopping just short of the garage. The automatic door ratcheted up at hourglass speed, until he estimated enough headroom to guide the car inside. He eased in slowly, twisting his head around back and forth to be sure the car cleared every possible impediment. Once in, he hit the garage door down button, stepped out of the car, and raced up the steps into the kitchen.

"Hi," Christine said, sitting on a stool at the butcher block.

"You're back," Tom said, "again."

Christine uncrossed her legs, recrossing them in reverse.

Mary's hurried breakfast preparation in the kitchen was the only sound. She glanced at Tom, making sure she was out of Christine's sight, frowned fiercely as she said, "I'll be back shortly, after I take Felix his lunch."

Tom placed both hands down flat on the block, knowing he had seen the last of Mary until he sent her the all-clear sign. He waited.

"Don't get bent out of shape," Christine said, "I'm just here to fetch the work we put in storage."

Tom nodded.

"I've been chatting with a few of my go-to buyers," she said, smiling slightly, a glint brightening her eyes. "There might be interest in the Myrcks and there's definitely talk happening about de Soto."

"Un huh," Tom mumbled, barely registering.

She stood up and positioned herself on the block closer in front of him. "Tom, I might be able to get your money back—well, not all of it, but most."

He stood still, trying to hold himself even keeled. "I don't care about the money, Christine. I thought it'd help give you a boost. If you get some back, that's great, use it to buy more. You know, I tried hard to like the art, really hard. But I could never get it like you do, not in a million years."

She sat back straightening up. "This is a good opportunity for you, Tommy, fiscally and maybe more important, socially."

He watched her lower her hands below the block where she could twist her fingers together unnoticed. She'd done it for years when she felt uneasy.

Tom took a breath. "You know I wasn't all that crazy about the big-time folks either." He dropped his head, fixing his eyes on the floor, "But I always liked you, Chrissie," he said, "it always amazed me that a class act like you would have me as a pal. I loved you for it," he said softly, then raising his eyes. "That won't ever change."

He bent over then, pushing himself up and away from the block. "Anyway . . . ."

"You know, you're very good at self-denigration," Christine snapped, "like you even believe yourself. You don't, of course," she said sounding impatient. "You could never be as successful as you've were—as you are about to be again, if you really try." Her eyes pierced him sharply, judgmental, a look he had seen so many times before. "I want to help you, Tommy, always."

Tom shook his head. "Thanks for that, really. And to tell the truth, at first I enjoyed rubbing elbows with the hoity toity. That was fun, you know? But now I want to do what I've always done, put down some decent licks with other guys. Play in a bar again, beers on the house for the band. I got lucky, sure. I don't have to worry about food or rent, the other shit. But I feel like it's all on the line soon. When we do play, if we don't knock them dead— if I don't knock them dead—it'll be over. All of it, this time, for good."

Christine's expression gradually shifted as he spoke. For the first time in years, she seemed to listen to him.

"Anyway, know that I care about you, I always will. But it looks like we're both going in different directions. So, . . ."

He stepped over and hugged her, "I'll be seeing you again soon," he said quietly. He held her at arm's length for a moment, then turned around to head down the hallway to the garage door.

Mary stood leaning on the hood of the Monte Carlo sharing a cigarette with Felix straddling the riding mower. He spotted Tom walking toward them, and quickly smattered unintelligible words to Mary. She handed him the cigarette, which he put out with the heel of his boot, then tucked the butt away in his shirt pocket.

Tom continued past them, only slowing down to say to Mary, "If she's still in the kitchen, please take care of her."

Mary nodded, but Tom was already past the swimming pool near the rehearsal room. After he closed the door behind him, she hurried back to the kitchen. She heard voices in the hallway, Christine's and others.

Mary went back to straightening up the kitchen when Christine meandered in. "The moving guys are here," she said, "getting the old paintings out of the attic."

"Right," said Mary, wiping the top of the cabinets counter.

"Tom really looks tired," Christine said.

"Yes, well," Mary replied, concentrating on the top. "You know, he's been very busy practicing and rehearsing. Doing other things," she trailed off.

"I understand." Christine leaned against the back of a stool. She lifted and dropped her shoulders, "Maybe you could persuade him to take a break. He looks so beat."

"Yes, well he's burning the midnight candle at both ends."

"Really?'

"Uh huh. New band, old songs, has to break them in."

"Oh. I didn't realize he had a timetable."

"Right, well he has this engagement coming up . . .."

"Yes," Christine said, "of course."

Seeing her perk up, Mary could shoot herself. "It's a small thing, nothing big."

"Sure," Christine said, "I get it."

Mary rubbed the countertop hard. Peeking up, she saw Christine wiping her eyes with her hand. She slowly lifted her head, and Mary quickly shifted back to rubbing.

"Right," said Christine, her voice slightly ragged. "Well, I can hear the guys bringing the goods downstairs, my cue to push on. Nice seeing you."

"Yes, same here."

Christine was gone, and Mary heaved a sigh, feeling very sorry for her. Oh well.

Tom flicked on the lights after entering the studio. Everything looked to be in order. The other players would arrive soon, which would prompt Mary to bring out the lunch. He hoped being left alone in the kitchen would nudge Christine on her way.

Billy and Frank arrived first, deep in conversation.

"She's good-looking, not great looking," Frank said. "She wears cool clothes, good make-up."

"The curse of the almost beautiful," Billy said.

"Out of the mouth of babes."

"Well, you know the old saying," Billy said, "'All's well that ends.'" Frank nodded up and down, then noticed Tom standing in front of the drum set.

"Hey Chief," Frank said, passing by to fetch his guitar from its stand. Billy stopped in front of Tom and rolled his right hand into a fist and pressed it into his left hand, lowering his head and saying, "Namaste."

"Likewise," Tom replied.

George barreled in, wedging past Tom.

"Hola, Mr. W."

"How's it going, Professor?" replied Tom.

"Beauteous, Boss, very extra-striata."

"Glad to hear it."

They all took their places on stools and behind the drums, waiting.

Don strolled in, flashed a pained smile, and headed for his seat next to the old roll-top desk.

Once everyone had settled in, Tom wheeled around in front of them and started.

"Okay, boys, we've been at this for a while, now. And for the most part, we've worked out the kinks. All that's left, then, is to see how we sound to a real audience."

He paused, both hands thrust in his jean pockets. He rocked back and forth, waiting.

"Yeah man!" Billy burst out, followed by George's "Damn straight!" and "That's great!" from Frank.

Tom stopped, grinning broadly as he watched them exchanging high fives.

"Where we playing?" Billy barked, "Yankee Stadium?"

Tom smirked as he started to answer when George chimed in. "You are the dumbest dumb asshole I know," said George, "and I met a few."

Tom stepped in. "Nothing like that," he said, "we're a few gold albums out from that kind of venue."

Now standing, Don said, "You guys know we're no way near that stage. We'll be playing here on the island, a small bar and grill with a good weekend crowd."

"Oh," Frank mumbled.

"What I tell you, knucklehead," said George.

"Don't rumple your stilskin shithead," Billy said. "We all expect to play the big stadiums someday. Otherwise, what the fuck?"

"Exactly," Tom said, slipping between George and the drum set. "First, though, we need to make sure we literally have our act together." Seeing open mouths, he said, "We need to practice our asses off."

"Oh yeah, man, 'course we do, number one on the hit parade." George paused, then said, "But where we playing, Tom, when we play?"

Tom twisted his head around to Don, who held his hands up, shrugging. Tom turned back to the others.

"Okay. We're playing at the Robespierre Hall in Patchoque, Suffolk County, not too far from the eastern beaches."

"Oh." The three sidemen exchanged glances, prompting Tom to continue, "It's a good place. Used to accommodate a lot of weddings back in the day. It still does a good weekend business for live music and dancing."

"It's a perfect venue for a tryout," added Don. "Good acoustics, plenty of room for our gear, and usually a well-oiled lively crowd."

The others again checked each other's take on the news. Then, Frank spoke out, "Well all right then, Twilight Zone here we come!"

"Uh, make that the Chi-lite Zone, brothers," said George.

Everyone roared as loud as they could.

After a vigorous rehearsal, the band dispersed quickly. Even Don took off without a cross word.

Twenty-Two

Tom whipped the Nova out and down the driveway, gunning it to Marbury House, hoping to beat rush hour traffic.

The plan remained the same; pick up Norah, hit two or three possibilities before dark, then catch a bite at a bistro on the way home. After a few weeks, both showed signs of fatigue. Norah remained obstinate, though. The more they traveled, the more impossible it seemed to him they'd find the magic combo of a comfortable residence close to her place of employment or near public transit, all at a reasonable rate for a social worker's pay. Good luck with that, he muttered to himself.

He pulled up to Marbury, suddenly surprised by the lack of parking on its street. He'd never had this problem before, another irritant to add to his present funk.

He spun the Nova around, cruising up the long block without luck. He turned the corner and coasted through the next street, also full up. Shite, he breathed.

Completing the long circle all the while still wondering where the circus was, he finally saw a Volkswagen bug pulling out halfway down the block. He stationed himself behind it, waiting. As soon as the car put-putted away, he ran the Nova up parallel to the car parked in front of the newly opened spot. Just as he stopped and turned his sight back to start parking, he saw another car right up on his rear bumper waiting for him to move on.

"Fucking . . . sonofabitch!"

Tom rolled his window down and stuck his head out.

"Hey! I was here waiting for this spot, pal."

The driver opened his door to stand halfway out holding his left hand up. He wore a waist-long, coal-gray overcoat and a cream-colored scarf hanging around his neck, al topped off by a woolen Irish cap.

"Sorry, friend, but early bird, worm . . . you know."

"Get the fuck out! I was here first. You need to move on, dude."

"Well, what if I don't?"

"Then—" Tom didn't know what then. Except he was livid. The guy had half the snout of his car—a Lincoln VIII, of course, — in the space. Tom felt like reversing into the other guy's grill, except he'd just gotten the Nova back from Murray's. Furious, he shifted gear and pulled slowly up the street, looking back and forth in his rearview mirror. He watched the asshole maneuvering his big-ass black sedan back and forth into the spot.

Tom wished he had a gun, also half-wishing he could bring himself to use it on that useless piece of shit.

Just then, a car pulled out of a space at the end of the block. Tom wasted no time whirling his steering wheel right-left into the curb. He straightened out perfectly, a half foot from the concrete and two feet from the car behind him, his front-end inches from the yellow line at the end of the block.

He quickly jumped out, pulled his guitar from the back seat, and shut the door all in a fluid movement. At the same time his eyes watched the driver of the black Lincoln walking down the street away from him.

Tom quick-stepped across the street and marched double time to catch up with the demon driver, ready to crown him with his ax if he had to. Then, to his utter astonishment, he watched the driver bear right up the Marbury sidewalk.

Oh, this is going to be good, thought Tom.

He stretched his legs, single stepping the sidewalk squares, shifting to skip up the stairs to barge straight through the entranceway. Buddy stood close inside holding the door open.

"Ladies and gentlemen," Buddy announced, "please welcome our traveling troubadour, Mr. Tom Weatherly!"

Tom held up, gripping his guitar by the neck next to his leg. The hallway overflowed with a cornucopia of people, black, white, brown, ruddy red, and tan. A few clapped while most of them wore blank expressions, obviously wondering who he was.

He searched frantically with his eyes looking for a familiar face. Instead, he saw a lean guy in a blue dress shirt open at the top and a pair of pleated twill pants. The natty Irish flat cap was gone, revealing black, curly hair complementing a carefully trimmed slim moustache. Tom stopped, wondering if he had the right guy. With a faintly light brown complexion, he could be anyone from anywhere. Tom suddenly noticed the guy staring straight back at him.

Tom quickly pivoted to Buddy and said, "Thanks, Mr. Rosen, I think it'd be better if I played later when everyone's settled in."

"That makes sense," Buddy said dryly.

Norah sidled up to Tom. "What the hell are you doing?"

His eyes back on the new guy, Tom spit out as quietly as he could, "That fucking asshole took my parking space!"

Rolling her eyes, Norah pulled on Tom's arm, saying, "Wow, a federal offense."

He stared down at her. "You're funny, but I'm going to drop that dapper dan even if I have to pop him with my stick," he said, shaking his guitar next to his leg.

"Oh, that'll be good. We'll visit you every month no matter how long you're in the pokey."

Tom held up. "Okay, then what am I supposed to do?"

"You can go over to him and politely tell him how you felt when he took your parking place." She pursed her lips, "And, if he tells you to pound sand, head to the refrigerator for a dozen eggs, take them out and egg his candy-ass car."

Tom cracked up, then quickly swallowed his laughter. "Okay, I'll mosey on over and register my displeasure. But I'm still taking my guitar with me."

"That seems reasonable."

"Okay."

He wended his way through the folks crowding the vestibule until he stood in front of the miscreant. Taller than he thought, Tom realized, looking fit too. Before he could wade into him, the guy spoke first.

"Hey there, Mr. Weatherly, I'm a fan of your music." He reached out his hand, which Tom grasped out of habit. His hand swam in the chilly paw of the new suit, an odd sensation for Tom considering his grip usually swallowed other people's.

"That's great," Tom said. He smelled good, too, some foreign fragrance perfect for manly men.

"Terence Able. Call me Terry. Yeah, I got me a few old cassettes, *Best of the Best 70's Songs*, *80's Hits*, you know? They got a lot of your music on them, two-three cuts at least. I'm wearing them out, you know?"

"Yeah, well maybe I'll play a few this evening."

"That'd be great, yes sir!"

Tom swallowed, "That's not the reason I came over here."

"Oh?"

"Yeah. When I drove up, I saw a parking space. So, I waited only to have you pull into it behind me."

"Oh, no, really?"

"Really."

"Oh, man, I'm so sorry 'bout that; if I'd known it was you, I'd gladly given up the space. My bad, really. So sorry."

"Uh huh." Tom said flatly, recalling how the guy—Able or whatever—stood halfway out of his car getting a damn good look as he sluffed him off with his "early bird worm" crap.

"Yeah, no lie," Able said. "If you want, we can go out, switch places now. I'm happy to go find another spot. That doesn't bother me."

"No," Tom said calmly, "I found a space just a few steps up on the opposite side."

"Oh, well that's great—no harm, no foul, right?"

"Yeah. Sure."

"Cool."

Norah came up and gently tugged at Tom's free hand. "Time to organize, gentlemen. The Marbury staff has put together stations around the house to update all our visitors. Can you come with me?" she said, looking up warmly at Tom's eyes.

"Oh yeah, that'd be great," Able said. "I think I'm supposed to be at a presentation about the younger kids."

"Sure, they're starting in the kitchen. Go through the east sitting room. The door to the kitchen's on the opposite wall."

"Great, Ma'am, I'm off. Don't want to be late."

He disappeared into the sitting room.

Tom turned. "What's with all the outlanders?"

"One of our open houses. To raise funds, also allow the kids some time with their parents, foster parents, and other caretakers."

"Jesus, you could've warned me."

"I know, I just . . . forgot."

"Huh. I would've come earlier if I'd known." Watching her shift to her other foot, he said, "or maybe a lot later."

"It really does get crowded," she said plaintively. "You should know you're welcome all the time."

"Okay." He moved the guitar to his left hand. "No songs today, right?"

"I guess not."

"I'll put me ax in me car, then." He started toward the door and stopped. "So, do you want me to come back later to look at apartments?"

"Yeah, I guess," Norah answered, "though I think dinner before won't be possible."

"We can get a bite afterward. I'll see you in a couple of hours."

She nodded up and down as he whirled out the door.

They managed to look at one place before calling it a night. The second floor of a warehouse cum open-space loft offered plenty of room and current cachet, just five city-blocks away from the house. Norah liked the polished maple floors a great deal, and Tom could see the place's potential if a few bucks were thrown into it. But it was out of reach given Norah's iron-clad financial blueprint.

"You don't have to be so fussy, you know," Tom said over his half of their Caesar's salad at Stu Mulligan's Irish Bistro.

Norah poked the salad with her fork, flipping her butter lettuce over and back.

"It wouldn't be a handout, just a break on the rent until you get a bump from Marbury. You can pay me back."

"Marbury could double my pay and I still couldn't afford that loft. Which is too much room for me alone anyway."

"Sure, but I have an idea that will take care of both issues. I want to invest in the space to make a studio out of it when the band gets rolling."

"But you already have a studio, your converted pool cabana. You showed it to me."

"It's a little bit bigger. It's fine for a mixed bag of rockers screwing around. But I could never get a full band in there, strings for example, recording equipment, a state-of-the-art engineer board. This place could give me enough room for all kinds of upgrades when we reach that level. In the meantime, you could sublet within your budget for as long as you like. It's a win-win proposition," Tom said.

"Sounds like a proposition all right," she replied.

He lowered his fork and sat back.

"C'mon. Go back to how we met. Ever since, we seem to be turning the wheel back. If you think I'm no more interested in you than that now, I don't know what to say. Or do."

"I know," she said, looking morose. "It's like, whatever you and I try to do . . . doesn't!"

He smiled, and they both began laughing.

"Okay," she said, "Enough."

"All right." He glanced at his watch. "It's late. Let's call it a day and a night, pack it in. Where to?"

She sighed. "Too late to go to Mrs. Landry's. Your place, I guess."

"Right. Next stop Chez Weatherly."

Twenty-Three

Norah woke up early as usual. At first, she didn't know where she was. Then, she did.

"Shit," she whispered.

After gathering her thoughts, she realized that she was in Tom's house. In his bed, not the master, but his guest bedroom where he piled up everything he used and maybe owned.

How did she end up here?

She thought hard, trying to piece it altogether. They arrived at his house at ten o'clock, her usual bedtime. Only they had a nightcap, a glass of pinot gris for her and two fingers of a single malt for him in a beautiful, crystal tumbler glistening in the ceiling light. Facing each other on stools at the butcher block island, they sipped and talked.

"Pretty good wine," she said.

"Yeah, I know a guy at a liquor store who lives for selecting upscale beverages for me that he can't afford. Sad, because I mostly can't tell the difference."

"Oh, I don't know about that," she said.

"Really?"

"Sure. Look at you, one sip and you still have your glass half full. Mine's almost empty."

He wrinkled his features. "That's kind of oranges and apples, don't you think? Your drink is about twelve to thirteen percent alcohol, while mine's fifty-one-point eight percent. So, one glass of wine doesn't even approach half the bang of my teensy-weensy dram of Laphroaig."

"Huh. Your glass looks half full to me."

Tom shrugged, "Just a matter of perception."

Norah sat quietly for a moment. She then said," I recall you saying that half-full or not, your glass is always shattered. Philosophically, I believe."

"Philosophical? Me?" His hand pressing his chest, Tom said ardently, "When I drink, half a glass coming or going is of no consequence."

"So, you're saying that deep inner thoughts about yourself don't pervade your life." Seeing him looking so dumbfounded, she said, "You know what pervade means, right?"

"It means your reading level is a lot higher than mine."

She burst out laughing, and he smiled.

"Yeah, I get it," he said. Your glass is always half full while mine's half empty. But you better be careful, though, because you might have a glass that's two-fourths full or even four-eighths. Then, you know what happens?"

He waited for it, downing another sip of the Laphroaig.

"What?"

"It goes to eight-sixteenths, and maybe even sixteen-thirty-twos."

"Whoa!" she said, feigning a backward fall. He reached out his free hand and righted her gently, the two of them laughing leaning close together.

Norah straightened up and gazed at him studiously, sipping the last of her wine. She finished and said, "Did anyone ever tell you you're the spitting image of Don Knotts?"

"Jesus Christ! Thanks for the left-handed compliment!" he brayed, his free hand pushing back in the air.

"Hey!" she said. "At the time I thought he was just short of being handsome."

"Right, when you were watching *The Andy Griffith Show*. What were you, ten?"

"More like four; I saw it in reruns, they ran them all the time. And lots of people thought he was cute. My mom loved him, and he was terrific on the show."

"Yeah, maybe," Tom said, finishing his drink. He reached for the bottle and poured another while saying, "He is a good comic, though his movies suck. I can see how people like him."

"Sure," she said watching him sip. She never liked scotch. She tried it once or twice before. Her mother always said it tasted like medicine, and she was right. But maybe his high-end stuff was better than bar brands.

"Back in the day, Tom said, "when we were just starting out, after a set people would come up to me and say I looked just like Sonny Bono. That's when I changed my pageboy and shaved my moustache."

She laughed aloud leaning off the stool into him again, pressing a hand against his chest to keep her balance.

"Hey."

"Okay, okay, you don't look a thing like Knotts or Bono, just your own runway superstar self!"

He laughed ruefully. "Yeah, well that's in the rearview mirror, too."

"Oh, is that so?" she said, exaggerating her scorn.

He smiled as he lifted his glass to her before taking another sip.

"Hey, pour me one, will you?"

He stopped, surprised. "Really?"

"Sure, why not?"

He shrugged and walked over to the cabinet to fetch her a glass, talking all the while. "I thought all this time I was just short of being handsome."

They raised their glasses, slightly clinking them together, and drank. At first its taste seemed oddly earthy on her tongue. Going down, though, it released an assortment of unfamiliar flavors, complicated but not distasteful, not at all.

"This is good!" she said.

"Uh huh," he nodded, "I think so, too." They laughed again.

"I don't drink the hard stuff too often," he said, "but when I do, it's hard to stop."

"You mean you have a drinking problem on top of everything else?"

"No," he said. "At least I don't think so. Vanity keeps me from that. I just need to get my shit straight is all."

"I see," she said, sipping more.

She paused once more, pulling back to take him in. He'd been good to her, driving her around the past few weeks without conniving to get anything in return. In fact, he seemed strange to her, this rock star with beaucoup bucks. He could still wow and woo the nubile groupies if he wanted. Yet, here he was, running her all over Long Island instead, for nothing.

She held her glass up, looking at his face fragmented by the crystal's angular pattern. So weird.

She drank, then asked, "Do you ever wonder what weird people think about us? Do they think normal people are weird? I mean, what is normal? Normal people aren't normal, they're just ordinary. Even mundane."

No answer.

Then she said, "Can you be lonely and happy at the same time?"

Studying his glass, he said, "Doubtful. If you decide to get out of a relationship, you're likely to feel empty, a gaping hole. Still, it's better than being dumped. To find out that someone you love utterly finds you unworthy. . ..," he shook his head, looking down at the floor.

"Aw-w," she said, noticing her voice sounding slightly slurry.

He straightened up. "It's late. Time to hit the hay."

"Oh."

"Yeah, and looking at the bottle here, it's not a good idea to drive. You're stuck again, I guess."

"Oh, Jesus. Fine, but can we switch bedrooms? Your master is so cold, sterile."

"Okay. Now you see why I camp out in a guest room."

"Yeah, you're weird that way."

"That is correct."

He turned sideways and bent over, gesturing with a sweep of his arm toward the hallway, "If you please."

Norah could not tell if he'd slept with her that night or in his master bedroom. She wore a St. Francis High School sweatshirt, which she swam in, and no bra. Now who took that off? At least her Hanes were still in place. But for how long?

Tom walked in from the bathroom holding a glass.

"Good morning," he said softly.

"Oh, I don't know about that."

"Hmm," he hummed. "How do you feel?"

"As if I was clubbed with a kielbasa."

"Ooh. I better make some coffee. In the meantime, here's some water that might help."

"Thanks," Norah said, quickly bringing the glass directly to her mouth.

"Okay," Tom said, turning around toward the door to the hall.

"Wait," she said.

He turned around.

"What happened last night?"

"Last night? You had your first taste of single malt. And your second, and third. In fact, we're now out of stock."

"Yeah, yeah, I know. But what happened here?"

"Oh. You crashed, so I put you to bed."

"Is that all?"

"Well, I gave you the sweatshirt, which you put on backwards. That's it."

"Really?"

"Yeah. You managed to remove your brassiere under the sweatshirt like Houdini in a straitjacket. Always amazing, quite the feat."

"That's it?"

He stared at her as though she was demented, until dawn blossomed in his eyes.

"Oh, you mean the wanton red-hot monkey sex we had over and over again, our privates raw without protection. By the way, if you're pregnant I don't know you."

"I see."

"Right. You removed your clothes on your own and dove under the covers."

"Really? You didn't help me."

"Nope. I rushed to the head to tap a kidney, maybe both. I poured a lot of booze down my gullet too, you know."

Norah squinted, furrowing her eyebrows. "Where did you sleep last night?"

"In the master bedroom. Chilly and empty, like you said."

"So, no red-hot monkey sex," she said.

"Correct."

Norah held up a beat. Then she said, "Why not?"

Tom immediately looked nonplussed. "I . . . we were both drunk, barely able to keep our eyes open."

"We've been drunk before," she said, sitting up. "That didn't stop us."

Tom stepped back near the big tallboy dresser.

"No, it didn't."

"Well?" Norah leaning against the headboard, her legs folded at the knees, feet together.

Without uttering a word, Tom leaned back against the tallboy, lifting an arm over his head to rest up on top.

Norah sat still, thinking.

"So," she said, "when did you lose your virility?"

He grimaced broadly, "At a very early age." Seeing her pout, he added, "Just keep this in mind; sex without meaning is meaningless sex. Or is it the other way around?" He put an index finger to his mouth as though he was wondering.

"I thought having sex was meaning enough."

"When it is, yeah. Unless it isn't."

Norah eyed him impatiently. Tom stared fiercely, as though out of sorts himself.

Norah sighed, nodding, "Looks like we spent a lot of time together drawing closer apart."

Stone-faced, Tom said, "I'm going to go make coffee now."

"Good idea, Tommy m'boy," she said.

He surprised her by whipping up a decent breakfast; eggs over easy, no broken yolks, bacon fried just right, wheat toast and real butter, of course, with a slice of fried tomato on the side, quite the flourish. And the coffee was strong.

Tom offered her the Nova or the Monte Carlo. He couldn't take her to Mrs. Landry's place for her to change clothes, then back to Marbury House. He would be late for practice with the band, which was starting earlier and going late with the big trial performance coming up in only two weeks. She chose the Nova as least likely to get her in trouble.

It had been a while since she had driven a car for any long distance. No one drove in San Francisco if they had a choice. Public transportation beat downtown traffic hands down. Oh, it took a while to get from Oakland to the Ruth Washington House, but she always brought a book with her for the commute. Her nerves stayed put while she happily added to her five percent knowledge takeaway from college.

She smiled at odds and ends brought to mind by thinking alone. A true pleasure in general, though loneliness sometimes threatened one's autonomy. Not like romance, though. That was the killer. Going through a half-dozen, two-year couplings in her past had built her resolve to tread lightly in matters of the heart. The dulling disappointment of signing off on another two-year bout of serial monogamy still trumped the soul-rending blues of true love ripped apart.

But this guy, this rocker past his shelf life, he presented a real problem. Tom Weatherly, aka Collins, contradicted everything she expected from a one-night stand. Here he was, still hanging around, ready to do anything she wanted, give her anything she needed or didn't need, without one thing in return—not even sex. What kind of rock'n'roller was he?

I'm the one who should be falling all over this guy, she thought. He's so good with the Marbury kids and her workmates. His one-man concerts were hilariously crazy. Who teaches elementary school kids to sing Bee Gees ballads as punk rock? Kids shrieking "How Can You Mend a Broken Heart" at the top of their screechy little lungs, enough to think about tossing in a stink bomb. But they loved Mr. Tom like crazy.

And here he was, making her crazy. No pressure, except she found herself longing for some. The status quo was just too damn static. The nicer he was to her, the more she wanted to jump his bones. Was this his game? Did it matter? Whatever he was up to, she was ready to box him in and bang his brains out.

She tightened her grip on the steering wheel and jammed the gas pedal.

Twenty-Four

"Okay boys," Don said, "this is the stretch when all of us need to show up, step up, and man up. Two weeks left before we step out and show if we have what it takes. We'll be opening in a small venue, no question. Believe me, though, its elite patrons are plenty mighty enough to spread the word fuckin' far and fuckin' wide. Which means we all have to be more than ready to give it more than our all."

Don paused. In the background Tom could see the young guys shifting back and forth on their feet, somewhat unnerved. Don started in again.

"Billy, step forward."

Billy moved up face-to-face with Don.

"Raise your left hand. Right on your heart."

Billy raised his hands.

"Now, repeat after me. 'I'—state your name—."

"I, Billy O'Reilly . . . ."

"–am a little baby girl—."

"Am a— a what?"

"Say it!" barked Don.

"Am a little …?"

"Little baby girl."

"Am a little baby girl—"

"In pink rubber underpants—"

"In pin—you gotta be kidding."

"Say it, or I get my rolodex for another drummer."

His features crumpled, Billy said, "In pink rubber underpants."

"And a pretty blue party dress—"

"In pink rubber underpants—"

"In pink—you gotta be kidding.

"Say it, or I get on my rolodex for another drummer."

His features scrunched up, Billy said, "In pink rubber underpants,"

"And a pretty blue party dress—"

"And a pretty blue party dress," Billy twisted around, saying, "Tom, really?"

Tom shrugged, while Don yelled, "Eyes up front, Mister!"

Billy turned back.

"Say it."

"And a pretty blue party dress,"

"Who will never become a superstar—."

"Who will never be a superstar—."

"On the cover of *Rolling Stone*."

"On the cover of—hey, man, what the hell you saying?"

Don stuck his tongue out followed by a Bronx cheer.

"Yeah, well, fuck you, too," said Billy, spritzing out raspberries of his own.

"Very good," said Don. "You may be seated. Frank?"

Frank stepped up, and Don began.

"I am a little baby girl—"

Frank started to say it, until both George and Tom burst into laughter. Don grinned and began laughing along with the others.

Frank smiled sheepishly, joining in, but Tom could see red creeping up Billy's neck and ears. Tom stepped over and threw his arm around Billy's shoulders while Don said, "C'mon Billy, you just got your formal baptism into The Weatherly Experience."

Billy coughed a laugh while Don reached down to pull up a bottle of Jameson Irish Whiskey. He poured out five shot glasses and passed them around.

"You've all proven your mettle," Don announced, "Now, rock'n'roll!" he bellowed, knocking his shot back.

"Rock'n'roll!" shouted the rest of them, throwing down their whiskies together.

"All right," Don called out, "time to man your posts. Break down the thunder!"

They almost ran to their instruments.

"Good. What'll it be, Thomas?"

Tom held his hands out from his guitar, palms up. "What else? 'Break Down the Thunder.'"

Don nodded, and Billy began thrashing his drum set, joined by Don's rolling deep bass. Frank carried the melody, with George hammering the black and whites. Tom joined in with power strokes.

Suddenly, they all dialed down to a common beat, repeated twice without interruption until Tom stepped up to the mike. He struck a heavy chord and began to sing.

> "I got freedom, freedom,
> freedom answers to me.
> I got freedom ready,
> ready to be,
> if all of you
> answer to me."

Tom sold the vocals as if it wasn't one of his first songs, a very deep cut on The Weatherly Experience's first album. In line with protestors at the time, "Break Down the Thunder" wouldn't have made it even on a 45's B side. The rockin' dirge only made the album because the band had produced it, and they were short on tunes. Hell, he still might have a hundred or so of the disks up in the garage attic, all that he saved after trashing the rest unsold. Could bring in a few bucks now, he thought, a rare collector's item. Worth more if they could pull off this comeback.

They came to the wrap up, with Tom hammering his Martin while shouting out the last verse to be heard above the others.

> "Break down the thunder,
> cry your battle cries,
> the world's gone under,
> though freedom will survive
> only if you all
> answer to me."

The band's full cast bellowed out one last shout "Break down the thunder!" They stopped, then broke into laughter together.

"That shook the cobwebs out," Tom said, smiling.

"No one napping in Patchoque now," George said.

"All right. Let's go down the list," said Don, "see what order we'll play in the show."

"Man, we're getting it down!" Frank couldn't hide his excitement playing a gig with a chart-making band, even if it was eons ago.

"Yeah, we got the beat," Billy said, "to beat the comp'."

"Oh, really? Plan on dislodging Prince anytime soon?" George said.

"He's old news, all washed up," Billy said, stretching back from his set, holding his drumsticks together with both hands.

"I see. Well, then how 'bout U2? Those boyos been around as long as any and they still number one."

"Not to worry," Billy yawned, "they're all fuckin' broads. Some of 'em are like two broads."

"I'm sure they all be happy to hear that," George said, "'specially from the likes of you."

"Yeah, well, just wait and see, my man. From now on we'll all be eatin' nothing but red meat."

"Man, that shit'll kill you," Frank said quietly.

Billy nodded, "Only a few diehards left; we're gonna die soon and die hard!"

They all laughed, even George shaking his head.

Twenty-Five

Tom felt good about the rehearsal, just two weeks before the big gig try-out. Despite goofing whenever Don called a break, the band seemed to be coming together at just the right time. At the end of the session, Don laid out the schedule.

"From today until showtime, double sessions. A week from Friday, we'll iron out any last wrinkles. We'll eat at five, then load up the van. We'll set up at the Robespierre around six and play our first set at seven."

"Yeah man!" howled Billy.

Don squinted. He raised his hand and pointed his finger in Billy's direction. "And, no booze, weed, snow, or any other pick-me-ups whatsoever that day."

"Aw, man," Billy cried out, "what a fuckin' killjoy."

"I'll kill you straight up if you come in lit up," barked Don. "I will happily blow your shit away."

Billy drew back, frowning.

"Hey, boy, don't fuck with the man," George said, nodding toward Don without looking. "He don't play. Keep in mind, there no turning back from a bullet."

"Oh, I'm so sure," Billy drawled sarcastically, looking spooked.

In a passable imitation of James Earl Jones, George said deeply, "Come to the dark side of the voice, Billy."

They all laughed, except for Billy and Don.

"Okay then," Tom said. "We're all set, right? Good. See you tomorrow."

They all grabbed a beer from the refrigerator and filed out the door.

Tom looked at Don. "All good?"

Don blew out a flat B, "As good as it gets with this lot."

"Yeah, well, ..."

After Don left, Tom wended his way back to the house, pausing to gaze around at the flower beds near the pool. Damp and bare marking the change of seasons, the grounds looked forlorn to him, almost yearning for spring to come, so far away it seemed now. That is, he thought, if flowers and shrubs could yearn.

He sighed, wondering if flowers sighed, too. Foolish, what the mind could turn to when preoccupied. Except, if it was preoccupied, what was it before other than occupied? Which came first, occupied, or preoccupied? If he'd thought about something before, then came back to it, did that designate the topic as preoccupied? If anything entered his thoughts afterward, would that qualify it as post-occupied?

Tom shook his head briskly, wondering what filled it now? The big gig? Felix's lagging on cleaning out the pool, and the flower beds nearby? Worse, was he becoming more like Billy, George, and Frank sitting in saloons wondering if submarines travel faster under water or on top? He shrugged, shivering like he was freezing. Bad, he thought, bad hanging around those bozos, soon to turn him into a bozo himself again.

He exhaled loudly, wondering what Mary had left to microwave and eat. Hitting the switch, he watched the garage door crank its way up to the ceiling, revealing the lawn tractor, the Monte Carlo, and next to them, his Nova. Norah was here, he realized suddenly, brightening up. He took giant steps up to the kitchen door and swung it wide open.

Norah stood at the island holding a cup of tea. She seemed mildly startled by his sudden appearance. She smiled slightly.

Tom stopped, still holding the door near the wall. Her beauty stunned him, her tousled brown hair, the slight crinkle of her brow as she eyed him with her sharp hazel eyes. She seemed utterly at ease, leaning against the block, comfortable in a denim shirt and dark-green khakis.

"What?" she said.

Tom caught his breath. "Nothing. I'm just glad to see you."

"Oh," she replied, nodding, "Me too."

He breathed in and out, "Yeah."

At that, Norah straightened up. "Are you hungry? Mary stocked some leftovers to warm up."

"Sure, I could eat."

They sat across from each other, spooning tomato soup conjured by Mary with late-ripening garden tomatoes and magical seasoning known only to her. Real butter spread on a warmed baguette and a half-full bottle of sauvignon blanc completed the perfect late-evening meal. Tom hardly tasted any of it, fixated as he was on Norah in front of him.

She sipped her wine, then said, "Enjoying the soup?"

"Yeah," he nodded.

"Mary is a sorceress," she said.

"That she is."

"Better than your mom?"

"I can't say that. Haven't seen her for a while. Talked to her on the phone around holidays. That's it."

"Wow. Really?"

He twisted his lips, and said, "Yeah, I'm a lousy son. My sister's a saint by comparison. She sees Mom on all the holidays, and her birthday. I just call. Sometimes I remember to send them gifts. But really, I am a shitty son and brother."

"And your dad?"

"With the angels."

"Oh, I'm sorry."

"It's been a while. I'm much older than you, don't forget."

"You are that."

"Hey, not that much," he objected.

She laughed silently, and he said, "What about your folks?"

"Both still kicking in, North Carolina. They moved to a seniors development near Wilmington, everything on the same floor."

"That's nice," he said, sounding somewhat forlorn.

Norah quickly said, "Hey, how about dessert? I think there's something chocolate in the fridge."

"No, I'm not that hungry."

"Okay. It'll still be there for breakfast if you want."

He laughed as Norah stood up and cleared their plates. While she put them in the dishwasher, he spoke.

"Listen," he said, "I know I've been delinquent in helping you look for a new place, what with the gig coming up and all. I feel bad about being away from Marbury, too."

"The kids miss you," she said, her back to him while she put leftovers in the refrigerator. "Especially Buddy—"

He laughed.

"—and Devon."

She turned around looking at him.

"Oh, shit," he said. "No excuse, just lazy. I promise I'll be over there tomorrow right after rehearsal. After that, I can take you to see some new housing possibilities."

Norah said, "No need," she said, stepping over to place her hand behind the nape of his neck. She whispered "Let's go—" as she lowered herself, gently pulling him to her mouth and kissing him.

Tom held her arms and kissed her back, deeply. Norah jumped to wrap her legs around his waist as she mumbled, "Mmm,"

Tom slipped his hands beneath her legs and lifted her up to wrap around his waist. Holding her closely, he walked her into the guest room and laid her down gently, sidling next to her. Norah never let him go. She started unbuttoning his shirt, then his belt while he lifted her shirt up to caress her back, kneading her gently down to her waist, moving his hands around and up to her breasts.

Norah pulled at his trousers, slipping one hand beneath his shorts. She worked her way down, pulling his pants and shorts off, mouthing him as she held him from behind.

Tom gingerly slid her up to him face to face. He kissed her, softly, then harder. He dropped down to her waist, removed the rest of her clothes, and nuzzled his head between her legs.

Following her lead, he plied her with his tongue and fingers. She guided him with her hand on his head, he moving more and more until she froze, emitting a tiny cry. He paused, then started again, several times until she stopped him with her fingers tangled in his hair.

"Uff Da," she rumbled. Then, she whispered, "C'mon up here with me."

He hiked himself up above her, and she guided him inside. Tom moved up and down in slow strokes until she said, "Go ahead, finish."

He did with a sustained grunt as she said "Ah."

He rolled off onto his side next to her. "Wow," he murmured.

"Pretty sweet all right," she said. Lifting herself up on one elbow, she pounded his chest, "Good job!"

They both laughed, tucking close together side by side.

After a while, he said, "So I'm thinking." He raised up on an elbow, gazing at her. "You don't want to look for another place tonight, right?"

"Not tonight," she said. She punched him lightly on his arm, "Now get back to work."

Later while lying next to her, his arm draped over his eyes, he wondered how this all came about. Again. After the first time, clearly an exercise in horniness, he had written off getting intimate with her anymore. Hope of that happening again occupied a very tiny part of his dreams, which made this night's activity complete, causing him to wonder if it ever would happen again. A one-off after a one-off again?

He thought about how it all came about and how it maybe was different from the first time. It certainly didn't play out like a case of "wham-bam, thank you ma'am." But the first time didn't either, though it did only go one round. This was different, too, in that he followed her directions. He seldom gave it a thought.

Back in the day, groupies seemed happy getting it on every which way. Norah seemed to enjoy it, too, though by this time he understood the quid pro quo of it all. Funny how you might not think twice about a groupie doing whatever, then turn around and admire a long-term sweetheart doing the same. Of course, he never had that many long-term relationships. Certainly not any like with Norah.

He moved his arm from his eyes back beneath his head. Only time would tell.

Tom suddenly sat up. Startled, she said, "What's wrong?"

"Um," he muttered, searching for how to say it until he finally mumbled, "I, uh," he sighed, "forgot to use a condom."

"Oh." She said nothing for an instant, then elbowed him in the ribs. "Don't worry. I dug up my diaphragm before I left Mrs. Landry's."

"Huh," he said. "Mrs. Landry's. You came here for a purpose."

She laughed, "I did do that!"

"Yeah. That thing, you on top undulating like that. . . it blew my mind."

She smiled, chuckling again, "Pilates with a purpose."

"I'll say."

They found it difficult to get out of bed except for trips to the loo or the kitchen. When she returned in again, huddling close with him under the comforter, she heard him humming a tune, familiar, but no words.

"What is that? I know it but I can't place what it is."

He began to sing:

> "'I got up this morning and while I was having my coffee,
> my woman came in, sat down by my side.
> With tears in her eyes, she said 'I've a confession to make'
> and I said to her 'Woman, speak what's on your mind.'
> She said, 'I've found somebody new to take your place.'
> I said, 'Don't feel so all alone, I've found someone of my own.'"

"That's it!" Norah cried out. "Man, that goes way back."

"Yup, 1971 by Frank Robinson, lead singer of the Free Movement."

"I never heard of them," she said.

"Yeah, they never had a hit after that one, so they split up."

"Huh, just like in the song."

"Well, sort of, I guess. But the song was a big hit, covered like a dozen times."

"Really?"

"Oh yeah. The King covered it." Seeing her puzzled expression, he said, "Elvis." So did some country singer, Cal Smith, a big hit. George Benson, too. Shit, even Hall and Oats sang it."

"Maybe that's where I remember it from," said Norah. "Seems like such a downer though, you know? They're both still unhappy breaking up, even though they've found other lovers."

"Yeah, could be. Or when he sings 'Don't feel so all alone, I've found someone of my own,' she's already said she found a new guy. So, maybe he's just saying he has, too, because he loves her so much. Maybe he wants her to think that he has someone new when he really doesn't so that she won't feel so bad."

"Wow," she said, "That's heavy."

"You never thought of this song that way?"

"No," she said wondrously. "Makes it even more morose."

He turned his head to face her. "You mean to tell me all the times you've heard the song, you never thought of a possible subtext?"

"Well, no. I haven't heard that song that many times."

He turned his head away. "God, I got to spend less of my time alone in my own mind. No wonder I don't get anything done."

She laughed, leaning in to punch his arm. "Once again, I' caught surprised that you're such a such a deep thinker."

He shook his head, "Yeah, I'm a fucking genius all right."

Norah smiled, laughing again as she snuggled up to him, "Works for me."

Twenty-Six

"Damn it!!" Norah spat out loud. What had she gotten herself into? Turning into a rock and roll camp follower? "God," she moaned, dragging out the epithet. She grabbed her head with both hands, which felt as large and heavy as a bowling ball.

"Ow," she whimpered. She closed her eyes, rubbing them as hard as she could, though the pain refused to recede.

She learned that her humble lover grew bolder every night they spent together. Back from one of his kitchen trips, he stopped to lean against the tallboy. Eyes closed, she could see him again, resting one arm on top of the dresser, the other draped over his shoulder like David, naked and nonchalant after whacking Goliath. Sloe-eyed, Tom asked her in a whisper, "Would you like to kiss me on the lips?"

Surprised, she opened her mouth laughing, but nothing came out. He dropped his arms and hugged her tightly, kissing her. He said, "This is comfortable for me. Let's stay like this all day."

She giggled as he pressed his lower body against hers. "Is that where you keep your loins?"

Norah barked another laugh, pushing him away, "Down boy!"

"Don't worry, I only have a quarter of a chubby."

"A chubby? Really?" she laughed.

"That's' what we called them back in junior high. I can go with erection if you prefer."

She boldly touched him below. "Seems like you could go either way."

"Um," Tom said, "next to you."

"Next to me."

"Yes."

"Without taking any liberties."

"Well," he said, "I don't know, I might have to hug you a couple of times. I tend to do that sometimes in bed."

"Of course, when you're with someone else."

Tom frowned, remaining silent.

"Then, no sex last night."

He shook his head looking morose.

She turned her head back and forth, barely shifting her eyes in time to the road. A school bus passed by with a half-hearted honk.

All mixed up; every visceral signal telling her she had to dump this guy. But why? Because he was a rocker, out of touch all the time and distracted by every shiny thing flashing past his eyes? Shit, here she was, driving alone in his big-boy toy Nova to Marbury because he had to have just one more practice for the big gig tonight.

Her head swayed again, involuntarily. He vowed out loud to her and himself that he'd be at Marbury every day that week. He knew the kids depended on him, all of them now, toddlers and teenyboppers alike, deep in his throes. When he showed up, party time. When he didn't, misery. The big kids played it cool, almost hiding their disappointment by shrugging it off. The little ones moped and complained out loud, crying. The big kids then told the little squirts to shut the fuck up, causing greater chaos, the grownups in the middle groping for their heads fresh off the guillotine.

But Devon. He showed nothing, which worried her. Children who displayed no affect often signaled deeper concerns hidden away. And that Able guy started coming around more and more often, spending time with the kids, big and small, particularly Devon. Not a surprise, Norah thought, recognizing that their little Dali Lama stood out. But Able taking over for Tom Weatherly, the Marbury Pied Piper? Not fucking likely—unless the Piper skipped the starting time. Which was why she could be so fucking mad at him all the time. Again, she wondered why she still thought so much about him.

True, the sex wasn't bad, even when it didn't go quite as planned, she laughed, remembering sitting on the bed naked, her legs folded beneath her.

She gazed down at him as he tried to get to it. Seeing his brow wrinkle in frustration, she howled, "Whoa, you lost your psych!"

"C'mon give it a chance!"

She started laughing, holding her fingers spread across her mouth. He looked down, alarmed, then back up at her.

"Now look what you've done!"

They both started in again, heads closer, laughing silently, too hard to speak. Finally, Norah gathered herself and said, "Maybe your libido lost its mojo."

"Well, what'd you expect—it's not just some faucet you turn on and off. I'm no teenager, remember."

"Oh right, the old codger Mr. Bojangles. Where's your dog? And when did you lose your virility?"

"At a very early age. Same with the dog."

"Really?"

"Yeah. He's gone, though. You know, my age in dog years. But he led a full life. Plenty of hip humping."

She laughed again, driving on. He could make her laugh.

Blowjob!" he bellowed one time stepping out of the shower.

"Excuse me," she said dryly, "I can only do so much at one time. What do you want first? Coffee, tea, or me?"

"Champagne cocktail!" he barked.

She sat back, smirking as she eyed him. "Again, priorities."

He hesitated. "I know I'll regret it later, but . . . coffee!"

He entertained everyone with ridiculous bromides and stupid made-up theories that had his audience laughing out loud while scratching their heads.

"Scratching is not a cure. It just makes you want to scratch more."

She shook her head.

"I'm pretty much glad that I'm straight. Makes life simpler. I admit, I like boobs, though God knows why. I just do. But I'm too self-conscious to be a boor. I keep my eyes up, too afraid to get caught looking."

She didn't have much luck trying to match his goofiness. One morning he pronounced, "I'm using my 'l' words today: 'Lassitude,' 'lachrymose,' 'lamentable'— 'lazy,' of course— 'lackadaisical'."

She parried immediately. "Really? Why so low?"

"Ah, quick, very quick," he laughed. "Right where my 'latitude' meets my 'longitude'."

Sometimes he just wore her out. Like he had to fill every void with something, anything, mostly funny, sometimes annoying after she brought something serious up. Like his sudden absence at Marbury.

"You said you'd come every day, and you haven't been there for the entire week. The kids are starting to think you've left them in the lurch, something too familiar to them."

"I'm sorry, I really am. It's just the rehearsals have run way long. The closer we get to showtime, the young prodigies seem to tighten up."

"I know," she said stridently, "but you made a commitment. A promise. You do whatever you want, but it matters to them. Especially the little ones— especially Devon." She said the last in a very small voice.

Tom remained quiet, still, his hands folded in his lap. She accelerated cleaning up the odds and ends after their sandwich dinner. "The astonishment comes from wondering where you are."

He grimaced, "'That's just great, Norah, just great. It grates on me, that's for sure. I'm a grown man, listen to me groan. I'm a wit! A lonesome wit. Still, better than a halfwit."

She threw a plastic serving spoon hard into the sink and snapped, "I never realized before what a rich exterior life you have."

"Well, you know how it is—Quoteth God: You want to be free, so here's your free will. Good luck with it.'"

"Oh, that is so profound, your grace, allow me to pull on me forelock."

"And thanks to you, Mrs. McGillicuddy."

"So, you think I'm an Irish buffoon, do you?"

"Absolutely not. Just Lucy O'Ball's mother."

She clicked her tongue again while leaving the kitchen, "Reruns. The bane of my existence."

When she returned an hour later, there he was, grabbing his head in his hands. He shook it back and forth. "What a fuck-up I am," he moaned silently.

Norah walked back into the kitchen. She noticed the open bottle of scotch and the tumbler next to it, empty. She stepped in front of him and said, "You know, I could just punch you in the head I'm so pissed at you."

"I know, he said. "I'm pissed at me, too."

"You're pissed, that's for sure," Norah said, nodding her head at the bottle. "Just what are you doing out here?"

"Talking to myself, and it's not going well. I'm not a good listener. It's like you said before; whatever I try doing . . . doesn't."

He peered up at her with watery eyes, "Do you know, every time after a shower, I clean the hair off the drain, thinking all the while I'm watching myself going bald. I'm starting to forget stuff, like my old man used to. People's names, or movie titles, like that. Then I get really fucking furious—if I'm going to lose my memory, why can't it be all the terrible shit happening to everyone on the planet all the goddamn time?"

He stared up at her. "And you know what's the worst. That I'm such a fucking crybaby about my sad, sad self, boo-hoo, boo-hoo." He whirled himself away from her, muttering "What a fucking dick."

Norah paused. "Okay. You're a dick." He looked back at her startled. "So's everyone one time or another. Make it right, make a point of coming over after rehearsal no matter what. Honestly, you guys have been at this for months. Odds are you're as good as you're going to get. So, block it out; come over after rehearsal this week, every day, even nighttime. Don't let in Don or the others—I'm sure you're the worst offender."

He flattened his lips together. "I guess I am."

"Well, don't let anyone or anything get in the way of seeing the kids. Every day this week. Play a song and see them to bed. They'll love it, and they'll love you all over again."

Tom nodded. "Okay."

Of course, he immediately walked out to his studio, and she wondered if he'd make it to Marbury even today. Well, she couldn't control everything.

Before she left, she headed over to the master bedroom to use the toilet. Sitting there, she noticed a V-shaped magazine rack crammed full of folded newspapers, *People* magazine, science fiction paperbacks, and various envelopes. His office, she noted.

She ran a finger through the paper morass, as much curious about what he read as finding something for herself to pass time. A crumpled envelope showed up. She plucked it out and read the front address.

It wasn't an address; it entitled the contents in light blue ink: *Fortunes*. She opened and pulled out a handful of small scraps of paper, some deep yellow from age. A smiley face fronted the first printed passage.

He that falls in love with himself will have no rivals.

Huh, she thought, a Chinese cookie fortune. She flipped to the next one, also led by a smiley face.

You may at one time be impractical, sporty, or intensely restless.

Followed by another smiley face. She read more.

You will discover the truth in time.

Listen these next few days to your friends to get answers you seek.

Now is a good time to explore.

An interesting musical opportunity is in your near future.

Do something unusual tomorrow.

On her drive to Marbury, she mulled over Tom's behavior. Man, she thought, who does this? This boy was so much more than the typical pop star. Sure, he enjoyed all the trappings, the money, the big boy toys, the fame, being roguish, the idolatry, and of course, the girls. But he was different than most of the others, he possessed a soul-saving quality too. Just out of reach in her thoughts, she settled on a revelation. He was nice. Nice to everyone, not a mean bone in his body.

"Boy," she grunted, pulling the Nova to the curb right in front of Marbury House, his favorite space, open of course. "How does anyone handle that?"

Twenty-Seven

He was late, late, late. Hard to believe how a band could screw up so much after playing together for damn near half a year. No lying about it, they were one screwed-up group.

He took a deep breath, just the heebie jeebies of a first-time lineup. Once in place, they'll come around, right after playing that first song in their first gig. He hoped to God anyway.

The street narrowed, packed by cars parked bumper to bumper on both sides. Tom cursed, wondering if he had to find a space three blocks away. But as he pulled up to Marbury House, once again fate smiled on him. He deftly whipped the Monte Carlo up parallel to the front car and backed in behind it in one smooth move. Sweet.

He hopped out, rolled around to the curbside door, opened it, and extracted his trusty six-string. Holding it by its neck, he balanced it on top of a shoulder and marched to the front porch.

As soon as he entered the house, he ran into Amelia squiring a small clutch of strangers around, donators no doubt, unable to attend the last open house.

"Oh, and here's another one of our heroes, Tom Weatherly," she said lusciously. "You might recognize him from listening to pop music on the radio; he knows all about green-eyed ladies."

"Sure," one Wall-Street suit said, "'Sugarloaf.' You were in that group."

Tom mentally pouted. "No, they were a little early for me, still in grade school."

"Oh."

An awkward silence followed until Amelia broke in, "Now, Tom here had a big hit with a song title like that. You remember 'Malachite Eyes', don't you?"

The visitor looked clueless for an instant, then said, "You bet."

"Yes, a real cool tune," Amelia said, quickly hustling them forward, "Let's get with the kids, they're all stoked to meet y'all."

Tom dropped his fixed grin and tapped on Amelia's shoulder before she could follow the visitors.

"Is Norah here?"

Amelia thought for a moment. "She was here this morning, then took off for lunch. Gertrude sent her out for some goods, I think. I haven't seen her since."

"Oh, okay, thanks Amelia."

She smiled over her shoulder as she hurried after the visitors.

Wondering where Norah had gone, Tom started searching for Devon and the other squirts. Typical fate, the day he makes it here to play, Norah's not around to witness it.

He moved through the right front sitting room, to the narrow butler passageway into the kitchen. A handful of preteens sat at the table in the middle doing their homework. They glanced up when he came in and broke into an incoherent ruckus until Jerome bellowed "Shut the fuck up!"

The other kids went silent.

"Nice to see you, Mr. T."

"Nice to see you, Jerome. I thought you moved on."

Jerome shook his head, ringlets bouncing off his brow, "Nope. Still here. You still layin' 'em down?"

"Not much lately. Getting ready for a new gig. Practicing a lot."

"Gotcha. But you playin' here today."

"Hope so."

The other kids broke in, "Yay," "You go, Mr. T," "Get down, B.B."

"All right, okay," Tom said, waving his hand. "I don't want to disturb you. Doing homework?"

"Some," one girl said, another following with, "Til *Law and Order* come on."

"Right. Okay, I'll move along. Meantime, keep an eye out for Ms. Norah, all right? Let me know."

Jerome nodded, and Tom turned to go back to the vestibule.

"Tom Weatherly, here you are again."

Leaning against the stairway post stood the Lincoln guy. He smiled wryly, slow-twirling waist-high a jaunty fedora straight off Frank Sinatra's hatrack. A cool, black corduroy jacket covered his purple dress-shirt tucked into fitted wool pants breaking perfectly over his black dress shoes. A hip, very upscale look, Tom noted. For someone ready to party a state affair, walk right in, but why? He also wondered why he was so mesmerized by this guy's cool-beans ensemble.

"Hey," Able said, holding out an open hand. Tom reached over reflexively, startled to feel a soft dead fish slip away.

He blinked, glancing up at obsidian eyes half-closed. Was this guy high, or just chill?

"How you been?" he asked, smile beaming, eyes gleaming.

"Good," murmured Tom, casually slipping his hands in his jeans pockets. "Busy."

"I'll bet. Everyone here says you're hittin' the road soon with your band. Gonna wow 'em again, huh?"

"Hope so."

"Well, good on you for not forgettin' Marbury, know what I mean?"

"Yeah, absolutely. You, too."

"I know! I came for a reason, but there's more here to see than I expected. I dig it, you know?"

"I do."

"Well, all right, then."

"Yup." Tom hesitated, then said, "Listen, I'm sorry, but for the life of me, I can't remember your name."

The tall man lifted his head up, staring at Tom for a moment. "Terrence Able," he said. He grinned knowingly, "Terry."

"Oh, good, thanks. I'm way past my memory shelf-date these days."

"Right, I get you, I get it."

"Yeah, listen, I need to go in and play for the little kids right now. You're welcome to come along if you don't mind hearing me torture a few golden oldies."

Terry's eyes crinkled as he smiled, "No, man, that'd be great. You got a big reputation here, you know?"

"Yeah, me and Tiny Tim."

Seeing Able's puzzled look, Tom said, "Never mind, it goes back to Johnny Carson and *The Tonight Show*. Anyway, we meet in the back sitting room to the left. I'll lead the way."

When they entered the old parlor room, the kids stopped what they were doing and swarmed Tom, like in a 1940s horror film, he thought.

"Okay kids, back around the sofa. Get ready to sing."

He scanned the room to find Devon sitting at the end of the old sofa next to the wall. Able sat next to him. He leaned over and whispering to Devon.

"All right, I'll start with an oldie that was big before any of you shot out of your momma's tummy. I'll sing some of it first, then you all can join in. Okay?"

They all howled an indecipherable roar. While waiting for them to quiet down, he noticed Able gently lifting Devon over to sit on his thigh. Tom shifted his eyes to Devon, who seemed no worse the wear.

"Good, now this is an old, sweet song I hope you like. Wait until I nod my head for you to join in."

He cleared his throat and strummed his six-string.

"Tip toe through the window
by the window, that is where I'll be,
come tiptoe through the tulips with me.

"Oh, tiptoe from the garden
by the garden of the willow tree
and tiptoe through the tulips with me."

Tom nodded his head, and started the song again, reciting the first line, coaxing his audience to accompany him.

"Glad to see you could make it," Norah said.

"I'm off to a great start," Tom replied.

"Here's hoping you can finish strong."

She raised her glass, which he tipped with his own, and they sipped.

"How do you like your Kool-Aid?"

Tom grimaced, shrugging, "I've had better. To be honest, I never liked the stuff when I was a kid."

"Really?"

"Yeah, really."

"Not even orange flavored?"

"Nope. None of that fake stuff. Can't beat orange juice."

"I guess that's true. Cherry?"

"Still artificial."

"I suppose. What do you like?"

"Yoohoo, of course."

"Oh, for the love of God." She raised her open hands, "Hello, does chocolate milk ring a bell?"

"Delectable!" he said. "But Yoohoo does have a fizz aspect going for it."

She grabbed the top of her head with both hands, "Chocolate milk and some soda water."

"I never tried that," he said, raising his index finger to his lower lip, his brow wrinkled. "It might just work."

Norah shifted her hands together atop her head, "For the love of Mary and Joseph," she uttered, "you're the strangest."

"Been said before," he replied.

They sat at a small corner table in the Marbury kitchen, eating dinner leftovers. The singing session had gone well. After dinner, Buddy ushered the kids upstairs while Amelia and Gertrude put the dirty dishes in the house's industrial-size washer, thank you GOBC. Ed Novicky's idea, of course.

Neither of them had much to say, though they tried, since spending time together had become optimal lately.

"You see that dude wearing the *GQ* outfit?"

"What? Who?"

"You know, Mr. Terrance Able from the last open house."

She squinted hard, trying to place him. "Yes. Good-looking guy."

"Not that good-looking. Anyway, have you seen him here since?"

"No, I don't think so."

"Yeah, well he was here today. Hanging around the sing-along."

"Huh," Norah said. She paused. "Maybe he's got a thing for you."

"Not bloody likely," Tom said, giving her the gimlet eye.

"Oh, yeah, he's obsessed. Got your attention by stealing your parking space, then fell all over apologizing. I remember him now. Better watch out, Weatherly, he's a real dangerous groupie."

"Get the hell—"

"You know how ardent they can be. Why, I bet he's gone commando beneath those snazzy duds just for you."

"Cut it out; you need a shrink."

"Oh, really? Well, here's a neutral man off the streets. Let him testify." She turned her attention to Buddy, who had just arrived from the kitchen. "Buddy, you remember the good-looking guy that Tom got all pissy about when he took his parking space? At the open house."

"The guy wearing the *Esquire* ensemble? He was here today. He's visited a couple of times."

"No shit?"

Buddy nodded up and down, "After school. He cruised around checking out the reprobates doing their homework. Looked in on the bambinos watching *Looney Tunes*. I never did have a chance to ask him, but he seemed to enjoy them as much as the kiddoes."

"I don't wonder," Norah said, "I mean, c'mon, Bugs and Elmer."

"Daffy Duck," Tom chimed in, "Yosemite Sam."

Buddy sniffed. "I prefer the savoir fair of Pepe Le Pew."

Norah and Tom both laughed at Buddy's deadpan expression as he left the room.

"Anyway," he said, "time to round up the little rascals, big ones too, herd them to bed."

"Oh, okay," Norah said, rising from her chair. "That's my cue," she said, gathering up their dishes. "I'm on the night watch with the Budsman."

"Hah, that's cute," Tom said, then shifted gears. "I thought you'd be coming back to the pad," he said, leering exaggeratingly.

"Not tonight, Hef. See you at breakfast, maybe."

"Awwh."

"I know, boo after hoo after boo. Anyway, you need to recharge, too, right? Practice for the show," she said singsongingly.

"Yeah, yeah."

"Well, all right then. Go home and rest. I'll come around tomorrow for brunch or lunch."

"Okay, okay."

She gave him a peck and started loading the dishwasher.

The week did not turn out as he thought it would. Norah called to tell him she had to skip lunch to do some paperwork for Gertrude. The Marbury Madam had discovered just how much talent Norah possessed, and rapidly exploited the same. Thing was, Tom fretted, Norah really liked pitching in.

He blew out air. Like he could complain. His own promise to see the kids almost daily looked to be hollow, at least next week. The young Weatherly players seemed to be locking up during practice, especially Billy. He could see the stick man's internal temperature rising, slowly building to set off a raucous explosion unless his bandmates could bleed some of his steam. Fat chance, especially if the group's so-called superstar seldom showed up.

He couldn't do it. He was a Marbury benefactor, not an employee or volunteer. Hell, he thought, he wouldn't be struggling with this if Norah didn't care. She held the lynchpin to his dilemma trying to be in two places at one time. What to do?

Huffing breath, he rubbed the side of his cheek, thinking.

Time management. He needed to block out next week's schedule to allow equal or near-equal time with both entities. Three entities, really, including time with Norah. And sleep. So, 24 hours divided by four equaled six hours each for Marbury, the band, Norah, and the rest, including driving time. Not too daunting for a single week. He'd done similar slicing and dicing in his past and was no worst the wear. Though he'd been a lot younger then.

Never mind, only a week. Start at 11:00 am, brunch and practice until 4:00 pm. At 5:00 pm, Marbury kiddie time until 8:00 pm. Dinner with Norah, in the sack by midnight. Friday practice and gig into Saturday. Repeat every day until next Friday.

Slightly bobbing his head up and down, Tom thought it could work. Of course, only if she herself went along with it.

Twenty-Eight

The best-laid plans, Norah thought, driving to work. Tom explained his problem and solution, which she understood and endorsed. She did doubt that they could follow the timetable one hundred percent, but it was only for a week. Just one week, which gave them both a little wiggle room, considering their slightly out-of-sync lifestyles. Every couple had to deal with conflicts of interest, she recognized. At least, so far. Still, here it was, already Wednesday. And were they really a couple?

In the aftermath of an open house, much needed to be done in the following days, especially after such a robust showing produced by the last gathering. Jerome won the lottery again, picked by an artistic couple offering to put him through school, college or trade. When he left, the Marbury staff retired to the kitchen to raise a toast. Norah noticed their eyes, doubtful above their broad grins. Jerome had been back and forth so many times before.

A few girls departed, too, youngsters and a couple of 'tweeners. Most of them never returned. Older boys did, though.

Anyway, time to reorder the house, including notifying other shelters and centers of the current openings. They went fast, the new kids usually arriving the same day. That's when the Marbury gang of four sprang into action, welcoming the newcomers, taking them on a tour of the facilities with a subtle subtext relating the rules. Very few fit in right away, though eventually all felt welcome. As much as they could, anyway, considering their circumstances.

She parked the car, being sure to lock it, and walked to the front porch. She opened the door to ultra-loud chaos, loving it.

Four-fifths of The Weatherly Experience sat in their chairs mesmerized by the fifth who sang standing at his post.

"Bob Dylan," Billy said. "Like a rollin' stone," he croaked, "in my nasal tone."

He stopped and said, "Frankie Valli," then shifting to falsetto. "Walk like a man, sing like a girl, walk like m-a-an-n."

"Okay, here's another; k.d. lang—" His voice rose to his top range. "Con–stant ku-vetching." He stopped, waiting for a reaction. Nothing.

"Well?" he said.

No one said anything.

"Oh, come on," Billy whined, "It's good, dead center!"

Don said, "Okay, this is what bothers me about everything." He stood up. "Instead of revisiting Billboard's Bottom Covers for the past half-century, why don't we try getting a passing version of our own shit?"

"Hey," George called out, "at least it ain't grunge."

"Or hip-hop," Billy shouted.

"What the fuck you know about hip-hop, motherfucker?"

"I know a lot about everything," Billy snapped. "I'm probably an autodidact."

"A what?"

"Autodidact, motherfucker. Knowing almost all there is to know."

"You're more like an autodi-dick!"

By this time George stood in front of Billy separated only by the drums. Don stepped in facing George.

"C'mon," he said, gesturing with his head.

George swallowed and returned to his seat.

Don turned to stare at Billy silently for a moment. He said, "What the fuck's wrong with you? We've got three days before we go on."

"Well, sue me," Billy said, "This is how I get ready. You don't like it, cut me loose."

Don stared, still as ice. Tom moved over before anything else might happen.

"Okay, everyone's tired, all wound up. Let's take stock for a minute, get back on track then."

Billy sat down behind his set. Don pivoted, turning around to ensure that Tom took notice of his outrage.

Tom spoke again. "Boys, we have just two practices left after this. We're lucky for that 'cause we could use another month. That's how we've regressed. We all know this, I think, all of us have short fuses. I say let's forget the small shit and zero in on the important stuff, playing the best we can this coming Friday night. I'm excited, and I hope you are, too. Let's leave the bad shit, the nervous nelly shit behind and get up front with what we've already proved we can do."

"Damn straight!" roared George.

"Hell yeah!" Frank yelled.

Tom watched Billy squirm and say, "I'm with you all. I'll do my damn best."

"All right," Tom said. "Don, ready to kick it off?"

Still burning, Don dipped his chin and played the opening note.

The practice concluded well enough, though they all still felt tension from the earlier outburst. As soon as the last man went out the door, Tom sidled over to Don.

"So?"

"I don't know, man. How can we keep this going while preventing our asshole percussionist from completely imploding? Worse, exploding!"

"I know, I know," Tom said, "he's scared to death. It's weird, not like he hasn't ever played out before."

"Sure," Don said, "but he's never worked with a rock-n'-roll star."

"Star? You know better than that," Tom said.

"Yeah, but he doesn't. Neither does Frank, George too. Though at least he knows he rules the ivories."

Tom pursed his lips, slowly nodding his head, "George does get down." He glanced at Don, "He'd be better off without Billy for sure. I don't know why he lets the little twerp drive him so crazy."

"George's a perfectionist, doesn't color outside the lines," Don said, "though his lines are pretty far out there on their own."

They both laughed.

"Yeah, Georgie can sweep us all into Nirvana."

Don glanced at Tom. "You know he'll be gone in a year or so, doing his own thing?"

"That'll be good," Tom grinned. "Hope he remembers to thank us at the Grammys."

"Hope we'll be around to enjoy it," Don said.

They laughed together and called it a night.

At home, Tom fell into bed at midnight, careful not to disturb the mound hiding beneath the covers on the left side. He slept on the right, closest to the bathroom. Lying there, he told himself he should get up and empty his tank. He also could drift off just for now, deal with the plumbing when the alarm below signaled Mayday.

Before he could dive into another world, the adjacent creature stirred, arose, and said, "Are you awake?"

"Now I am," he mumbled, "if I wasn't before."

"Oh. Sorry. Go back to sleep."

"Doesn't work that way."

"Oh, I'm so sorry, honey," Norah said.

"No, no," Tom said, working his way upright. "I'm awake. What's up?"

She reached her arms over to envelop him in a big hug. She felt warm, he thought, cozy.

"You can't sleep?"

Norah shook her head until realizing he couldn't see her. "No," she said quietly, "Not really."

"Oh. So, what's wrong?"

"I don't know," she said. "The place was a zoo, new kids arriving. Everyone trying to keep business as usual while welcoming our new charges, most buttoned down fearing a new place—again."

"Oh man, and we thought we had a bunch of young punks to straighten out."

"Yes," she whispered, "As the world turns."

"So, who did you lose?"

She sucked in a breath. "Shailene, Effy, and Vanita so far—Rashan."

"Rashan? No shit. I thought he'd been sent back here for the duration."

"Nope. He can be charming when he wants."

"Huh."

"We'll probably see him back soon enough. He gets antsy, followed by outrageous."

Tom sighed, "That's tough."

"Yeah." She spoke her words carefully. "There are others still under consideration."

"Really? Any I know?"

"A couple of 'tweeners," Norah said, "I don't think you know them; they came and went pretty fast."

"Uh huh."

"And, um," she hemmed.

"What?"

She turned to him. "Devon."

Tom didn't move or speak.

Norah forged ahead, "A relative, it seems, wants to adopt him."

After what seemed to be endless silence, Tom's voice floated.

"Who?"

Norah gritted her teeth before answering. "Terrance Able. He claims he's Devon's uncle." She waited in the dark, wishing for some light to appear.

"No," Tom whispered. "That sweet boy's uncle is Terry Able? That can't be right."

"I don't know," Norah said, "Gertrude tells me the paperwork looks to be in order."

"Terry," mumbled Tom, "'Everybody loves a sharp dressed man.'"

"I don't know," Norah said, almost equally upset. "He seems to be stable."

"Really? The guy comes in alone. Where's his family, his wife? Doesn't the kid need a mom?" Tom bleated.

"C'mon, Tom," she said. "There are lots of kids with single parents, good ones. Lots of single fathers."

"Yeah, I suppose," Tom said. "I don't know."

Norah said, "I'm turning the light on." She quickly faced Tom, startled to see him almost forlorn staring down at the bedspread. She expected him to be livid, his features viciously distorted by outrage. Instead, he looked wounded. Hesitant, she came to the realization that he wasn't one to explode in fury, she was. She would rather scorch the earth, which usually put her out of work while leaving the earth scorched. Never an antagonist, Tom was everyone's ombudsman; save the day, live another day.

"Right," she said, "You're exactly right."

"Oh? About what?"

"You know, keep on keepin' on."

"Oh, okay." Tom paused. "How do we go about that?"

"I don't know, maybe call him out somehow."

"Sure," he said, "I guess. But what if he's legit? If he checks out with Gertrude, we have to let go."

Norah grimaced, biting her lip. "Really? That's all we can do?"

Tom sighed. "I don't know. You know better than I do how these things fall out. I'm just a monkey with a squeeze box."

He could see her start to crumble. "Okay, neither of us know how this is gonna go. Let's sleep on it, then drive to Marbury first thing and ask Gertrude what's up."

Norah snapped to. "All right. But if it doesn't go our way, I'm not sure what I might do."

"Yeah, I'm not surprised. I'll hold your coat."

She punched him hard on his upper arm exactly where it hurt the most.

"Jesus Christ!" he shouted. "That really hurt!"

Smiling slightly, "Just so you know."

"Fuck yeah I know," he replied, rubbing his bicep. "C'mon, we need to sleep if we're leaving at dawn."

"Of course," Norah said, pushing him back on his pillow. She straddled him, saying, "Right after I turn out the light."

Twenty-Nine

Norah nudged him awake. "It's morning. Time to get up."

Tom remained still.

"Did you hear me?" Norah asked, poking his side.

"Yes," he droned.

"All right."

Tom remained still.

"Tom," she said louder, "Get the fuck up."

"Okay. I'm going to get up now."

A few minutes passed, and she said, "You mean now or," she raised her hands, "now?"

"One of those 'nows.'" Before she could go for him, he said, "Live in the now . . . at least for now. Well, for now. Putting one 'now' in front of another."

Just as she raised her fist to rap him, he slithered out of bed onto the floor. "Okay. I'm going to get up this now."

He stirred and failed.

"C'mon," she said standing in front of him, "I'll beat you to the shower."

"You win," he said, now sitting.

Despite the short night, they managed to leave the house at six, out before commuter traffic squeezed the road. Tom drove the Nova as fast as he could while cognizant of his shaky body, worn inside and out. He did notice Norah turning her head back and forth from the road to him. He kept his eyes on the road.

At length, she asked, "How you feeling now?"

"Like I was mugged. How many fingers am I holding up?"

She cut short her laugh.

"We're here," Tom said, stating the obvious to break the sudden silence.

"So," he said, "now what?"

"Now we go find Gertrude and ask her about Devon."

Inside, the kids passed by saying hello, or ducking their heads as they moved into the dining room. Norah and Tom followed them, peeling off into the kitchen to Gertrude' office, what used to be a modified butler's pantry. Amelia sat at her desk, clicking a mouse as she concentrated on the monitor screen in front of her.

"Hi, Amelia, how you doing?"

Amelia looked up, "Well, hi, Norah. Nice to see you, Mr. Tom. You're here early."

"Yes, we were inspired," Norah said.

Amelia laughed, "Well, then, praise be!"

They laughed. When it tapered off, Norah asked, "Is Gertrude here?"

Amelia shook her head, "She's not. She's off to CCCNC in Garden City."

"CCCNC?" Tom asked.

"Child Care Council of Nassau County. She goes after every open house to check backgrounds on a few potential foster parents we met at our open house. She should be back by suppertime."

"Oh," Norah said. "Well, then, I'm glad I came in early."

"Me too," Amelia nodded. "Plenty going on here right now."

"We noticed. I'll hang my jacket and get going."

"Great," said Amelia, "you, too, Tom."

"Oh, is Buddy around?" Norah asked.

"Upstairs. Rousting the stragglers."

"Good enough, I'll see if he needs a hand."

Buddy met them halfway down the stairway.

"Hello, fellow travelers. Early rise for Bedlam?"

"Hi, Buddy," Norah said, "I see you're at your morning best."

"Cheery as a fledgling in a cat's mouth."

"Oh, why so glum?"

"Because it's Thursday morning, not Sunday, my day of rest. And why are you so bright-eyed, bright eyes?"

Norah pressed her lips together, then said, "Do you have time for a quick talk?"

"For you, I have all of the time left in the world. The children are in the dining room, so how about the front parlor?"

He led them into the sitting room next to the vestibule. Tom wasn't used to seeing the room so clean, or the TV off for that matter. He glanced over at the door to the back room where he held his ad hoc concerts. He sighed just as Buddy stopped.

"What's up, friends?"

Norah hesitated a second, then spoke. "Buddy, you know the kids who are transitioning out of Marbury."

"Sure. I saw the list. I'm changing only half the linen in the boys' wing. I'm sure we'll be seeing certain individuals back in a few days. In fact, the renovations boys have a pool going on who returns first, if you want in," he turned to Tom, "including your associate Mr. Novicky."

Norah shook her head, "No thanks, Buddy. We're not here for that action. It's about Devon."

Buddy's insouciant expression morphed gravely. "Oh," he said flatly.

"You know, then."

He lowered his head, "Ms. Amelia told me. She said he was being adopted by his uncle, maybe next week." Saying it, he winced, quickly resuming his smooth-stone bodhisattva face.

Norah said, "That's what we heard, too. Amelia told us Gertrude was on her way to the Garden City to check backgrounds at the CCC. Do you think that includes Devon's uncle?"

"Who's that?" Buddy asked.

"The uncle," said Norah, rolling her eyes up to his. "Mr. Savior Faire." She waited. "You don't know, do you?"

"Know what?"

"The so-called uncle is Terrance Able." Seeing his puzzled face, she said, "Terry Able, Mr. Cool in his Madison Avenue duds. You know him, he's been hanging around Marbury for a while, now. Maybe a month."

Buddy still looked stymied.

Norah raised her voice, "He drives a black Lincoln for Chrissake."

"A Lincoln VIII," added Tom, "fast as hell."

Dawn broke on Buddy's face. "Yes. I remember him." He eyed Tom directly. "He took your parking space."

"It not exactly my parking space," Tom muttered, "but yes, he did take it, blatantly."

Looking annoyed, Buddy said, "Oh, he's not a savory gentleman at all. You can tell the first time you see him." He shook his head rapidly, "I know, believe you me."

"Well, we do, Buddy," Norah said, "but what can we do? Gertrude's at the CCC in Garden City checking out his bona fides. And if he's got them—if he really is Devon's uncle—that's it. Game over."

Buddy rubbed his chin, "Oh, I doubt that happens. You don't want just anybody taking our precious little boy. The Marbury House manifesto would come crashing down entirely."

"I hope you're right," Norah said in a small voice. "Amelia says Gertrude should be back by dinnertime."

"Well, then, we'll know then," Buddy said.

The little kids swarmed into the front parlor shouting, spraying little bits of breakfast in the air.

"Children behave," Buddy called out. "If you're going to spit food, do it in the music room."

Tom felt a warm wave flush through him. The music room doubled as the general depository of all the kids' stuff. Sobering, he noted.

Devon ran up to Buddy, hugged his kneecap, then pivoted to hug Norah's leg. He swung over to grab Tom's legs in a double take-down. Tom gazed down at Devon's fabulous hair, a thicket of soft umber ringlets crying out for fingers to knead. Which Tom did while he could until Devon broke away.

He dashed over to the picture window's large blinds lowered until the sun moved over the roof. Pushing a slat up as hard as he could, Devon said, "Hello, reflection."

While still talking to the other children, Buddy sidled over to the front window to raise the blinds.

"Hey," yelled Devon, "don't shine that light into my eyes or I'll go blond!"

The three adults laughed loudly, happy for the relief.

"I'll usher the rest of the restless into the music room," Buddy said, "You can bring the young master along with you?" he asked Tom.

"I'm afraid not," Tom said. "Tomorrow night's the big gig, so we're practicing our derrieres off getting ready."

"Oh," Buddy replied. "Then, I'll take the little prince with me now. Come along, Devon."

He gently moved Devon toward the back door to the music room, shutting the door behind them.

Norah and Tom walked into the vestibule, where she faced him.
"So, you're going back now."

"I have to, Norah," Tom said slightly plaintive, "A few of the new players are getting antsy, up tight. We need to practice them into rote playing so they can't screw up even if they try."

"I see."

"Right. Which means I won't be able to come tomorrow. We'll play all day, take an early dinner break, then head out to the Robespierre."

"Okay."

"I promise to be here every day from here on in. I swear."

"Sure. Until the next gig. Or maybe a tour."

He felt the thunderclap. What you get when you live for the day every day. He stepped over and embraced Norah, his chin resting on her head. She remained still, so he hugged her in place.

"Listen," he said, "I'm not doing this if it means losing you. We baptize the band, and I set the dates from here on in, few and far between."

"Okay," she said, "but what about tomorrow night? I don't have a car."

"You do," he said, smiling hard while trying not to let it show. "The Nova."

"The Nova? That's great, but how are you going to get back to your studio? I'm here all day and night."

"I said you can drive the Nova."

"And the gig?" How will you get there?"

"You take the Nova. The band's going in a van, so I'll take a cab to my house and ride with them. You can meet me there, and we'll go home together."

"What about the other players? You'll leave them to load up the equipment and everything? I thought it was part of the band codicil, everyone pitches in."

Tom grinned, "The perks of being a superstar, even emeritus. I get to go to my hotel room to tear up while the rest deal with the woofers and tweeters."

"Hotel room?"

"True in this case. I'll diverge if you'll be my groupie."

She punched his arm, "Not now, not ever."

He rubbed his bicep, "I get it, bad joke. And quit hitting me on the arm; hurt me and I might not be able to play."

"Fat chance. And what about Don? You expect him to pick up those heavy speakers? He's your age, you know."

He stopped. The first time she ever said anything about their age difference. He never thought about it himself unless at a funeral. Walking around town, he noticed people passing by who didn't look young, who seemed to be middle-age or older, then shocked when he realized they probably were younger than himself.

"I'm too immature to be my age," he said quietly, "I'm too young to be so old."

Seeing her face redden slightly, he quickly said, "Don's rock-star number two. He needs to stay there to orchestrate—see how I worked that in—he orchestrates the loading and unloading of the equipment to be sure nothing is damaged or pilfered. He doesn't lift a thing, though he'll still be tired." He glanced at her, then said, "He's also three months my senior."

'Oh," Norah said, relieved that he had so supplely passed over her gaff.

"Right. Everyone goes back to the homestead where the young lads pick up their rides and go home. Don puts the van in the garage, locks it up, and drives home himself."

"That's a long night for him."

"Morning more like it. I could ask him to stay over if you like. Though he's used to the routine." She frowned a little, and he said "I'll tell him to head for home. He'll be fine."

"Oh, I'm sure he knows the drill quite well, Mr. rock 'til you drop."

"Hey, you said it. I'm too old to be a rocker. Unless I'm not."

She laughed as he pulled out the keys to the car and handed them over. "I'll call you a cab," Norah said, clasping him by his neck to kiss him. Cool and dry but lovely, he thought, waiting for the cab.

Thirty

After a four-hour snooze Tom felt better, almost human. He splashed around in the shower for five minutes, hoping for the best. Mary handed him a mug of coffee outside the bathroom, averting her eyes even though the door stood open just a crack.

"Ta, Mary, I need this bad."

"I know. I have a sticky bun at the ready and a full carafe for when you go."

"Yeah, well, I'll be spending the rest of the day in the studio tuning up the band. We'll load the van and take off just around dusk."

"Oh, you're not taking your new friend?"

"No, she's really busy at Marbury. I gave her the Nova last night to get to the show this evening after she's done at work."

"Oh," said Mary. "Well, I hope she doesn't spill anything all over your new car."

"Yeah, it's more like a vintage car than new. I'm sure that she won't spill anything either. She's very neat."

"Maybe so," Mary said, her voice sounding a bit brittle. "I'm sure you paid a pretty penny for it nonetheless."

Tom stuck his head outside the door. "Jesus, Mary, you sound like your gramma talking to the next-door neighbor. Or is this your insinuation gambit to get a raise?"

"Not at all, Mr. Collins, I'm very well remunerated, thank you. Maybe even too much, given the hours, days, and weeks that go by without me even boiling an egg, you being the traveler you are."

"Yeah, well, that's because I don't like boiled eggs. Over easy, I say."

"True, many a confidence man has appreciated your being over easy."

"Sheesh!" Tom yelped. "I better get dressed before you steal my duds and sell them."

"They wouldn't bring in much, even at a thrift store."

He tsk-tsked, "You're not sounding like my dear departed father right now."

"I should hope not! I only have six years on you for heaven's sake. Considering your mileage, I'd say we're twins."

"Yeah, Irish twins."

She shrugged. "So, what do you want to eat."

"Something to go. The boys will be here any minute for a quick run-through. I can get something later before I leave for the show."

Mary nodded, "All right. Scrambled egg on a bun with some bacon and cheese to lift it up."

"Perfect."

"And juice, too."

"Spoken like my resolute nutritionist."

She feigned a pout and left for the kitchen.

By the time he crossed the lawn to the studio, Tom had scarfed down the sandwich and drained the juice, a sweet nectar he couldn't quite identify. Only the coffee remained, something of a grown-up binky for him, considering that Felix made a full crock of exquisite coffee in the studio every morning. Always tiptoeing on Occam's Razor of groundskeeping, Felix managed to avoid unemployment through his masterful skill in brewing coffee. Three carefully measured quantities of French, Indian Mysore, and Blue Mountain beans ground on site led to a nirvana of addictive, caffeine delight. People who drank it and left, Tom fantasized, called all their discriminating friends to rave about it.

"Felix, we'll be practicing in the studio into the afternoon. So, I ask you to limit your work to quiet clean-up tasks. No heavy equipment: don't start any major projects today, and please take yourself home before sunset. Is that agreeable to you?"

"Sí."

"I'll take that as a yes."

The bandmembers showed up on time, which gratified Tom and Don. Surprisingly, Billy seemed all business today, though his attire spoke otherwise. Except for his engineer boots, his all-denim outfit accented all over with glistening spangles shouted out rhinestone cowboy. He topped it all with a stovepipe hat that Lincoln would have liked. No matter, during the first few breaks, he said nothing provocative. Instead, he pulled a three-fold newspaper out and read silently, occasionally sipping iced tea from a can.

The others appeared more rocker orthodox in their outfits. George wore a dark-purple satin dress shirt, tail out over his shiny black pressed slacks to disguise his girth. A pair of slick velvet zipper boots and a vintage Borsalino pulled down to his eyes finished his cool look.

As expected, Frank showed up in his usual throwback hipster style, flannel shirt tucked into well-worn patched jeans flaring out over his beat-up Air Jordans. A wool tweed cap served as his only flourish, proof positive of his Irish roots.

Don wore his usual all-black ensemble, altered only by the time of year, long-sleeve in winter, t-shirt in summer. After twenty years performing, he knew the only crucial element was rock and roll.

So, where did that put me? Tom wondered two decades later. A blue-striped Arrow shirt, gray chinos, and black loafers served as his going-out-in-style uniform. In short, he fit the fashion plate sported by the Jackson Brown, John Denver, Bruce Springsteen set. Though his stage persona bordered on the James Dean model—if James Dean could sing that is, and still be alive. On the other hand, retro could mean raw rock'n roll. Or utter failure; too late to start over.

He whipped his head around and said, "Let's get it going."

Don nodded and struck a note.

They ran through the first set without a hitch. And they all knew it. Billy jumped over to the refrigerator and pulled out a handful of cold brown bottles. Tom felt his stomach flop until Billy passed them out, root beer. He knocked the cap off on a well-worn sideboard and took a long sip as he surveyed the others.

After scarfing down a sandwich, Billy dug into his knapsack and pulled out a copy of the *National Enquirer*. He spread the pages across his drum set and began to read.

Frank watched him for a while, then said, "Anything of interest there?"

Without moving, Billy said, "Lots. There are 51,864 rockets with nuke payloads around the world, for example."

"No shit!" Frank said. "That's pretty scary."

"Better than the '80s," Billy mumbled, "61,662 back then."

"Yeah, like decommissioning 1,000 missiles makes a fuckin' difference," George muttered.

"Could be worse without nukes. Global warming's already fucking up our food and water sources."

"Bullshit," George said. "They say that's a hundred years off, plenty of time to fix it. Not our generation's problem."

Suddenly Don intervened. "You don't think so? You believe all those bogus scientist deniers know anything? Don't they know that someday the glaciers are going to melt? Where will they be then with their long coats? There's your worst fucking daymare; nukes need not apply."

"All right, all right," George said, holding his hands up shielding his head. "I don't know all that much."

Don huffed. "You know plenty, George, plenty enough."

The studio remained quiet until Billy leaned over to face Frank. "Bogus. Now that's a weird word. Where'd it come from?"

"I don't know," Frank said.

"Huh," Billy said. He wrinkled his forehead, "Is the plural of bogus bogi?"

"Bogus is an adjective," Frank said. "It'd have to be a noun."

"So, in Spanish, you would pluralize it—"

"All right," Tom said. "Time to play the second set."

Billy glanced back at Frank "See how well one mind works when it works together?"

The trip from the studio to the Robespierre Hall took 45 minutes depending on traffic. Don built in a good half hour extra to account for safe loading of the equipment van, and also Tom's fraying nerves. He sat in the back seat to save himself from dwelling on the speedometer and the clock. Instead, he fixed his sight on the passing landscape.

George sat next to him, whistling a little, switching to humming then back to whistling to end the tune. After a moment of silence, he'd start in again, a new number. Always soothing though, Tom thought. Not enough to drown out the ongoing exchange between Billy and Frank sitting in the middle seat.

"Look at that sign."

"What? 'Long Fence?'" said Frank.

"Yeah, 'Long Fence.'"

"Sure. So?"

"Long Fence—is that the name of the company or the actual length of the fence? Or both?"

Frank's brows furrowed. He scratched his head, "We can't tell unless we walk the length of the fence."

"Exactly!" Billy said.

"We could look it up in the phone book."

"Sure. But we still wouldn't know if it was this Long Fence."

"R-i-gh-t," Frank said.

They went quiet for an instant. Tom sighed, watching trees, ponds, and billboards flash by. Telephone poles too.

He must have dozed, he thought, awakened by their chatter again.

"The BoogerMeister: for those hard-to-get nuggets up your nose," Billy said in his best voiceover delivery. "Seriously," he said in his own voice, "I saw Suzanne Somers on deep cable pitching them. She starts with asking, 'Are your fingers too big to get to those deep solid greenies?' 'Are your knuckles too thick to get past your honker holes?' Then she goes into how the BoogerMeister easy-flex comfort padded prongs can be custom fitted to go up your nose without a rubber hose!"

Eyes still closed, Tom heard the raspberries coming from George.

"C'mon, man, grow the fuck up."

"I'm telling you, she said it. I saw it on late TV, a remote channel showing old episodes of '*SCTV*.'"

"Aw, well," George said scornfully, "You probably saw Catherine O'Hara doing a bit sending up Suzanne Somers."

Billy scrunched his eyes. "They did that kind of stuff?"

"Oh, man . . .," George trailed off in disgust.

"We're here," said Don. "Get ready to saddle up, boys."

They rolled out of the van parked on the Robespierre's backside, barely lit by a silhouette of splashy neon figures and script welcoming all comers.

Don and Tom led the way to a door near the middle of the dark, wooden building, which opened immediately to the first knock. A quick conversation, and Don motioned for the others to start unloading the van. In the meantime, Tom walked inside.

The Robespierre Hall looked as spacious as ever, the perfect venue for all sorts of musical events. Black varnished tables skirted walls around a dance floor the size of a small basketball court. A stage three feet high ran the breadth of the floor opposite a long bar and stools. A single door led to a bar out front with gangs of big screen TVs broadcasting favorite sports hung for all patrons at the bar and in booths to see. One big, burly man graciously greeted guests paying for the stage show, while gently guiding inebriated patrons back to the bar or out the door. Only occasionally did they toss a customer hands and feet from the premises, and all were welcome back the next time, tabula rasa for a do-over.

Tom slipped his speaker off the hand truck and proceeded to plug in the power and his Stratocaster. He strummed a few notes, barely able to hear them while the others humped speakers and mics to the stage with the locals, who helped wiring everything as well. Satisfied, Tom leaned the Stratocaster back in its stand and reached for the Gretsch when he saw a few people entering the hall. He smiled when he picked out Mary and her husband coming in, waving languidly to them. They waved back at him vigorously along with a third person he couldn't make out. A friend of Mary's maybe. He shrugged and returned to checking out his guitar. After propping it up, he bent down to hop onto the dance floor. As he walked to the table close to the back door, the overhead bank of lights dimmed, replaced by an array of chandeliers glowing above. Hence, the Robespierre Hall.

Closing in on their table, he grinned, waving again at Mary, her Bob, and—Christine. He stopped; his smile frozen until he spoke.

"Hi, everybody, so happy to see you all. Now I know the show's already a success."

They all chimed in with encouraging words he couldn't make out.

"Only a hundred or more to go," he said, triggering a joint laugh. "Thanks for being here, it means a lot to us, to me." Again, more warm reassurances, which he acknowledged until he pardoned himself, heading back to the stage.

Up top, he donned his denim jacket while standing next to Don.

"Everyone settled in okay?" Don asked, brushing back his gray-streaked black hair.

"More than expected."

"Oh, really?"

Tom nodded, "Mary and Bob. And Christine."

"Christine? She's here? I thought she was out of the picture, so to speak."

"So did I," Tom muttered.

"Oh man," laughed Don. "What about Norah? She's coming, right?"

"I think so," Tom replied, "at least until now."

Just then George showed up, trailed by Billy and Frank. "You guys ready? Stage manager says they opening the door. We need to get our butts behind the curtains for the big intro."

"Yeah," Tom said absently.

George looked at Don. "What's up?"

Still gazing off stage, Don said, "Christine's here."

"No shit. You invited her?" George said, gazing at Tom.

"No."

"Huh."

Billy said, "What's up? What the fuck's going on?"

George said, "Mr. Tom cat here, he invited his old flame Christine to the show."

"Yeah? So what?" Billy said.

"You heard of Stockholm Syndrome?" Don said. "She suffers from Scarsdale Syndrome."

George cracked up, joined by the others.

"Shopping Syndrome," said Frank. Surprised by his chiming in, they all broke out laughing loudly again.

The Robespierre stage manager leaned into the microphone bent over to his mouth.

"Ladies and all you other hipsters," he announced, "it's good to see you tonight for the long awaited, first performance in two decades of the classic, real deal, genuine rock and roll band—put your hands together—for the one and only Weatherly Experience!"

Jimmy placed the mic upright and walked backwards to the side curtains, all the way clapping and whistling without looking. At the same time, the Weatherly players took their places as Tom took over the front microphone. He held still while the audience, at full capacity, whistled and shouted standing up for a full ten-minutes.

"Thank you for coming. We hope you'll be staying."

Thirty-One

Without a break, the band cranked out three of their best broadcast dance hits in a row, one heart-pounding beat after another. As they played, Tom took note of how the audience reacted, swaying in rhythm to "You Make Me Wanna Move," lurching to "Rock 'n Roll Fandango," and finally blasting the irresistible "Get Down or Get Out." By then, Tom saw that everyone standing on the dance floor was seriously getting down.

As they started in on "Shakin' While We're Neckin'," Tom felt happy, sort of. They finished the tune, and Billy started to put down the opening beat to "Don't Know Why," when Tom waved to him to halt. He caught a glimpse of them all looking befuddled, which he ignored. Instead, he grabbed the mic with one hand while cupping the other above his brow to block the kliegs. Leaning toward the audience, he searched for Mary and Bob's table. He saw them behind a cluster of people standing and shifting, then Christine. Another peek, but no Norah.

He fretted. Where was she? he wondered.

"Hey," Don whispered loudly, "what's up?"

Tom raised the mic. "Sorry, ladies and gents, I was searching out our manager. He has a habit of slipping away when things go south."

The crowd laughed while he pulled a face, saying "I'm sure he's just in the loo." They laughed again while he signaled to Billy to start up.

His interruption made him decide to restart their engine with a few numbers they planned for the second set. They knocked out "Guns on the Run," then followed with "Don't Know Why," and "She's Back Again, Again." Before the applause subsided, Tom silenced them with "This Old Place," one of his signature ballads off his very first LP.

After finishing the song, he waited for the clapping and sporadic shout outs to tail off. He leaned into the mic and said in a deep voice, "Thank you. We'll be back after a brief massage."

The audience laughed a little, then turned to crowd the bar. Tom swiveled to the front door and saw a few couples leaving. Same with the back door. Not terrible, he thought. He started for the steps down to the floor, a little bit startled that he was last on the stage. The rest of them had headed straight to the bar. Don stood in front of Mary's table.

Tom moved over next to Don and waited for an opening in their conversation.

"You were good," said Christine, right in front of Tom looking up from her seat. "Great, really," she said. "I didn't know you still had it in you." He slowly rolled back his head. "You do have it. Maybe you should've done this before. I mean," she said, sweeping the floor with a gesture, "you just had a fantastic night!"

"Night ain't over yet," he mumbled.

She burst out laughing, "Too true. But c'mon. You know what I mean."

"I do," Tom said. "A lot, I guess, coming from you."

A grimace flashed past her smile. "Well, you know me, Tom, I'm a straight shooter."

"You are," he said. She had dressed for the occasion, very hip in a black shirt and slacks ensemble showing off her indisputably fantastic figure.

"Listen, I have to get moving, we need to start the next set in about five minutes."

"Of course," she said. "Don't worry, I'll be around."

Tom slipped by Don to speak softly to Mary. "Norah's not here?"

Mary shook her head, "No. Is she supposed to be? I thought she might still be on duty at Marbury."

"No," Tom said absently, "She said she was coming," he said plaintively. He turned to Don, "Do you have that phone of yours with you?"

"Yeah," Don said, reaching to pull it from his belt, flipping it open. "I don't know if I can get a signal out here in the wilderness."

"Try this number."

Tom recited the Marbury phone number and waited impatiently.

Don listened, closed the phone, reopened it, and punched in the number again. After a while, he raised his head and shook it.

"Damn," Tom uttered.

"We need to get back on stage," Don said. "It's getting late."

Tom nodded, then said, "What about Margie? Can you call her, see if she can get Marbury?"

"Margie's with her mom in Toronto. She bought the ticket way before we booked the hall."

"Oh, yeah."

"Anyway, I doubt I'd get a signal calling her, either. We're in the Long Island boonies, you know."

"Yeah, yeah."

"Look," Don said, placing a hand on Tom's shoulder, "Let's get a drink and head back to the stage. We can try her again after the second set. A signal's easier to get later at night."

They headed to the corner of the bar, forcing smiles to the happy, well-oiled fans grinning as they made way for the talent.

Don ordered a Coke with a small splash of rum, then turned to Tom. "Johnny Walker Black on the rocks," Tom said. Don seemed surprised.

They made their way to the stage and propped their drinks on separate speakers. Tom stepped up to the mic gazing out at the floor crowded once again.

"Thank you for coming back. I didn't know we all had so many family members. Lots of cousins, many twice removed." They laughed again, while he said, "Of course you know, if any of you do go, that'll be the end of you. Remember, freedom answers to me!"

Before they could react, he signaled Billy to hit it. Billy bashed his drums, causing a glance from the others, who joined in hard themselves on "Break Down the Thunder." The audience roared, all writhing together on the dance floor until they stopped to join in on the final, full-throated battle cry.

"And now," Tom said, "for something completely the same."

He switched to the Gretsch and glanced back at Don strapping on his Les Paul. Without looking up, he sharply stroked the opening notes as Don joined in seamlessly singing the classic lyrics.

"Shake it up baby,"

The rest harmonized, "Shake it up baby,"

"Twist and shout,"

"Twist and shout,"

"C'mon, c'mon babay-a-ay,"

"C'mon baby,"

"Work it on out,"

The band followed the audience as they sang along, dancing a clumsy, beer-fueled jitterbug.

Except something was wrong. Tom couldn't figure out what. He stole a look back at Don singing, who jerked his head sideways. Tom followed Don's eyes to Billy hammering his drums.

Shit, he thought, as he finished the song.

The crowd didn't seem to mind, clapping like crazy accompanied by a few piercing whistles from the back. He moved up to the mic.

"Thank you very much. And props to the Isley Brothers and the Beatles for filling out our catalog. Without them, we'd a wrapped this gig up in fifteen minutes."

Laughs ensued again, slowing as they all waited for what the band played next. Tom wondered what, too. A lull descended, disturbed only by a few quiet conversations, almost inaudible. People shifted in place.

A middle-aged woman broke the silence with a tiny, little voice.

"Malachite Eyes," she peeped. Then again, more boldly, "Malachite Eyes."

A few others joined her, forming a small, mellow movement.

"All right, all right, you've beaten us down. Just remember that it never sounds like it does on the radio. Come again, they never play it on the radio anymore."

Already switching to his Martin six-string, Don subbed the Rockabilly fiddle opening on the original LP with precise, yearning notes. Then, Tom started in:

> We search the world for the love of our lives,
> mine was a girl with malachite eyes.
> She magically sang, she danced in the air,
> the sheen of her eyes, nothing compared.

The band joined in the refrain.

> Malachite eyes, malachite eyes,
> my heart fell apart in her malachite eyes.

> She laughed when I told her I loved her so,
> "You're a common fellow so full of yourself,
> Not handsome, not strong, no eyes that possess,
> Begone in an instant and never be missed."

> Malachite eyes, malachite eyes,
> my heart fell apart in her malachite eyes.

Tom grabbed the mic from its stand and pulled it in.

> Look high at the midnight sky
> and see a million stars fly by,
> the shards of my heart shattered
> by my love's heartless goodbye.

> Malachite eyes, malachite eyes,
> my heart fell apart
> in her malachite eyes,
> the love of my life lost
> in her malachite eyes.

To his surprise, a choir of voices from the crowd sang the refrain for the last two verses. When he finished, he gazed out at them, all still for what seemed like forever. They burst into applause.

Tom tried to speak, but the noise drowned him out. He craned his neck to the band, each shaking his head, grinning.

He pivoted back to the floor, and the applause faded, eager faces looking up to him, waiting.

"Uh, thank you," Tom said, "t'anks a million." He hesitated, then said, "I can see you all been drinking heavily."

Everyone laughed.

"Makes me want to follow suit." They seemed to chuckle this time. "Shame we have to clear you all out, but it's time for our floor show."

This time he saw confusion and a quick mood swing.

"Joking, just joking. Here's another tune from deep on our first album." He heard Don murmuring. "Our second album?" Tom said. "Excuse me, it's on our second album *Don't Do That Anymore*." He strummed once saying, "And here we go."

As he played, he lifted his head to survey the table; Mary and Bob were still there with Christine. But Norah was missing.

Thirty-Two

They finished the set, and Tom watched the band's young sidemen traipse down the stairs on their way to the bar. He hesitated, then crossed the stage toward the steps himself. Running a soft cloth over his instruments, Don stopped and said, "So, what do you think?"

Tom halted. "What do I think? I think I need another drink. What about you?"

"Our drummer is a fucking trainwreck."

Tom sighed, "Yeah."

"I mean, you have any idea what the fuck he was doing?"

"I don't know, man. He has issues for sure."

"Yeah," Don said, "nothing a frontal lobotomy won't fix." He gave the Martin a vigorous rub as he said, "Like Ralph Kramden put it, the dude is a total mental case."

Tom replied, "Something like that."

"So how're we gonna get through the last set?"

"Fast," Tom said.

Don laughed coarsely. He said "It doesn't really matter. Our favorite oldies, the graybeards, called it a night. They got their nostalgia hit fix, then it was time to go home."

"Sure, I guess."

"But we burned a lot of numbers having to do Malachite like that."

Tom shrugged while gazing over to Mary and Bob's table. They just stood up and looked in his direction, smiling at him. Ready to go, he thought. He didn't see Christine, though. Maybe she'd already split.

"You got any thoughts?"

Tom said hurriedly, "I don't know, play more deep cuts and some covers. Those still here just want their load on."

He turned, "Listen, Mary and Bob look like they're ready to leave; I want to say goodbye."

"Sure, pal, knock yourself out."

Tom ignored the wisecrack and hurried down the stairs. He loped over before Mary left, though they did have their coats on.

"Going so soon?" Tom said, throwing an arm over her shoulders.

"Yes, if you want breakfast tomorrow."

"Oh, c'mon, make it brunch."

"That's fine, but Bob might get hungry."

"Oh, hell, Bob," he said with a grin, "you're lousing up my diet."

"Go on," Bob said, smiling widely, rosy cheeked and round, "my avoirdupois won't suffer much from a slight contouring. Mary's the one who calls the shots."

She punched him on the arm, which he grabbed as though in enormous pain. "Thanks for the compliment," Mary barked.

They laughed, Tom following up with, "No Felix, huh?"

"Nah. Felix, lives in a world of his own."

"Don't I know it. And Norah never made it."

Mary immediately seemed sympathetic, "She didn't. Probably something going on at Marbury. I never gave it a thought."

"Sure, right," Tom said, though both understood without a word. He surveyed the hall, saying, "Looks like Christine took off."

"Seems so. We didn't see her leave."

"Yeah, well anyway, safe home you two. See you when I see you."

"Sure," Mary said, followed by Bob, both gushing in unison, "You were great!" "Like the good old days."

"Ah, thanks. It means a lot that you came and had a good time."

After final hugs and goodbyes, they left. Tom pirouetted, wondering what to do next, when a young woman in black slacks and a black t-shirt emblazoned with Robespierre Hall on the front stopped in front of him.

"Can I get the talent a beverage?" she asked. Cute as a high school cutie, though he knew she had to be of age to work here.

"Yeah," he said, "Single malt, the smokier the better. On two rocks."

She smiled, open mouthed. "Well, okay then. You are a rock star."

"It's fake," he said, "all fake."

"Don't listen to him," Christine said, "he is the real deal."

He turned, and there she was, right in front of him, smiling.

"You didn't leave," he said.

"Of course not. You're great, really terrific. I'm not going to miss any of your comeback. I'm sure if I wait, I'll be paying through the nose to see you perform again."

He felt his ears burn slightly, annoying him that he still could succumb to a microcosm of flattery from anyone.

The waiter returned with his drink. Seizing it with one hand, he put a ten spot on her tray with the other."

"No, no, Mr. Weatherly, on the house for band members."

"Not for this booze," he said. "Anyway, that's for you getting it."

She blushed, mouthing a thank-you as she slipped away.

He took a healthy sip as he glanced back at Christine.

"She forgot to see if you need a refill."

"No worries," Christine said, "she knows who's who here. I'll get something when she comes around again."

"All right. Good. I gotta go."

He pealed out, hearing her say "Break a leg," for which he grimaced. Hopping back up on the stage, he placed his drink on the amp box and strapped on his guitar, calling out "Rock My World, Baby."

They finished the last set watching those left on the dance floor gradually melt away. Tom turned to Don, who nodded his head. Tom swiveled gazing out at the vast hall.

"Thank you very much, folks. We appreciate you spending your Friday with us—date night to us, though we didn't get no dates. You were our dates, like a dream come true. We hope you'll spend more of your time with us when we play again. Thank you!" he shouted at the end as the 20 or 30 hangers-on gathered in front of him, clapping as loud as they could.

"Goodnight!" Tom yelled, striking up "Rock Out the Carousel."

After crouching on the stage to chat with the last few fans, Tom wished them a goodnight and safe home. He stood up and started to step over to Billy's kit, but Don was there first.

"What the fuck did you think you were doing?" Don snapped furiously.

"Knock'n 'em down, pardner," Billy said in a lazy drawl.

"You're a fall-down drunk, you know that? You suffer from acute alcoholism."

"You mean I'm cute when I'm drunk."

Tom abandoned them for the only table still occupied, Christine. He sat opposite her, and as if by magic a tumbler filled with tea-colored liquid and two ice cubes appeared in front of him. He twisted his head up to see the young waiter again standing before him.

"On the house Tommy, this time."

He smiled broadly as she walked away.

He took a long sip. Superb.

"I'll bet that hits the spot," Christine said, sipping out of a cocktail flute.

Tom nodded, "It did. Crazy night. First, a mop-tops mob scene, then the Gobi Desert. Never mind our drummer freaking out."

"No way!" she said.

Moving his head up and down, "Curds and way."

Christine yelped a laugh, immediately stifling it seeing his look.

"The kid needs a 12-step program," she said.

"A 12-step program for a shit," he said. "Twelve steps dropping him off a cliff."

Christine chuckled some more, then said, "You're being a little hard on the kid, aren't you? He's just a boy, and he sounded fine most of the time. You guys all sounded fabulous."

Tom shook his head, "Not good enough for big time."

"Okay, but c'mon. You're still breaking him in. He'll get it."

"I don't know about that. He has a learning curve that's like a loop-de-loop."

Christine laughed again, "All right, all right. He's a baby left on the church steps, but he's your baby."

"Yeah, maybe." Tom wrung his hands, and she followed up.

"What's the matter, Tom. Why so glum?"

He hesitated, then sighed, "Norah." He lifted his head, "Someone I've been seeing. She was supposed to be here tonight," he shrugged his shoulders, "but she didn't show."

"Oh," Christine said softly. "Mary told me about you and her. Quite a few burning fires."

He threw his head up, "Ah, Mary. I wish she'd keep my life to herself."

"Sure, but she worries about you. She thinks maybe Norah isn't a good fit for you. Maybe your lifestyles are too different. Especially if you plan to go on the road again. Do you think that'll work for you both?"

Tom raised his eyes again, "Ah, shit, fuck, howdy."

Another full tumbler of single malt appeared in front of him.

"Last call," the waitress said to him. "We'll be closing in 20."

Tom stared at the glass. He mumbled, "Uh-oh."

Thirty-Three

Norah drove fast while crying. She glanced at her watch for the nth time, miserable at how slow time passed now after running herself around at Marbury for the last twelve hours. Way past midnight and just on her way to Tom's, never mind his gigantic coming-out show in Patchoque of all places, the far side of the Island. Hell, the world.

She envisioned a terrible encounter with him when she arrived. He'd either burst into a riotous rampage or shut down completely, buried in disappointment for her no-show at the most important occasion in their time together. Terrible itself, he will fall apart completely when he hears the reason why.

"Oh my God!" she cried bursting into tears again. "My God, my God," she wept, "how can I tell him? He'll die!" she said to herself.

But it all played out again for her as she drove. The crowd at Marbury, the children seated in front of the TV instead of doing homework. Marbury's staff standing in small groups, whispering to each other, Gertrude talking to two men in suits with pads in their hands taking notes. Amelia and the cook Lamar, hugging each other, wiping moisture from their eyes.

What had happened? Everyone was quiet, no workers hammering above, very little noise from the TV in the parlor. The little kids sounded like they did every morning, but the older ones were quiet.

Norah made up her mind and moved over next to Amelia and Lamar. As soon as they saw her, Lamar lowered his head and left for the kitchen. Amelia, sobbing, threw herself into a hug with Norah.

"What's wrong, Amelia, what's the matter?"

Amelia held close to her while whispering in her ear.

"Norah," she said, her voice uneven, "It's . . . it's Devon." Norah felt her body roiling. "What? What do you mean, what are you saying!"

Amelia drew back to see Norah's face.

"Devon," Amelia said, "he's gone."

"Gone? Gone? You mean dead?" Norah cried out.

Amelia shook her head, "He's disappeared. No one's seen him."

"My God," Norah asked heavily, "What happened?"

"It's bad, Norah," Amelia said, her eyes impossibly wide open, "It's really bad." Seeing Norah's stark expression, Amelia shifted back, gripping Norah by her arms. "Buddy's missing, too."

Norah tried to draw back, but Amelia held her close. "The police are interrogating Gertrude about where he might be." Amelia began crying again, "The police think Buddy might have taken Devon away."

Norah tightened her grip on the steering wheel, forcing herself to concentrate on getting there. When she arrived at Robespierre Hall, she cried out loud, this time in frustration. She turned the Nova around and started backtracking to his house. Stewing all the way, she fretted about missing Tom's big gig, leading to dread about Devon and Buddy. How had all this happened?

Despite blowing off the speed limit, she couldn't drive fast enough to get there in time. Tom must be so hurt by her no-show, but he'll be crushed when she tells him about Devon and Buddy. Crushed.

Minutes away from Tom's house. She tried gunning the Nova faster, but the winding curves of the residential blacktops slowed her down. She finally found his gate, 84 Cove Road, wide open. She turned onto his driveway and gunned down past the pond to the garage doors. Without looking down, she whipped out the remote to raise the door for the Nova.

A car was in the space. Puzzled, she didn't give it a thought, instead backing up and moving forward to park the car behind the door for the mower. Getting out and slamming shut the door, she figured a member of the band had crashed at Tom's, too inebriated to drive any further.

Norah bounded up the garage steps to the kitchen door. She flew inside, dropping the car keys on the butcher block as she hurried to the hallway down to the guest room. She heard mumbling as she opened the door. But no one was there.

More muffled talking came from farther down the hallway. Norah turned and walked slowly to the master bedroom, the door slightly ajar. She stopped and lifted her hand to slowly push the door open.

A lamp on a nightstand revealed two intertwined bodies, naked. One of them was Tom flat on his back, a knee up, the other stretched out. The other was a woman embracing him with one arm across his chest, and a bent leg straddling his waist.

Norah held her breath, staring at them. They moved slightly about each other, more like trying to find a comfortable way to rest together. The coitus part of the night seemed to be over.

The woman noticed her first, and raised herself on one elbow, fully facing the door. Norah recognized her then, the artwork vendor. What was her name?

"Oh," Christine said quietly. She tugged a sheet up to her shoulders.

"What the fuck!" Norah snapped, her voice an audible whisper.

"I'm sorry," Christine said, "so sorry."

Tom lifted his head. "Oh, for the love of fuck." He tried to raise up, but only managed to prop himself up sitting next to Christine.

"You stupid, stupid shit!" Norah spit out. "Here I am, worried to death about hurting you for missing the gig, dreading to tell you why! And you're such a dumb-fuck rock star, you couldn't do the same for me? Instead, you rush to bang this kewpie-doll fashion plate?"

"Now, hold on—" Christine said.

"Shut the fuck up before I brain you," Norah bellowed. She shifted back to Tom. "What were you thinking? I didn't have a good reason for missing your big gig? You didn't give me one bit of credit for maybe having a priority that kept me at Marbury?"

"No, no, Norah," Tom said, folding his hands together, "this all happened crazy. I missed you so much I got drunk."

"You got drunk," she said mockingly. She gestured at Christine, "an excellent excuse for fucking this bimbo."

Christine opened her mouth, then shut it.

"Well, I've got news for you, Tommy boy. I couldn't make your rock star wet dream tonight because all hell broke loose at Marbury. Buddy Rosen snatched Devon and ran off. No one knows where they are."

By this time, she was weeping.

Tom straightened up. "Buddy took Devon?"

"He kidnapped him!" Norah yelled. Looking down, she said softly, "at least that's what the cops said." She lifted her eyes and said, "I can't believe it. None of us can believe it."

Tom pulled the blanket up and started to wrap it around himself while trying to stand up.

"Stay put," Norah said, sticking up her hand, palm out. "There's nothing anyone can do. Nothing more you can do."

She looked around the room absently, as if an answer, any answer could be found. Then she turned to Tom again, next to Christine in the bed.

"I'm going now. I'm taking your Nova. You can come pick it up later. I'll leave the keys with someone at Marbury."

Norah walked out into the dark hallway.

Tom slumped over. He turned his eyes to Christine. "How in hell did this happen?"

Staring at the dark hallway, Christine replied, "You were shitfaced. I felt for you, your being stood up and the like." She swung around and said, "To be honest, I didn't think she was going to show up."

"When were you ever honest?"

"Oh, excuse me. I thought an understanding was reached when you were straddling me in bed."

"I know I was drunk as a skunk," Tom said, "but I believe you were the one straddling me. I don't think I was in any shape to move."

Christine sighed heavily. "Details, details." When he didn't react, she said, "C'mon, we've been fuck buddies for a long time."

"Not a lie," Tom admitted, "but it makes me sick to think of it now."

Tom dragged himself over to the guest room while Christine stayed put. Things hadn't worked out the way she thought they would. At the concert, Mary mentioned her surprise that Norah never came. Not that she blamed her, Mary said, noting Tom's many quixotic romances. He'd fallen in love so often, he should have been married and divorced at least a baker's dozen times. The lad needed to settle down, sighed Mary.

Christine wasn't worried, just tired. She'd weathered many of Tom's other true romances through the years. When they went south, he returned to her ready for the brutal truth. Sometimes she was more brutal than truthful.

Tom relished her good looks, impeccable style, and the limits she seemed to set with her cool demeanor. Whenever sharing punchlines and linens, they were boon companions. But considering their shaggy dog history together, Christine saw the long game as her best bet.

Norah surprised her, though. The Marbury counselor did not depend on endearing warmth to win Tom over as so many others tried before. Norah seemed to care for him genuinely despite the deep depth and breadth of his foibles. Christine realized that when Norah corrected course with Tom, he went along for the ride. Amazing, Christine mused.

When Norah failed to show up at the concert, she saw a chance. Now, lying on Tom's huge king-size bed in the master bedroom all alone, she faced the cold facts. In one hasty move, she might have undone all she had ever achieved in winning Tom over. By trying to displace Norah, she managed to fuck up everything for herself and Tom. And Norah. Staring in the dark at the enormous shit sandwich she had served up, she understood that she would have to consume it all alone. She, alone.

Thirty-Four

Tom rolled out of bed onto the floor, which awakened him. His head felt full, expanding with dull pain punctuated by the sharp bang on the floor.

Oy, he mouthed silently, which hurt. He sat up despite the shifting agony. He sat still, slowly reviewing his cognitive functions starting with the need to pee. As simple as this seemed, he shunned it, unable to choose between mobile distress and bladder relief. Then, he began to remember despite trying not to; Norah; Christine; good God.

He slapped both hands over his ears as he got up to rush to the toilet. After throwing up, he stood and pissed into the bowl, not missing by much. He staggered slowly to the bed and sat down.

Nothing could be as bad as it is now, he reflected. Norah is lost to him, forever, while he cannot seem to lose Christine no matter what. He lowered his head and propped it in his cupped hands, not thinking; rather, reviewing the entire fiasco of last night. What to do, what to do?

After what seemed the length of a funereal watch, he raised his head. Amends, he resolved, piece by piece, shard by shard. He arose and slowly walked back to the bathroom, first flushing the toilet that he'd neglected before. He flushed it again and stepped into the shower. He twirled the spigot, standing stoically beneath the freezing water until it warmed, then turned hot. He washed and toweled himself dry. After putting on clean clothes, he left the bedroom for the kitchen.

Mary was nowhere in sight. Of course, it was Saturday, her day off. So, all the talk last night about breakfast then brunch was wishful drinking thinking. Nonetheless, a large glass of red juice topped by a celery stalk a piercing wax paper cover stood on the butcher block. He adjusted his course, lifted the paper and celery from the glass and took a long swallow. Virgin Mary, he determined, perfect. God bless Saint Mary, he thought. Then it dawned on him again that Mary was off. Christine must have made the drink.

He sat on a stool and sipped while wondering what to do.

Devon had been kidnapped. By Buddy. He shook his head; that can't be. At least about Buddy. But why did he disappear, too? To search for Devon?

Tom realized he had no idea about what happened, or what was going on now. The best he could do was drive to Marbury to find out. Also, throw himself down at Norah's feet begging for forgiveness. Like that would work.

He went back to his bedroom for the Monte Carlo keys and his wallet. He walked up the hall to the master bedroom and knocked on the door. No answer. He gingerly opened the door to find that Christine was gone. She must have left in the middle of the night. He shook his head slightly, another fuckup to try and fix. Well, later.

He hustled through the kitchen, picking up a thermos of cold coffee brewed by Mary yesterday before the gig and bounded down the stairs into the garage. The Super Sport hummed beautifully; he whipped it out under the garage door and gunned it all the way to Marbury House.

When Tom first cruised down the street searching for an open spot, he saw a double row of cars in front of Marbury. He did his best to find the closest spot but ended up four blocks away. He hopped out of the car and jogged down to the house as fast as his aching head would allow.

He finally reached the front walk, where a small host of police stood around. As he approached the porch, an officer stepped in his way.

"I'm sorry, sir. Only qualified personnel allowed entrance."

"I am qualified, I volunteer here almost every day."

"You have to be an employee, sir."

"Hey, I work the hours, singing songs with the kids."

"Listen, if it was up to me—" the officer said, then cut off by a sharp yell.

"Officer, he's okay," Gertrude said, coming down the stairs. "He's a regular. Hi, Tom."

"Hi, Gertrude. For a moment I thought I was persona non grata here."

"Well, you are," she said brusquely. "Somewhat. Come on in, maybe you can give the detectives more information."

"Oh, okay. I'll do my best."

She led the way into the vestibule. "Wait in the music room. I'll get one of the cops to come over."

She entered the right parlor room as he shuffled left. Inside, he inspected the familiar old couch, it's green fabric close to the color of the walls. Kitty-cornered rested another beat-to-death threadbare maroon sofa. The old TV stood in the corner across from the doorway. The rest of the space was filled with chairs wherever they fit. Tom sat down on one near the front picture window, drapes closed to keep the kids from daydreaming.

How many times had he come into this room to fool around with the youngsters? Or in the back room where they would sing? Still so familiar, the place seemed strange to him, foreign now that he'd earned pariah status. He exhaled, mouthing a silent 'fuck.'

"So, you don't know anything about Buddy Rosen?" Detective Hayes asked. He seemed to be an affable guy, the opposite of aggressive law enforcement officers on *Law and Order* and other police procedural shows. "Nothing about where he might be?"

"No sir," Tom said. "We worked together at Marbury House. Buddy was usually here at night, and most every day, too. Really, he was committed to the kids like no one else. Except for Gertrude, and Amelia Evans. Marilyn Shrewsbury, too, the head cook here." He glanced back at Hayes, "Norah Kealy. She's the newest counselor here, but she has a lot of experience in social work."

"Yes, Ms. Weintraub filled me in. Buddy Rosen was the second longest employed here."

"Right," Tom said, mumbling afterwards, "That makes sense."

"You implied that before, Mr. Weatherly. Others here say that Mr. Rosen considered you to be a close friend."

"Oh sure," Tom said. He smiled sardonically, "I'm everybody's best friend. You know, a hundred miles wide and three inches deep."

"Really? Most of the staff here consider you to be a very warm person."

"Ah, you know, Officer—excuse me, Detective. The rock star phenomenon. Everyone thinks they know their favorite celebrity until they don't."

"Huh. You're a celebrity?"

Tom shrugged, "Well, maybe not in your crowd."

Hayes nodded. "But you and Mr. Rosen got along well together."

"We did. He's sort of a beautiful human being."

"Uh huh. So, you don't see him taking away a young boy like Devon Nelson."

"Absolutely not. He's ironic about the kids he works with, but it's obvious that he cares about them all."

"Interesting," replied Hayes. "And you do not know where Mr. Rosen might have gone?"

"Not a clue. I don't know anything about where he's from. I'm surprised that he left Marbury, or why. He couldn't possibly have done anything related to Devon's disappearance. In fact, you might want to talk to Devon's uncle, Terence Able. He's petitioning to take Devon back in his custody."

"Yes," said Hayes, "he's here in fact. Dr. Weintraub phoned him immediately after Devon's absence came to light."

"Oh," murmured Tom, "that's a surprise."

"Uh huh, he's quite upset apparently."

"Right. I can imagine."

Silence ensued for a moment.

"Okay, Mr. Weatherly, thank you for your help. Here's my card. Please call if you hear anything about Devon. Anything at all."

Tom nodded as Hayes stood up and left the parlor.

He wondered what he should do. Talk to Gertrude? Amelia maybe. He rolled his head, wishing that Buddy was still here. Except he wasn't, and he might actually have news about Devon.

"You're here?"

He gazed up to see Norah standing in the doorway.

"I cannot believe you'd show your face here."

"Norah—"

"Shut up. I don't want to see you anymore, I don't want you to be at Marbury. I talked to Gertrude about this, and she agrees."

"Oh. I see."

Tom stood up, and she backed out from under the door frame. He moved slowly into the hallway close to the front door giving her a wide berth. But he couldn't help himself.

"Norah, I'm so mortified; there's so much I want to . . .."

She backed up to the stairway, her face full of fury.

"Don't. Just don't."

He slumped. Nodding his head, he turned to the door and slowly opened it. Holding the knob, he started to speak but she cut him off.

"I'll get someone to drive back the Nova," she said coldly.

Slowly, he lowered his head. "Keep it."

Before she could answer, he left.

Thirty-Five

Staring at the new buds punctuating the ornamental shrubs outside his bedroom window, Tom registered no emotion stirred by such signs of an early spring. Instead, he nurtured a funk of misery fueled by equal parts of hopeless hope and self-condemnation. He vacillated between one sensibility to another. Trying to convince Norah that black stars aligned the night of the gig, enmeshing him in behavior in which he seldom participated. Or prostrating himself at her feet abjectly imploring for her undeserved forgiveness. Neither daydream persuaded him that it would work.

Mundane matters slowly interfered with his mourning. Two days after playing Robespierre Hall, Don came over to discuss the band's next move. George and Frank tagged along. Only Billy was absent.

Tom hadn't summoned them, but after seeing him fall apart piece by piece, Mary took the initiative by calling Don. Don instantly called Tom and suggested the meeting.

When they showed up at the front door, Mary had to roust Tom out of bed as though he'd been on an epic bender. More like time in solitary confinement. Nothing appealed to him. Mary really had to chide him awake even though he couldn't sleep. She finally captured his attention with a cup of coffee, swearing it had an Irish whiskey bump.

He dragged himself out of bed and picked a pair of jeans off the floor to put on. As he tucked his feet into a beat-up pair of slippers, Don slid through the doorway and tip-toed over to perch on the end of the bed.

"Pain of the head, or just of the heart?" he asked in a carrying whisper.

"What do you think? Both."

Don nodded, "I can almost feel them myself. Catching?"

"I don't know. Did Joanne leave you?"

"Not yet."

"Well then," Tom mumbled, slumped over.

Don flashed a devil's grin. "Bunkering down in your office isn't necessarily the way to deal."

Tom raised his eyes full born skeptical.

Don went on, "You can't let the other parts of your life atrophy beyond repair."

"You mean the band."

"Well, yes. Of course."

"I don't know. To tell you the truth, Don, right now, I don't care."

"I understand, but there's reason to alter your course."

"Oh, really."

Don leaned over to Tom. "Jimmy O'Donnell called. He said the gig was a big hit, and he'd like us to do it again." Seeing little response from Tom, he continued, "Maybe make it a regular date."

"Yeah, who wants that?"

"It's a step in the right direction. Jimmy said he'd pay us top of his budget. We could try out new stuff while getting paid."

"Wow."

Don pulled back. "Look. I know you're miserable. Welcome to my world, that's why I take pills. But think of the other guys. This could be great experience for the youngsters."

"You mean George, right?"

"Okay, not George. But the snotnose boys."

"Billy too? I thought we agreed to include him out."

Don pulled a sour face. "If we do that, we're months behind breaking in a new guy."

Tom shifted his pursed lips to one side.

"Anyway, they're all here."

"What? Why?" moaned Tom.

"We all know we need to practice. And the boy scouts know they're on the edge of a cliff."

"Oh, for the love of . . . fuck." Tom hesitated, then said, "Let them in the studio. I'll be out in a bit, after a shower and a pint of coffee."

In the studio, Billy held court while they waited for Tom to show up. He stood in the doorway, listening.

"In the vanguard of avian flu prevention," Billy said, pausing for effect. He pronounced the answer, "Geeks."

The groan in the studio was universal, followed by Billy's objection, "Hey! What do geeks eat? Birds! And how much do they get paid? Damn near nothin'!" They all moaned again.

"All right, my next pearl of wisdom; answer me this; if a tree falls in Brooklyn, does anyone say 'Yo'?"

"Jesus Christ in heaven," George called out, "is there no relief from this assault?"

"Seriously, man," Billy said, "it's great to be in my mind when I'm in one of my manic phases."

"Yeah, but couldn't you at least make earplugs an option?" followed George.

"One more, one more," said Billy. "If you're the president, then leave office, does that make you the pastident?"

Billy ducked the empty beer can whipped at him by George, saying as he straightened up, "I gotta lot of energy, so I would be the 'pepsident.'"

George stood up, ready to jump.

"Wait a minute, don't do it. I need to be careful. I have what they call a deviant septum."

"It's 'deviated septum,' jerknuts," George bellowed, "unless you got your nose up someone's ass."

"Okay, last one, last more. If a snail races a slug, do you think its shell slows it down?"

Another empty beer can flew past Billy's ear. He ducked and sat down behind his kit.

Tom took the pause in action as a good moment to walk over to his place. He ran his eyes over the array of guitars shelved behind his seat and lifted off an Ibanez RG550. As he turned around to perch on his stool, Don said, "You haven't played that for a while."

Tom said, "It's good for making a lot of noise. Let's get going."

"What's it going to be," asked Don.

"'Sweet Assassin,'" Tom replied.

"Makes sense," Don said.

They tore it up for an hour, one deep cut after another. Tom played out of his mind, hammering tense riffs endlessly on his guitar. The others tried to match him, but he played too fast and far ahead for anyone to keep up. At last, one of the Ibanez strings snapped.

"Well, shit," mumbled Tom.

"Right," said Don. "God keeps fucking with us. Quantum physics."

Frank chimed in, "Yeah man, I dig it." When they all looked at him puzzled, he continued, "You know. When the string snapped, was it a wave or a particle? Or both?" Noting the general befuddlement, Frank muttered, "Never mind."

The rehearsal went well enough. Mary brought in an array of sandwiches, which thrilled the group like a bunch of school kids eating PB and J. But Mary's sandwiches bordered on gourmet. Everyone dove in with both hands except Tom. He sipped a Bartle and James wine cooler while staring beyond the others as they dined and dished.

Don slid over next to him. "You all right, kemo sabe?"

Tom sighed. "Lovesick. It's like malaria, subsides a bit then comes back."

Don briskly swung his head back and forth. "I'm so sorry for you, Tommy. There's no way to deal, except one foot in front of the other."

"Yeah, I know." Tom moved to face Don. "Let's call it a day. Tell the fellows we'll rejoin tomorrow."

"You got it, pal."

Don whispered into their ears one by one. After listening, each of them pulled on his coat, nodding to Tom as they left the studio.

Don came back. "Anything else I can do?"

"Yeah, help me bus the glasses and stuff to the kitchen."

"No, I can get it all. You go ahead, do what you want to do."

"All right. Please tell Mary I'll eat out, so she can go on home now."

"Whatever you say, Tom. You want some company this evening?"

"No, thanks man. Go home, give Joanne a squeeze for me. And I'll see you tomorrow."

"All right, brother."

They strolled together to the garage, parting when Don trotted up the steps to the kitchen to say hello to Mary, while Tom slid into his car. He revved it up and backed it out to spin around to the main drag. Sparing no fuel and oblivious to the speed limit, he gunned the SS over Cove Road to 25A, took a hard right, then hammered down to Northern Boulevard. He slowed down considerably to elude any bored local cops. Finally, he came abreast of the Marbury front door, in plain view due to the empty parking space right in front.

How lucky, Tom thought sadly. He stopped the car halfway up the space and expertly parked in one fluid motion. He slid over to the passenger side, got out, pushed the lock button down, and slammed the door shut as he walked to the porch. He hopped up and rang the doorbell. Nothing. He knocked on it hard, and still no answer.

Well, fuck.

"Yo, what the fuck?" a voice shouted from above. Tom stepped back gingerly down the front steps to gaze up, shading his eyes.

"Hey, look what the cat dragged in."

Tom squinted at the silhouette leaning over the roof.

"No shit," Tom said, recognizing the big man perched on the roof. "What tears you away from Cali, Ed, too balmy for you?"

Ed Novicky laughed, saying, "Too much rain for me. And you're still at Marbury, Tommy?"

"Not exactly, though I contribute."

"Spoken like a good student. Wait there while I climb down."

The big blond man came down on a ladder propped against the side of the house. He strolled over to Tom and grabbed him by both shoulders to bring him in for a hug.

"Great to see you," he said, then leaned back, his hands still on Tom's arms. "You look a little peaked. Working too hard?"

Tom shrugged, "You know, pissing in the wind."

"Ah," Ed nodded, "Urination in our nation."

"Something like that."

"And the lady you squire," Ed said, standing back, "the one with the beautiful, musical eyes."

Tom almost burst out crying. He held back, saying evenly, "In the wind."

"Ah, a shame."

"So, what are you doing, up on the roof? I thought you'd taken care of all that."

"Ah, these fucking old houses. Fix one leak, out pops another. Come spring, I fear we'll have to pony up for a new roof entirely."

"Oh, I see. Too bad. I hope you won't be up there again."

"Not likely. I'll have to find some other rundown cause."

"Yeah, well they're plenty available, I'm guessing."

"No guess. They're there."

"Yup."

The talk dwindled, and Tom shuffled toward the door. "Okay, Ed, always a pleasure. Hope I'll see you again soon."

"Sure, Tom," Ed said. He leaned forward and whispered, "Seriously, though, if there's anything I can do for you, give me a call. Anything."

Tom was touched by his sincerity. "Thanks, Ed, that means a lot. Ditto for me."

Ed grinned, gave him a slap on the back, and whirled back to the ladder.

Tom went to the door and turned the knob. Unlocked, he noted as he walked inside.

The vestibule was empty, but he heard muted sounds from all around, upstairs, and both parlors. He took a deep breath, exhaled, and entered the right parlor.

Amelia looked up at him, slowly.

"Hello, Tom. We miss you."

He stumbled slightly. "Oh. I'm surprised."

"Yes, well, we knew we couldn't keep you here for long. What with your musical career and all."

"Oh, yeah."

"Norah said it went really, really well. Congratulations."

"Yeah, thanks." He rocked back and forth slightly. "Uh, did she say anything else?"

"No. Only that she'll miss you, too."

"No kidding. Is she around? I'd like to thank her myself."

"I'm afraid not. She's back in her digs, getting some travel clothes together."

"Really? She's leaving?"

"A break. I don't know if she'd ever take a vacation. But she and a friend are driving back to San Francisco to get the rest of her things. Bring 'em back here."

"Huh."

"Yeah," Ameila said, "I thought you knew about this, that she'd tell you."

He squinted, "Not necessarily. We're on a little break ourselves right now."

"Oh," Amelia exclaimed, "I didn't know."

"Yeah, with the band traveling and all."

"Sure."

"Yeah," he murmured. Then, he said, "Say, anything about Devon—or Buddy?"

Amelia's face almost collapsed. "Nothing. We're still trying—Mr. Wilcox is here right now with the detectives, reviewing things with Gertrude."

Tom's face tightened as he tried to hold back his distress. "Oh, Amelia, I'm really sorry to hear this," he said in a singsong, almost crying.

"I know, Tom," she said full of emotion herself, "we all do. We know how close you were to little Devon."

"Yes," he choked out. He sighed, "Okay, I'm going to go out front and wait, see if I can talk to Gertrude."

"I'm sure she'd be glad to."

He walked heavily out to the front porch and sat on the oak bench, waiting for Gertrude. But mostly holding back tears.

Thirty-Six

Norah slid into the front seat of the Nova after meeting with her new old landlady, Mrs. Landry. Apprehensive about the reception she might receive, crawling back after so many months elsewhere, she was very much relieved by the proprietor's warm greeting. Absolutely flabbergasted in fact when Mrs. Landry ushered her back upstairs to the attic bedrooms.

"Still seeing that musician fellow?"

"Professor Harold Hill?" Norah said. "No, he's out of the picture."

"Shame," said Mrs. L. "He seemed okay, treated you with respect."

"Not completely," Norah uttered.

"That's all men," Mrs. Landry said. "They are who they are. You would think I'm a widow the way Mr. Landry acts."

"You're not a widow?"

"Heaven's no! He's retired, not dead. Sits downstairs in the basement, wedded to sports, sports, sports, any kind of sports. Never comes up except at bedtime. I bring him food downstairs. There's a toilet in the corner, he can pee or sit, still watching the game with the big mirror on the bathroom door."

"Does he bet?" Norah asked.

Mrs. Landry pursed her lips, shaking her head. "Too cheap. He hates to lose money."

"Oh," Norah said.

"Don't worry, we have enough. He gets a pension for being a steamfitter for 50 years. I have a TIAA annuity from teaching little squirts in grade school. We own the house, so we don't need much. I like to have boarders for a little extra and to have a chat."

"Uh huh, that's very nice."

They reached the top floor. "Right. Here we are, same as before. No one else here now, so you can use both rooms. If someone comes, you'll have first choice. And, like I said before, I never rent to anyone of the opposite sex. Boy-boy, girl-girl, so no worry."

"Well thank you Mrs. Landry. It's good to be back."

"I think so, too."

"Yes, here's two months' rent—it's the same rate, right?"

Mrs. Landry nodded, "Nothing changes."

"Right. You should know that I'll be making a two-week trip soon, back to San Francisco. I'm going to pick up stuff I left behind. I hope that's okay."

Mrs. Landry shrugged, "Two eggs for breakfast instead of three."

"Right, I'll be back with some stuff to store—and more clothes."

"No problem, we have plenty of room up here."

"Wonderful. Mrs. L., thank you so much for letting me stay."

Mrs. Landry spread her hands, "I like you."

And here I am, Norah sighed, all over again. She laid her knapsack on the floor and flopped on the bed. Mrs. Landry was a doll. And Mr. Landry a complete surprise. She forgot to ask Mrs. L if she had any kids. Well, another time. They'll be plenty of other times. In the meantime, Marilyn flies in tomorrow, so she'll have plenty to talk about on the trip back. After that, she didn't have a clue about driving all the way back alone.

She felt guilty about the car, too. Tom loved his new old Nova, yet he never asked anyone to fetch it. At least, anyone she knew about. Nora cringed, too, wondering how beat up the car would be after a round-trip close to 6,000 miles or more. She shook her head, thinking he probably wouldn't care. He was in bad shape. She knew because common friends volunteered his condition to her. She knew also because she was in bad shape, too.

She sighed a heavy breath. She missed him. she felt she was spinning on a hamster wheel, loving and hating him at the same time. He was sweet, also equal parts thoughtful and thoughtless. Like the time he sidled up tight next to her on a narrow sidewalk. "Let's walk abreast," he said luridly. When she called him out on it, he replied, "C'est moi."

"Oh, French now. I didn't know you were a polyglot."

"I didn't know you know what a polyglot is. What is a polyglot?"

"Somebody who can be an idiot in multiple languages."

"Oh," he said. "I thought it'd be something like glutton parrots. Or many brands of gluten bread. But you're right, c'est moi."

Yes, he and his stream of unconsciousness. He'd start in on the middle of something, saying something impossible to track, causing him to lose his impatience filling in the blanks.

"Man, everything is fraught, you know?" he said once, shaking his head."

"Everything is fraught?" she said. "What's everything fraught with?"

"Everything is fraught with . . . fraughtness!"

"Man," she said, "did you ever get up on the wrong side of the Earth!"

They laughed together, bumping into each other often when they laughed. He'd say something serious, deadpan, and make her laugh.

"People say to love someone, you have to love yourself."

"So?"

"I'm trying to figure out if I love myself enough."

"What about making love," she said. "Who do you love then?"

He replied straightforwardly, "Some men equate happiness with pleasure."

"And that includes foreplay?" she asked.

"Oh, I take that much too seriously to call it play."

She moved her head back and forth, he was so goofy thinking, irresistibly of course.

"I fear many things I see coming before anybody else does."

"Oh, really? So, you're omniscient."

"Yeah. I guess."

"Then if you're so omniscient, how come you don't warn us beforehand about bad things coming up?"

"I can't bear to look."

She laughed, "All right, you sound like a born-again Buddhist. Do you believe in an afterlife?"

"I'm willing to give it the benefit of the doubt."

Norah laughed again, wiping tears from her eyes. Stream of unconsciousness indeed. He was the most unassuming person she'd ever known, the most fun, the most sensual. Remembering all the things they did, kidlike adults with all the mature liberties. Like getting all hot and bothered. Which spun her back to the starting point on the hamster wheel. How could he fuck the first woman to come along, she thought, because I was late?

Tom started inventorying everything out loud. Women's perfume: In the 70s like a potpourri of herbs, heavy on the herby musk scent. In the 80s, 90s, like clean scrubbed soap. And the top hits, at least as far as he was concerned at this very moment: "Reflections of My Life" by the Marmalade.

"All my sorrows," he sang, "sad tomorrows. Take me back to my old home. The world is a bad place, a bad place, a terrible place to live," following with "Oh, but I don't want to die."

"Second place most mopey song: "He Ain't Heavy" by the Hollies." He shifted on his stool and began to sing again. "The road is long, with many a winding turn, that leads us to who knows where, who knows where"—it should be 'when,' but for some unknown reason, they went with 'where' twice. Can't tell you why, but anyway—," he broke into song again, "But I'm strong, strong enough to carry him, he ain't heavy, he's my brother."

"And finally, the wimpiest sad song of all: "Diary," by Bread." He started in again, "I found her diary underneath a tree, and started reading about me. The words she'd written took me by surprise—"

"Mother-fuckin' A, can you take a break?" George moaned, "Or give us a break. We're dying here."

"Sorry, I can't. This is how I feel right now. Bereft. You can shut your ears or wait in the kitchen."

"C'mon man."

"The world is," Tom sang sorrowfully, "a hard place, a terrible place to live in."

"Those aren't the lyrics," Frank said quietly.

Don shook his head, "Doesn't matter. Here, let me try." He moved down in front of the drum set and whispered into Tom's ear, "Are you done?"

"I was done until I was undone. I coulda been a tenor, a counter-tenor—Requiem for a Heavyweight. I'm remiss; I've committed the sin of remission."

"Jesus, Tom, what're you on? Have you been taking uppers?"

"Proactive or Prozactive? How 'bout Prose-active?"

"Anything out of the ordinary?" Don said, growing increasingly concerned.

"How about dirt of the earth? I changed a near-life experience into a near-death experience. All in one swelt foop. Or maybe swell foop."

"I know man, you're hurting. I'm so sorry how it worked out."

"That's life, Donny. It's like everyone knows about a prenuptial whereas the sadder but wiser wish they could've had a postnuptial."

"Yeah, another time and a million bucks from now," Don said.

"Céad mile fáilte," uttered Tom.

"Caid millay faulta? What's that?"

"A hundred thousand welcomes in Irish."

"Irish. Okay, how do you say a hundred and one thousand welcomes in Irish?"

"I don't know," muttered Tom, "Why don't we just go with a hundred thousand and call it a day?" When Don failed to respond, Tom said, "You know, years ago I ran into a stop sign on my bike and said 'Well, at least I obeyed the sign.'"

Don lifted his head to the ceiling to hide his rolling eyes. He looked around at the others in the studio. Then he said, "Let's take a lunch break."

Alone with Tom, Don said, "Buddy, what'd you do? Have a few drinks for breakfast?"

"Think so? Me too."

"Yeah, well we can't continue this way. Suppose we call it a day, meet again tomorrow."

"Same Bat-time, Bat-station?"

"Exactly. Get yourself some sleep, and no liquid breakfast."

"Okay. Bloodless Mary all the way."

"I'll be sure to give Mary the lowdown," Don said.

The next day, everyone arrived early, wondering how Tom would shape up. Don went to get him and returned quickly with Tom trailing behind. All noted silently that the Weatherly namesake looked like death warmed over.

Tom turned front and center to address the rest of the band. Despite his ashen face, he spoke without any speech impediment or insane observations.

"Gentlemen, I apologize to all of you and hope for your forgiveness. I was wasted, no question, and I wasted your time, a mortal sin particularly to myself. I promise from this day, this moment forward, I will never subject you to such outrageous behavior again. Please forgive me."

The four men listening quickly extended their sympathy and absolution in unintelligible words crowded together. Don finished by suggesting another deep cut, "Fight for Your Love," as their first number.

The morning went well, and all were glad to be on task again. Mary signaled the break with a tray full of sandwiches, nuts, and chips. Billy sauntered over to the refrigerator and fetched two handfuls of Gatorade bottles.

The Weatherly Experience talked little between bites and swigs. First finished was Billy, who laid his clean plate and empty bottle on the table. He stretched, then said, "I suppose all of you are up to speed on the Penis Fly Trap?"

In mid-munching and drinking, they all stopped for an instant.

Don said, "The what?"

"The Penis Fly Trap. Also known as the Circumcision Conspiracy."

Everyone returned to their meal while George replied, "Now, what the hell you talkin' about this time?"

"Simply one of the greatest travesties in history, and I do mean his-story." Billy looked up to see who was listening. Seeing everyone facing him, he lowered his sight and read out loud.

"Today's physicians continue to float the notion that circumcision is healthy to prevent a multitude of medical menaces, such as penile cancer without any supporting data. In reality, circumcision makes male members more palpable."

He looked up. "They must mean 'more palatable' to women."

Everyone burst into laughter except Billy. "What?" he said, but no one answered.

They played another set, solid but not sensational. Everyone spread out around the table sipping beers.

Billy had his feet up on an empty chair. Taking a deep sip, he said, "Say lavy, Dudes."

Don stood up and took the remaining two beers off the table and walked them over to the refrigerator. He exchanged them for two bottles of iced tea, handing one over to Tom as he sat down.

"Ah, c'est la vie," Tom smacked, accenting the accent.

"What's the difference?" Billy said.

"En francaise, la Rive Droite is where we learn and la Rive Gauche is where we lounge. Also, if you're not careful, where you stand up to your eyeballs in detritus."

"Detritus? What, is that French for malaria or something? Don't they get dengoofever in some of those French places?"

"It's dengue, pronounced with a long 'a,' at the end," George said.

"Dengay? The frogs are all gay?"

"Don't be an ass," Don snapped.

"Oh, c'mon. You know how those Frenchy dudes dress, they gotta swing both ways, right.?"

"That's just stupid," Tom said. "Anyway, what difference does it make?"

"Hey, maybe it causes that dengay shit going around."

"You are so fuckin' ignorant," George snapped.

"What? I don't have anything against them."

A common groan circled the studio.

George stood up, his chest pushed out, and said, "Okay, jackass, then what am I? Straight or gay. Which is it?"

Looking uncomfortable, Billy turned to Tom. "You're the boss here, you should know," he said. "Is George gay?"

Startled, Tom's eyes widened. "Gay?" he said, "he's so gay he's ecstatic!"

Everyone exploded into laughter except Billy and Tom.

"Seriously, though," Tom said, "I'm not the one to ask. It's a very delicate matter, privacy and all. So, if any of you need to know, I think you should call up your sweethearts and wives and ask them."

They all laughed again. Even Don grinned a little while Tom sadly smiled.

"Okay, okay, just asking," Billy said. "I don't mind if he's a gay or straight. I was just wondering." The others grumbled incoherently.

"All right." Don said, slipping his bass strap over his shoulder, "let's pick it up."

Thirty-Seven

Tom made it through the night without imbibing or partaking of any hallucinogenic substance. He felt relatively well after a night's uninterrupted sleep, chemically induced or not. Otherwise, his mind and soul were shattered. Still, the band was on its way for a high noon meeting about their future. So, he drank coffee black, though he hated its unadulterated purity. Usually, he liked disarming it with plenty of cream and sugar. Today, though, he drank black.

Sitting on a stool in the kitchen, he watched Mary silently prepare toast and fruit for his breakfast, all that he could get down. She knew from experience, including the element of silence. Nothing to hear there, he understood.

Felix must have been using his manual weed-whacker, tipped off by Mary, Tom guessed, to keep the decibels down. He appreciated their care, familial rather than class observant. They knew his origins and cared for him like a prodigal son. The only family he had locally; he loved them dearly.

The doorbell rang. Tom glanced at his watch, 11:00 am. Who could it be at this time?

"Shall I get it?" Mary asked.

"No, that's all right. I'll stretch my legs."

He hopped down from the stool, almost teetering over. Catching hold, he straightened up and strolled out to the front door. He opened it to see one of the least likely people to be calling on him so early—William "Billy the Kid" O'Reilly, the band's wild hair.

"Billy my boy," Tom said half-heartily, feigning bon homme. "You're extremely early. Or did you sleep over here somewhere? One of the pool changing rooms?"

"No, Tom, I got up early on purpose to come see you alone."

"Alone?" Tom repeated. He wondered if Billy had an inkling that he and Don were deciding whether or not to send him down the road.

"Okay," Tom said, "let's go into the living room."

He led the way while calling out to the kitchen. "Mary, could you bring some coffee to the living room?"

Tom ushered Billy into an empty and immaculately clean room, a sign of its infrequent use. He pointed to an easy chair on one side of the fireplace for Billy to sit down. Tom sat in the chair opposite.

"So, what's up, Billy?"

Billy's mouth tightened, then relaxed as he started in.

"Tom. I know you and the others see me as a buffoon, or as I put it, a life well wasted. It's true, I search out the outrageous and cling to it. But I'm not utterly crazy, and I know a troubled friend when I see one."

Tom shifted one leg over the other, fearing what he might hear next, an intervention by a character whose own behavior has him crying out for help every waking moment of every day.

"Here's the thing. I understand you've been crushed by the loss of your loved one. Let's face it, it's clear from yesterday's outburst that you are suffering deeply, man. I know, I been there."

Every waking day, Tom thought.

"But I got help. Which did me an enormous amount of good. And because of it, I have an answer for you."

Tom sighed audibly. "You do, huh? What could it be?"

"My mother." Seeing Tom's confusion, Billy continued, "She's not just my mother, Tom. She's possibly the world's greatest psychic that ever lived."

Tom did not even try to disguise his skepticism. Seeing his doubt, Billy hurried on.

"I'm not joking, Tom, she's done me a world of good. To be straight with you, I tried to end my life three times. Three times, mind you, twice with overdoses, and once with a gun and some quaaludes. I was lost completely, Tom, until my mom stepped in. She straightened me out, Tom, convinced me I was worth something in this world. She persuaded me to give up the bad shit—coke, 'ludes, and the rest—so's I could embrace the good all around me. And you know me well, Tom, I'm clean except for a beer now and then. I'm well and ready to rock the world as you know."

Tom was pretty sure he did know, not the way Billy described it, however.

"Now, my mom's registered with the West Coast Psychics—they've been around forever. You know, the commercial jingle on TV, 'The Joy of Being Whole.'" You can call her; here's her name and number. Or you can go and see her, she lives in Jericho off of 495, maybe twenty minutes from here. Here's her number and address."

He reached into his jacket pocket and handed a scrap of paper to Tom, who took it robotically.

"I'm telling you, Tom, she can straighten everything out for you. And really, what have you got to lose?"

Billy grinned broadly and said, "I'll go wait for you and the rest in the studio."

"Never mind," Tom said. "I'm too bushed. I'm canceling today's get-together. Felix can give you a ride to the bus terminal or train station. Don and I will let you know when we reschedule. And thanks for thinking of me, Billy."

Mabel O'Reilly puttered around her house trying to find where she left the newspaper. After fussing in several places several times, she held up and forced herself to retrace her morning trek after waking up. Not upstairs in the bedroom or adjoining bath. Downstairs in the kitchen, nothing there. Finally, the half-bath off the living room. She scurried to it and found it folded to the very story she'd read halfway through. But where were her reading glasses?

The phone rang. She picked it up, and said "Mabel O'Reilly, Master of Past, Present, and Your Future." She waited, then said, "Oh, hi, Loverboy, how's the world treating you? Still playing with the old rock star? Oh, that's good. Wait, really? Really? When do you think he'll call? That doesn't give me much time to prepare—that is, summon the spirits. So, tell me some things about him. Uh huh. Uh huh. What's his girl's name? Uh huh. Uh huh. She's seeing someone else? So, he cheated on her, and she caught him at it. And she's on a trip out West? Okay. Really? A fellow named Buddy and a little boy named Devine? Devon. Okay. Enough? Enough for now, I suppose. All right, m'love take care of yourself. Come over this evening, I'll make some chicken potpie."

She hung up. A sweet boy, but not very observant. Back to the newspaper.

The phone rang again. She picked it up and answered professionally, "Mabel O'Reilly, Master of Past, Present, and Your Future."

"Mrs. O'Reilly, I'm Tom Weatherly, a friend of your son Billy. I, uh, I'm interested in your advice."

"Why, yes, Mr. Weatherly, you want to know about Norah Kealy."

"Yes," he said, somewhat coolly.

She quickly followed up.

"Yes, Billy shared your story with me. He's very distressed for you. Perhaps you could come here and we could discuss your situation."

"You have time to meet?" asked Tom. "No other engagements?"

"Well, I do have a full calendar. But I could tell from Billy's call that you need help now. So I rescheduled all of my other appointments knowing that you would call right away."

"Oh, that's very impressive," he said flatly.

"Yes, I'm free right now. Here's the address and directions. I'm easy to find." She rattled off her address and highway directions.

"Okay," Tom said, "I'll be there in about an hour."

Tom hung up and wondered where he'd put the pellet pistol he'd received as a long-ago Christmas gift from his brother Joe. He was ready to put it to his head right now.

He skipped looking for it, instead calling Don to postpone the band gathering. When Don asked why, he mumbled, saying he'd tell him later. In the Monte Carlo on his way to 343 Walnut Avenue, Jericho, Long Island, NY 121749, Tom practiced a new mantra, Tom You Idiot.

Norah looked around her living room one last time, and the bedroom and bathroom, the toilet, shower, and basin, all somehow jammed into the space of a confessional. The aged woodwork of the unfinished walls emphasized the effect. Still, it was better than barracks shared with dozens of others, she thought.

She seemed to have all she needed without overpacking. The less she brought now meant space for more junk she could spare. True, she needed to make room for her fellow traveler Marilyn. When she met Marilyn at the Ruth Washington Home, they hit it off immediately. Like Norah, Marilyn had gone through a series of loser men before calling it quits. She still had an off-on thing going with a guy in Oakland. After another fierce spat, Marilyn also thought it would be a blast to go cross country with Norah. Plenty of time to fill in their respective gaps over the years. Also very cool to go from New York, where Marilyn had never been. Pretty great to do it with a friend who knew the ins and outs. "Pedal to the metal, man," she said over the phone.

Marilyn was to meet her at JFK Airport, then spend the weekend in Manhattan with her, doing the museums, Central Park, and a few clubs up town—jazz, punk, and new wave. After that, back to Marbury to hit the road, San Fran here we come. Taking the south route to avoid seasonal weather in the mountains, Norah figured they could make it to San Francisco in six days or so unless they decided to sightsee a bit more. So, return to Marbury in two weeks, good enough.

Tom would get his classic Nova back well broken in with an additional 6,500 miles on his odometer. Served him right, she thought, followed by a pang. She shook her head briskly; she needed to get over that bullshit.

"Hey Norah," Mrs. Landry called up from the stairway. "You gotta phone call."

Norah scrunched her brow. Who would be calling her here. "Can you take a message?" she yelled down.

"I don't know. Sounds pretty urgent."

"Oh. Okay, I'll be right down."

"I'll leave the phone on the counter. Give you some privacy."

"Thanks, Mrs. L."

Who could it be? Gertrude with some news on Buddy and Devon? Oh, God, she thought, I hope not if it's not good. Marilyn running late? More like that, not Tom wanting his car back.

Well, here goes. She sucked in some air and tap-danced down the stairway, noting on her mental list to get a phone put in upstairs.

"Hello," she said, leaning on the counter, the receiver held to her ear. "Oh," she said, straightening upright. She listened quietly for a short while. Then she said, "I must admit, you're the last person I expect to call me. What do you want?"

She bent to lean over again on the counter, listening.

Thirty-Eight

Tom felt ridiculous in every possible way. His spanking brand-new medium listened to him cry like a baby, moaning and whimpering, until she'd heard enough. "All right," she snapped, "get a hold of yourself."

Shaken, he immediately. stopped talking He took a deep breath, and almost choked on the foul smell permeating her living room. And dining room, and most likely the crawl space beneath the house all the way up through the cobwebs in the attic. Trying to place the stench, all he could think of was bad breath in dogs seasoned by age-old fur odor saturating the house for at least two-decades. Proof of his analysis came from continuous scratching and howling behind a closed door that he assumed led to his hostess's boudoir.

She sat in one of the four wooden captain's chairs encircling a round Mission style table covered with a worn fake Persian rug, a single potted plant, possibly a geranium, and a crystal ball. Mrs. O'Reilly wore a shawl covering a flannel shirt and the top of her blue jeans. On her orange-red pageboy-style haircut she sported a dark-colored headband. Tom noted rings on all her fingers and thumbs. Possibly antennas to the future?

She continued, "You got an awful lot of self-pity going on there, mister. You need to get a grip. Stop feeling sorry for your sorry ass and start thinking about how you can undo what you did."

"That's impossible."

"Nothing is not possible. I had a client come in here, get divorced, get re-married, divorced again, then re-married—all to same person! As bad as it is, your situation is easier to rectify by far than the marrying spin-cyclers. But you must take responsibility for your immasculine sins."

Immasculine? He'd never heard that before, though it seemed to fit his situation.

"To start reclamation, you must do due penance."

Do-do?

"Your transubstantiation teeter-totters on mortal sinuation—you must reverse it through significant action. You must start with a pilgrimage."

Tom felt his face fall dramatically. "Pilgrimage? How the heck can I do that? Who does that anymore anyway?"

"People north, east, south, west. Seeking peace for the spirit and the soul. You need inner spiritual healing before you can correct your outer misfortune. Only then can you once more be a presence to Norah."

Norah. He couldn't remember if he'd told her Norah's name. Maybe Billy prompted her. Either way, it didn't matter. He would do anything to have any kind of chance with Norah again. Anything.

"So, where does this pilgrimage take place?"

"West. Norah is going west. You need to follow her spiritually while you reconstruct your spirit. If you commit absolutely, you will be able to confirm your transcendental transformation. Your truly restored aura will be fully revived."

This is nuts, he thought. A lot of mumbo-jumbo featured in 1950's zombie movies. Except for one thing: at the end of this crazy psychic tour, he would have the green light to approach Norah. That was the thin thread he grasped turning the whole crackpot trip into a voyage of hope. He filled his lungs carefully through his lips and released the longest sigh of his life.

"Where am I going out west?" he said quietly, tamping down his resentment as much as he could.

She hesitated. "Your decision."

"My decision? How can it be my decision? I know the big venues in California—LA, San Diego, though nobody goes there, too many flattops, not enough freaks. San Francisco could be good except I have no clue of where to start there. I know generally about mountains and deserts in Vegas, hot like 115-degree days. That's it."

He listened for her reply, which did not come. While waiting, he watched her rustle papers below the edge of the table. What the hell? he thought.

"Okay," she said abruptly, startling him. "Do you have an internet account?"

"Sure."

"All right, look up Death Valley National Park. Follow directions to the Furnace Creek Visitors Center. If you drive, you can park there. Go inside and choose a trail. Park rangers can give you maps and advice on which ones to take. You should seek out those that will allow you to purge your Atman."

Tom drew back. Atman? "My what?"

"The closest thing to a soul in Buddhism. Though in Buddhism there really is no soul after death."

"Oh. Great."

"I advise you to go now, since time is limited."

Don't I know it, he thought. "Okay, thank you very much. How do I address the check?"

"Oh, just make it out to Mabel O'Reilly. That'll be $250."

Tom glanced up at Mrs. O'Reilly for an instant, then back down to finish the check.

"Thank you very much," she said in an efficient sounding voice. "If you need more guidance, feel free to call me at any time. And good luck with the Spirits!" she said brightly.

"Oh, I'll call all right. And thanks for the good luck," Tom said, rising and leaving the house as fast as he could. Outside, he took a long deep breath, savoring the cold, clean air while also weighing the daunting crusade ahead.

After flying the redeye to Las Vegas, Tom boarded a puddle-jumper to Beatty NV, a small airport 40 miles or so from Furnace Creek. Originally an enclave upgraded by Borax Company executives in the 1920s, an adjoining airport had been constructed near the Furnace Creek complex as well. However, years of neglect had made landing on Furnace Creek's sole runway an iffy proposition. Larger planes with durable tires occasionally flew out of Furnace Creek. But inbound planes were virtually nonexistent. Rather than chance a landing at Furnace Creek, Tom reserved a charter flight to Beatty, CA, followed by a car ride.

He arrived at Beatty at daybreak. He tripped down the short ladder, the only passenger on the plane. Outside, almost withering dry heat descended upon him. And Beatty was at a relatively high location. Shaking off the thought, he pulled his Aussie breezer hat forward onto his head and quick-stepped to find his ride to the Furnace Creek Visitors Center. Inside, a sign directed him to the sole rental agency's back door. There five feet away he saw a single white Ford Explorer parked behind a concrete bumper block. Beyond the vehicle a stretch of dun-colored mountains formed an end-to-end horizon framing a stunning sunrise sky. Quickly lowering his eyes, he made out the silhouette of someone leaning on the Explorer's driver side. Tom draped his backpack over his right shoulder and walked up to the SUV.

"Hey," he said, "I'm Tom Weatherly. I reserved a ride to Furnace Creek. Are you the driver?"

A shambles of a man stepped forward, tall and potbellied, white skin burnt red from his t-shirt sleeves to his hands. A panhandler hat shaded his face, still pink but darker beneath the brim. Suspenders over his sweat stained t-shirt held up his faded jeans, riven at the bottom to expose his well-worn leather boots. Close to Tom, he pulled out a handkerchief from his back pocket and used it to wipe his brow, pushing his hat brim up in the process.

"I'm your driver. Barron Leslie at your service."

He stuck out his right hand, which Tom grasped, retrieving it quickly to avoid any broken bones.

"Tom Weatherly."

"Is that your tucker bag? Anything else to carry?"

"Nope. I intend to get some things at the Visitors Center."

"Huh. You travel light for a city fella. Hope you're not looking for a lot from the Furnace Creek store. They got a lot of stuff there for tourists. O'course not so much for prospecting anymore."

"Huh. I didn't know there were any prospectors left."

"There aren't."

"Oh."

"Yeah, gold around here's been pretty much tapped out. Nothin' but waste rock and tailings. Folks like to go to museums about them."

"Sure," Tom said. "Listen, I don't want to rush you or anything, but I'm in kind of a hurry."

"Oh yeah, right on Mr. Weatherly, hop in."

They took off, working their way onto what looked to Tom like a long, flat, two-lane road to nowhere. They turned left onto 374 West. After that, the road stretched flat narrowing to infinity somewhere in the distant mountains at the edge of the earth.

"Goin' to Death Valley for work or fun?" asked Leslie eyes fixed on the road.

"For a pilgrimage," Tom said, "a nonreligious one."

"You don't say," Leslie said. "My grandmom on my mom's side of the family, she went on a pilgrimage in Ireland." He turned his head to look at Tom for a moment. "She was Irish."

Uneasy, Tom replied, "Oh, yeah?" shifting his eyes straight ahead to the road.

"Yup," Leslie said, "up a mountain on her knees. Some saint's day. O'course, that was religious. Seems crazy to me, though."

"Yes, me too."

"But yours isn't?" the driver said, more of a question than a statement.

"Mine's nuts," Tom said. "Nothing to do with religion, more a matter of the heart."

"Oh, I see," Leslie said, now concentrating on the road which never changed, running uninterrupted flat and smooth, unbroken desolation on both sides.

"Too bad," Leslie said. "My experience with them kind of pursuits is that those involved come up empty. Still, they feel pretty good no matter the outcome. They feel good anyway about doing it."

"Yeah, I'm not sure that's how I'll feel. I'm worried as hell about this, and I haven't even begun yet."

"Well, you're about to, "Leslie said.

They rode along in silence for a time straight on a two-lane highway narrowing amid the distant mountain chain along the horizon. Children might think the two sides of the road joined further down the road, not knowing they never would. Only later, as adults who paid attention to their teachers would know the illusive nature of parallel lines and the fact that they could never come together. He knew this because after his junior year he had to repeat both trig and physics in summer school.

He wondered if Norah knew. Where Norah was now, and what she was doing. Laughing uncontrollably at jokes she might have shared with him. Marveling at the stark beauty of this portion of the great western landscape. She might ask him to pull over to look at some of the flowers, their beauty muted by

They passed 'Welcome to Nevada' signboards on both sides of the highway. Strange, he thought, they seemed to be in Nevada since they left the airstrip. Rendered in waves of blue, pink, and sandy colors, the splashy signs looked out of place amid the barren landscape all about them. Only the blinding Klieg-like sunshine bleached the endless stretches of brown and black sand and stone into lifeless, over-developed positives.

"We been driving on NV-374," Leslie said, "Deaf Valley Road. We crossed into Cali, same road 'cept it's now CA-374. In Nevada, it's named Daylight Pass Road."

Not a surprise, Tom thought.

The road continued flat and monotonous, except for scrub subtly scattered here and there. Scarlet hills slightly pinked closed on both sides. They came upon a vividly lettered Death Valley Park sign made of concrete and stone resting on painted woodblocks. Tom noticed bas relief letters at the bottom, 'Homeland of the Timbisha Shoshone.' After that, more barren stretches of road, rock, and scrubs.

Slowly passing the sign, Leslie steered the car straight past a left fork to another road marked by a sign for Beatty Road.

"We're on Daylight Pass a bit more 'til we get to Scotty's Castle Road. We cut left there, then a quick bounce over to wheel right onto 190S. That'll take us all the way to Furnace Creek."

Furnace Creek. Death Valley sure sported a shitload of cautionary names, thought Tom. Right out of the handbook of dreaded destinations – Hells Gate, Badwater Salt Flat, Desolation Canyon, Devil's Cornfield, Tarantula Ranch Camping and Luxury Sites, The Tow Truck Company, Devil's Golf Course, and where they were bound naturally, Furnace Creek. Even as he wound down the list of daunting destinations, he stood in front of the Furnace Creek Visitors Center watching Leslie peel out going north on 190S.

It was hot, he realized. Not ungodly so, but certainly around the Devil's degree. He picked up his backpack filled with hiking gear, all newly bought from L.L. Bean and Timberland, and turned to face the complex.

The center seemed ordinary, a conventional civic structure, which immediately faded into the background when he happened to look past it to his left. He did a double take at what he saw behind the center.

An oasis, he realized, much more developed than anything he imagined about Death Valley. Much more beckoning than his expectation of a barebones, wooden lean-to manned by rangers indistinguishable from dusty mean bears.

He wandered over to a wooden fence bordering a thriving grassy lawn. He got a good look at signage for The Furnace Creek Ranch, Founded 1927. Amid a variety of healthy foliage including Palm trees, he could see large, manicured stretches of green populated by tiny triangles flapping on slender poles—a golf course! Shaking his head, he turned back to the Visitors Center, built of bricks like sixties elementary schools. He stopped, hiked up his trousers, took a deep breath and walked inside.

A young ranger stepped out from behind a high counter.

"Can I help you, sir?" she said.

Tom noted how fetching she looked in her green uniform and her jaunty, broad-brimmed hat. Also, how she could be his granddaughter if not his daughter. Somewhere in between Norah's generation.

"I'm here to hike," he said, wondering if his Downunder breezer with its green plastic screen between brim and top looked ridiculous.

She grinned without laughing, replying, "Well, you've come to the right place. Do you have an idea of anything you might like to see?" She gestured with one arm behind her. "We have displays of many interesting sights marking Death Valley's colorful history."

"Here's what I wanna do," he said. "I want to hike all day and all night on a trail I can start from here and return by next morning."

"Huh. That's a tall order," she said, "or should I say long?" Tom didn't reply, so she continued. "Do you have any hiking experience?"

"Lots," he lied.

Thirty-Nine

Colorful history, the Ranger said. Bullshit. All he could see was rock, brown rock, dark gray and black rock, surrounded by gravel, sand, a few stickled pale green plants, and white-hot light so bright it seemed as though the sun floated above him attached to a cable. So much for the Back-Door Roundabout. Ranger Marcy said it was an intermediate trail for beginners except for a few hills. Bare-ass mountains, she should have said.

When he started out, he forced himself not to turn his eyes back to the lush haven of Furnace Creek Center. He did not want to see its picturesque paths beneath its impressive canopy of shade-spreading trees.

He could have crashed there for the night and started early in the morning. After a shower and a restaurant steak followed by a good night's sleep and a hearty breakfast, he would have been much better off. So much better than flatfooting around rocks and dirt, forever hot in his sweat-wet hat and knock-off shroud beneath an unimpeded, unforgiving sun. Its searing rays would only subside when the sun god gave way to the stars and moon, which would martial their freezing temperatures, compelling their victim to fervently wish and yes, ironically pray for warmth. That's when the wayfarer would yearn for the clothes he stashed beneath a bin behind the Center. But even if he made it through the night, the sun would be waiting for the tortuous march to continue come morning.

And what would all that mean to Norah? If he took the easy way out but edited out the lux breaks he might take, what kind of devotion was that, physical or metaphysical? No matter what he chose, soft beds or nails, he knew he would feel the same, deep in the chasm of misery, lost from Norah.

Tom trudged on, weighed down by two gallons of water on his staff, one across each of his shoulders. When Marcy suggested a pair, he puffed up his chest, pronouncing that one would be enough. Then she added another water jug to his load. At least he nixed trail mix, figuring he'd only be two days and a night away from the Center.

He passed a small crossing for the Texas Springs and Indian Village Roads down to a curve toward 190S. Though he couldn't see it, he knew that the Furnace Creek Inn stood only a few football fields ahead. Not to be confused with the Center, the inn boasted a mini-opulent sanctuary lavishly displayed in its sales brochure. A smaller but still impressive canopy of trees bordered the Inn, fully shading its sidewalk and cool, blue swimming pool.

Once again tempted by his resident devil, he weighed spending the night at the Inn, barely a mile from the Center. All desert cruelties could be thwarted, Tom thought, simply by booking a room at the Inn or hell, even just a manger. One with a fan and a faucet, heavenly spirits be good, with air conditioning and a mini fridge. More blandishments threatening his risk of body and soul to win back the unknowing lover who had spurned him.

Sighing, he turned away from the Inn down onto the Badwater Road. He was the culprit here, he had to pay the price whether Norah cared or not. And he had no time to waste, even if it meant wasting away.

He reached his first landmark—a sign for Breakfast Canyon at the mouth of a trail that snaked up the mountain to a dead-end escarpment. The worn wooden sign fronting the canyon entrance reminded him of the trail he had turned down at the Center. He shrugged, swallowing sandy phlegm.

He plodded ahead to his next marker, the Golden Canyon Trailhead, three and a half miles from his starting point. He huffed a breath and turned left onto the path that would take him across the low mountains to other manageable routes down the other side. Plenty to get lost on too, he thought.

Tom soon found himself climbing slowly up steep slopes. As he ascended, he felt both taxed and, not surprisingly, hungry again. He had sworn off solid food as another sacrifice on the trail, he estimated that thirty hours or so fasting wouldn't be fatal. But Marcy's trail mix could really hit the spot now if he had it. Another reason among so many others to kick himself in the slats.

The wind picked up just then, blowing hot air and sand around him as he trudged along on the never-ending trail. He had left his wristwatch behind, knowing otherwise he would be checking it endlessly. If so, he would be constantly disappointed finding out that his estimate of a long hour of walking added up to just five minutes.

He drank water frequently, which meant stopping to lower the staff off his sore shoulders. Every time he imbibed by freeing a plastic gallon jug to raise high, slurping and spilling precious water. The first time he drank from one of his jugs, he put it back on his staff, lifting it over his shoulders only to fall over himself. Now what?

After a few minutes of thought, he poured water from the full gallon into the other until they matched waterlines. He hoisted them onto his back, gratified this time by the easily rebalancing on his staff.

He pushed on, up higher and steeper for at least an hour, he imagined. Or thirty minutes—which probably meant twenty. The rocky outcroppings on both sides of the path looked sharp, black and gray rising out of dusty sand covering the trail. Except for the few piercing points hidden mid-trail by collars of pulverized granules. Every time he trod down on one, he felt a jab in his instep or heel, dully discomforting. Considering the damage that might have occurred wearing sandals, he thanked heaven he'd sacrificed verisimilitude for his Timberland boots. And the goofy breezer hat.

Norah would have collapsed laughing at the hat, never mind her complete disregard of any fashion style affecting her attire choices. Comfort ruled her collection starting with the looser the fit, the better. Another wonder of Norah's; she looked great in whatever she wore. Fabulous, in fact.

Tom heaved another big breath, a sad reminder to keep breathing at all. At the top of a ridge, he felt thankful for seeing the path straighten ahead of him. He stopped to look over a vast, arid plain stretched out below, disappearing into the distance seamed with cracks where water might have been. Death Valley proof. Norah would have loved the sight. He thought of her standing next to him, leaning her head on his shoulder as they surveyed the exquisite panorama of nature. Feeling hollow again, he marched on.

The hills seemed a bit cooler, he thought, unless twilight was on its way. He stopped, put a hand on his brow, and squinted at the sun above. Still high in the sky, he thought, shaking his head. Lowering his sight, he saw distant mountains, burnt red in color, rippled with horizontal folds carved out by the elements. Immediately below him, he viewed bare-bone mountains all around, high but not towering, reduced by wear and tear heat and other brutal elements over unfathomable time.

He came upon a junction of two other paths. A sign provided confirmation, Badlands Junction, followed by Gower Gulch Loop to his right and Zabriskie Point to his left. His hiking brochure showed Gower Gulch doubling back to the Badlands Road. Zabriskie Point, he decided.

Tom drank more water before marching on, noticing that his staff felt much lighter. He made a mental note to ration his water as much as he could without risking dehydration. He also cursed himself for spilling so much earlier. Sighing, he thought maybe he would find more at one of the centers around the park. Fat chance.

The wind whipped particles around him, in his mouth and eyes. When he rubbed them, they lodged in his teeth and his eyelids, hurting like hell. He spat on his hands and wiped them carefully on his shroud. Then he carefully licked his hands again, and gently worked around his eyes removing the grit. He spit as much as he could, difficult in the hot, dry air.

At twilight, near the bottom of the hilly path, he saw a sign next to a jumble of wooden beams and rocks. Hurrying around to the sign front, he read the headline printed in red:

Danger! Abandoned Mine!
Unsafe Mine Shafts–High Walls!
Cave-ins – Decayed Timbers!
Deadly Gas – Lack of Oxygen!
Unstable Explosives!

He looked past the sign and the debris, shifting so he could see the front. There was an entrance. When he worked his way to it, he saw a threshold inside a yard deep and wide. He could sleep here out of any wind. He'd be safe from wild animals too. Except maybe for lizards and rattlesnakes. And scorpions and black widows. Some harmless beetles at least. But maybe coyotes? Lions and tigers and bears, oh my. He gave his face a slap. Get a grip, he said to himself. Norah would have enjoyed the fancy of course, if they avoided that kind of menagerie in real time. He blew out another sigh.

The wind whirled again, sending a chill down his spine. He suddenly realized that he was exhausted. Still leery about the mine, he asked himself what choice did he have?

He worked his way past a few broken four-by-fours into the mine's entrance just beneath its low ceiling. There was enough room for him to stretch his legs out width way. Two yards lengthwise from the head of the mine, he felt space below. Reaching down at the lip, he couldn't tell how far the edge dropped off. He rubbed his chin, then left.

Outside, he found a few broken four-by-fours in the pile near the opening. He dragged two inside and wedged them together at the back edge. He prodded them, and they stayed still. Satisfied with the makeshift speed bump, he stacked his water jugs against the side of the mine, rearranged his shroud to cover as much of him as it could, and clutched his staff to his chest and between his feet. Resting his head on another piece of broken wood, he felt like an ancient Japanese samurai. Except, he didn't have an exotic hairdo.

In the morning, sunlight poured into the mine well before Tom wanted it. He rubbed his eyes with his fists, engaging the grit left over from the twilight incursion the day before. Swearing at himself for not thinking last night of where the morning sunlight would hit, he felt like poking his eyes instead of relieving the scratchy pain. He reached over to one of the plastic water jugs and poured a tablespoon into a cupped hand. Carefully placing the jug down, he wet two fingers in the palm of his hand and once again gently wiped his eyes.

Better, he thought. Better than boring bugs and black widows, scorpions and snakes too. Or falling down an abandoned mineshaft.

He sat straight up, facing outside to survey his vast empire.

A scruffy looking coyote sat in front, gazing into the mine directly at him. Tom froze, fixed in place. The coyote blinked, turned away and trotted off.

So much for stark fear, Tom thought.

He got up, hung the water jugs over his shoulders, almost too light now, and started back to the trail. The sun was up, though the heat wasn't intolerable this early in the morning.

He had to be near the final leg to his turnaround, he figured. A mile and quarter to Twenty Mule Team Canyon, then up-hill another three miles or so back to 190S, this time going north. Then, all the way back to Furnace Creek, twelve miles overall.

Tom pursed his lips and blew a silent whistle. He was not sure he could make it. He needed some kind of sustenance and more water. Shaking his head ruefully, he put the staff and near empty jugs over his shoulders and marched on.

Fifty yards downhill, the trail surface turned from sand into macadam. Coming out of the boulder path, he found himself slowly strolling down to a plain surrounding the Zabriskie Point Parking Lot. Twenty cars occupied the lot, along with SUVs, pickup trucks, and a few Winnebagos parallel parked on the road. All centered around a small cabin restroom with a water spigot between two doors.

Elated, Tom picked up his pace as he headed down to the lot.

A car cut in front of him, its driver hitting the horn at the same time. He slowed up, seriously pissed off.

The driver rolled down the window and said, "Where you going, pilgrim?"

He stopped dead, staring at the dusty gray Nova and the two women sitting up front.

"You look like you could use a ride," Norah said. "Hop in."

Forty

The Ranch at Furnace Creek proved to be as cracked up as its billboards claimed, Tom thought. As soon as they pulled into the parking lot, he reserved two luxury suites chockful of amenities, including a well-stocked minikitchen. A sitting room with floor to ceiling windows overlooked the pool in front of distant mountains. And of course, along with a luxurious bathtub and shower, a jacuzzi beckoned.

He took full advantage of everything, eating blueberry muffins and onion bagels while sitting splay-legged in the spacious tub filled with room-temperature, beer and wine on a side table he dragged in from the sitting room. While he dined, Dan Hicks and His Hot Licks blared throughout the premises at top volume "I Scare Myself."

Tom felt that way, examining his red face and ankles, thank heaven for his all-encompassing shroud, and to hell with the Aussies' fucking breezer. Listening to his oldie favorite, he longed a little bit for a joint, gone from his palette since 1980, when he decided to go full out promoting the Experience. Joe told him to quit then, persuading him that the pigs would be all over him if they found just one stem in his possession. Picturing that and time in a federal prison chilled him to the bone. He knew that Joe wanted him to quit smoking anything, but his suggestive scare tactic worked this time for good. He shrugged in the tub, recalling how he quit tobacco, too. Why not? Depravation could only go so far. He couldn't be more miserable then, just like he was now. Only "now" was worse; the worst. Norah was here, in an adjacent suite with her Calli friend. She might as well be in India, for as much attention as she showed him, scooping him out of Death Valley notwithstanding.

He took a swig of his Lagunitas IPA, wondering if Joe spilled the beans to Norah about his trip. He put the bottle down and grabbed hold of the telephone he had dragged into the bathroom.

"Joe Collins," answered his brother.

"Did you tell Norah where I was going to; Death Valley?"

"I'm well, thank you for asking. And how's your sunburn coming along? By the way, I lost all of your money. Thus ruined a fine family fortune."

Tom grimaced, then said, "Sorry. This is important to me. I just need to know."

"Oh," Joe replied. "I did not tell anyone anything. That includes Noreen, whom I have not met yet."

"It's Norah. Norah Kealy. And you told me not to introduce you to any woman I showed up with unless wedding bands were announced."

"Yeah. So, you're marrying this girl?"

"No. I don't think so. Not in a million . . . but—"

"She's important to you."

"Yeah."

"Well, I'm sorry, I haven't heard from her."

"Huh."

"Listen, if there's anything I can do . . . ."

"For sure, Joe. I'll give you a ring."

"All right, my brother. Anything."

"Thanks, Joe. Really."

"And your Lawrence of Arabia trip? You speak Arabic now?"

"Of course. Looking for oil wells and the like. Got sunburned, that's all."

"That's plenty enough. You've got some strange impulses, Tommy, m'boy."

"I do. But I'm okay. Give my best to Maggie and the kids."

"Absolutely."

He called Don next, who knew nothing, though he sounded happy that his lead singer was alive.

So, who's left?

He called Ed Novicky.

"I never talked to her. Your business, not mine."

Tom hesitated, then said, "Of course you're right."

"I hope you see her again, sort everything out."

"Right. Me too."

"On another matter, your call is copasetic. I have that other information you were looking for. It took some doing, but it's all there."

"Man, that's great! But I'm here in Death Valley."

"Oh. Well, can you find a fax machine there? Maybe the hotel's business office?"

"Yes! Excellent idea! If I find one here, I'll call and leave a message. If not, I'm sure I can use one in San Francisco. Lemme get out of the tub. I'll call you as soon as I know."

Tom signed off and rushed to dress and get out the door. He quickly walked to the front desk. They immediately ushered him into their business office, where he called Ed back with the fax number. Ed said he would send the information at once.

Tom took a seat next to the hotel's fax machine waiting for the buzz to notify that the fax was arriving. Tom watched the printer move back and forth dot-printing each of the document's pages.

The machine was old, maybe a model dating back to the first used in offices. While he waited, he stared out of the picture window in the office facing the hotel's main corridor, watching its guests passed back and forth. Including Norah and her friend Marilyn, joking and laughing as they strolled by. Seeing Norah so relaxed brought back times when she carried on like that with him, poking fun at each other.

"How can you eat so little with all that's available to you?" she said seriously while laughing, "The world really is your oyster."

"I eat them sometimes," he said.

"I don't believe you. Look at you, you're like a living mummy!"

"Don't be talking about my mommy. She spoiled me in the best possible ways."

She burst into laughter again, "Not your mommy, a mummy, like Ramses, or Tut."

"I don't know what those guys ate, but my mom fed me very healthy meals. She was extremely careful about too much red meat and high blood pressure. She learned that from my grammy."

Okay," Norah said, "let's hear your grammy's blood pressure."

"What, after she died? It was zero."

He said it straight faced while she laughed and laughed. They could carry on like that all day and night.

Tom felt like he could let go of the breath he held all the way down. Now, none of it seemed funny at all.

The fax machine finally finished its slow emission, like those ten-ton borax wagons that made Death Valley a vacation destination. Back then, those borax-loaded wagons simply meant broken backs of nameless men further weighed down by heat-burning monotony.

Tom read the fax, which again had him praising Ed Novicky's lean thoroughness, and almost crying at what Ed reported. He folded the document in three and stuffed it into a rear pocket. He sent Ed a brief email confirming that he had received the fax and thanking him again. He left the office then to join the women.

Tom took them to dinner at the Ranch that night, where they savored the fare flown in by the excellent chef who had abandoned the madness of NYC for the quiet of Death Valley. The conversation held fast to the breezy level, everyone being cordial and warm. After dinner, they strolled around the grounds, gazing at the astounding display of stars fixed in the blue-black sky crowding the horizon. All astounded, they retired to their rooms, gliding to bed virtually asleep already.

The next morning, they made quick work of breakfast, fresh fruit and tamales. Norah and Marilyn gathered their gear into the Nova's trunk while Tom paid the bill. He joined them then, climbing into the back seat.

Behind the wheel, Norah turned her head to him and said, "What, not even a toothbrush?"

"I'll get a new one in San Fran. I got my hiking gear," he said, patting his backpack next to him on the car floor.

"What about your shroud and your saucy hat?" Marilyn said, smiling brightly.

"For some weird reason, they don't fit anymore." He shrugged his shoulders, "Maybe the next wayfarer can use them."

"Or the hotel dog," Marilyn said, causing them all to laugh.

They made it to San Francisco in nine hours as expected, eating lunch halfway, plus a making a couple of bathroom stops. When they hit San Francisco, though, Tom felt tension growing in the front seat, ever since Marilyn mentioned leaving the car first to visit her old-new friend Trey. They drove across the Bay Bridge to Oakland, continuing for half an hour, Marilyn giving directions all the way. They pulled up to a two-story craftsman house in need of a paint job, but otherwise well kept.

Marilyn opened the car door to get out, while a tall, thin, bearded guy with dirty blond hair dashed out of the house and down the stairs to pick Marilyn straight up in his arms. They hugged and smooched, which made Tom feel sharply awkward. He glanced over to Norah, who sat still.

Marilyn and the big fellow, Trey by name, broke their hugs to walk back to the car. Norah stepped out to open the trunk for Marilyn. She handed a bag to Trey, then turned to receive a ferocious hug from Marilyn. Norah slid back behind the steering wheel, while Marilyn went back to the passenger window, leaning on her elbows.

"Norah, thanks so much for the ride. It was really out of sight," she grinned. They laughed as she turned to Tom, "Thanks, Tom, you are one cool dude, you should know it."

He smiled, genuinely warmed by her sweetness.

"Okay," she said, straightening up. "I'll call you later once I get the lay of the land." She giggled and Norah laughed, too. "Good luck," she said, following Trey into the house.

Norah turned the key over, starting the Nova up. She didn't look back as she said, "I suppose you'd like to sit up front."

Surprised, Tom said, "I would."

He worked his way to the passenger side and pushed the seat over to climb out of the back. He sat down looking straight ahead.

Norah said, "We can drive over and crash at my old place and load my stuff in the car in the morning. Then I'll take you where you want—the airport, train station, buses."

He gazed back at her. "Seriously? You're going to drop me off, then drive alone in my car 3,000 miles give or take, from here back to Long Island? You think that's okay with me?"

"I thought it'd be better for both of us," she replied, her voice tight.

"Yeah, well, you need to think twice," he said, a bite in his voice as well. He sighed, and relaxed. "Look. You certainly deserve to have nothing to do with me. That's not what I'm talking about. I just want us to get home safely. We both can do what we want after that. Can you agree to that at least?" He whined a little at the end despite himself.

Norah sighed loudly. "We'll go get my stuff and drive back to Long Island."

"Good," he said flatly, "Great. Though, there's something I have to do."

She turned her head, completely puzzled.

"Eyes on the road, please."

Forty-One

They crossed back over the bridge out to a suburb close to the city. Norah drove as though by rote through windings and hairpin turns as if she had never left the Bay area. They pulled up to a brick building ten stories high. She engaged the emergency brake and turned off the car. They got out, and she walked over to Tom.

"Second floor," she said, "can of corn."

He followed her into the old but well-kept building. The green and tan linoleum squares still shiny, and the pink walls glowed as if painted yesterday. Norah trotted up the stairs next to the elevators, and he followed. Exiting the stairs, he saw her smack in the middle of the hallway turning the key in a lock.

"This is it," she said, "my old pad."

The apartment was small, with one side of the living room dedicated to a kitchen counter and sink. A small refrigerator stood on the left, an oven on the right. A large window on the opposite side allowed sunshine in, though the brick wall of the building next door seemed close enough to jump to the opposite windowsill. A sofa below the sill displayed a number of throws that together harmonized like a brash quilt. In front, a host of magazines and newspapers covered a low coffee table. Lamps situated on side tables also vied for space with books and papers piled high.

"If you need to go to the toilet, it's straight down the hall."

"Okay, thanks."

He went down the hall past two doors, one on each side. Two bedrooms, he imagined as he relieved himself, Three tenants? Someone new already?

He walked past old posters on the hall walls for Mr. Natural and the Fabulous Furry Freak Brothers. A Peace sign hung on the opposite wall next to a poster of Robert Smith backstage at a concert of The Cure. Next to that, posters for the Clash and U2.

Back in the living room, he said, "Your roommates have quite an array of rock'n'rollers through the ages."

"Oh, yeah. We came to most of them later when we weren't teeny boppers."

"Right." A decade younger, he remembered, a cosmic fathom apart.

"Anyway, here're my things, ready to go."

He peered down at a few boxes and two suitcases unmatched. "That's it?" he said.

"Well, yeah. When I first moved, I took what I needed day-to-day with me. This is the rest."

He tried his best not to look amazed and skeptical. "Okay, you take a box, and I'll get the two suitcases. We should be able to make it in two trips."

"Really? You think? The suitcases are heavy."

"If they don't have any barbells in them, I should be fine."

"Well, they do." He stared up at her. "Both of them."

They laughed together.

"Okay, double hernia here I come," he said grabbing both suitcases and lifting. They were heavy, but not Olympic weight heavy. Not gallon jugs over the shoulders heavy. Still, he said, "Let's take the lift."

She picked up a box and led the way to the elevator, which they rode downstairs. In short order, they had filled the trunk with her boxes, suitcases, and travel bag.

"All right," Norah said, "thanks. So, do you want to drive?"

"I do," Tom said. "But we need to make another stop."

She glanced at him, "What? Where? Why?"

He pulled the fax out of his back pocket. "Read this. You'll know why."

Tom started the car and waited.

When Norah finished reading, she looked at him, alarmed as he expected.

"How did you get this?" she asked.

"Ed Novicky. You remember, the Good Old Boys Club? He fixed up the Marbury." Seeing her memory dawning, Tom continued. "Ed figured it out. Here's a map. If you can plot our way, we should get there before rush hour."

She looked at the map, and said, "Laurel Canyon. Man, we should've done this before coming here."

"I know. But I didn't want to involve Marilyn. From the way she and Trey greeted each other, I'd say I was spot on with that decision."

She laughed, "Yeah. They get together, then they don't. Crazy about each other except . . .," she trailed off.

"Yeah," he said.

They made it to LA.in seven hours, tired and hungry even though they'd bought drinks and sandwiches to consume in the car. Neither of them said a word about stopping, other than for bathroom breaks and gassing the Nova. They arrived at Laurel Canyon just before sunset, thankful that they still had light to wend their way through the labyrinthine hills of the valley.

Along the steep drive they saw a field of mailboxes covered by old bushes and trees at the heads of driveways dropping down below. Taking the last shift behind the wheel, Tom slowly passed them all, occasionally doubling back when the street dead ended. After several false starts, just as the sun set they finally found what they were looking for, 1432 Crescent Road. Tom steered the car down the short winding driveway leading to the house, a typical two-story split-level, dull gray in need of a paint job.

"This is gonna be weird," Norah said.

"I know," Tom said. "But we have to do it. I just hope our instincts are right on."

"And Novicky's directions." She smiled awkwardly, "You think it'll be safe, right?"

"I do." He said, hoping he was right.

They got out of the car and walked up a short set of steps to the front porch. Tom took a deep breath and rang the bell.

They heard thumping inside approaching the door until it opened wide.

Buddy stood in the frame, still holding the knob.

"Oh," he said flatly, "you're here."

He looked the same, wearing loose painters pants held up by suspenders over a faded red cattle-drive shirt, sleeves pushed halfway up his arms— Except now he had a gray beard.

Tom and Norah said nothing.

Buddy gazed at them a bit, waiting. At length, he stepped to one side. "Well, come on in. It must've been a long ride."

Norah and Tom glanced at each other, then stepped inside. Buddy closed the door behind them.

"C'mon, relax, have a seat. I'll get some iced tea."

He gestured for them to sit on a couch against the wall between the front door and the kitchen. Both feeling self-conscious, they sat down on the bulky couch. While waiting, they looked around, first turning their heads toward a large painting depicting stock Indian warriors on horseback brandishing rifles and spears, surrounding fallen calvary men in blue. At dead center stood a stylized rendering of General George Custer on the top of a small, grassy rise carefully aiming a Colt .44, clearly depicted as heroic as hell. To their surprise, someone had planted an actual dart directly in the General's eye, perhaps executing a counter-culture correction. Either that or boozy inspiration.

Tom looked all around, taking note of other hip décor—a concert poster for a psychedelic 70's band *"The Watsons": We Need You!* next to a beautiful copy of *Christine's World* above a dark stained sideboard. Opposite, a couple of easy chairs and table lamps flanked an old, oval braided rug in the middle. Given all the other vintage knick-knacks everywhere convinced him that the living room décor hadn't been changed much through the years, maybe even decades.

Buddy returned with a tray of tea-filled crystal glasses and a plate of Lorna Doone shortbread cookies. He leaned over for Norah to take a glass and a cookie, then to Tom, saying "Take two." Tom did, and Buddy placed the tray on the coffee table in front of the couch. He sat down in one of the easy chairs opposite his guests, reached for his tea, and sat back.

"Well, it's very nice to see you both after all this time. What is it, three months?"

"Yes, I think that's right," said Norah, warmly, overly loud.

"Buddy," Tom said, pausing. "I mean—what the fuck?"

Buddy's features became solemn. "Right, Tom."

"Where have you been? Or should I say, why?"

Norah filled the cooling air, "We were just worried, Buddy, so worried about you—."

"And Devon," snapped Tom. "Where is he?"

Buddy sighed. "He's safe."

"Really? Where? Where is he safe?"

"Upstairs. Taking a nap. He gets so excited at school, when he comes home, he falls asleep wherever he is. Standing up at the table, sitting in front of the tube. So, I have him take a nap right when he gets here." Buddy smiled, "After he has his snack, of course. You know, kids."

Tom and Norah glanced at each other again. Tom swung back to Buddy. "Why did you take him? What were you thinking?"

Buddy seemed to clench his teeth, pressing his lower lip out. "I had to," he said, staring down at his hands, folding his fingers.

"Had to? What do you mean you had to?"

Buddy looked up. "You have not one idea of what was going on. Not a clue."

"Buddy, you kidnapped him! You could go to prison for a long, long time!"

"You think I give a fiddlers' fuck?" he snapped. They leaned away from him, surprised by his anger. "I know! I went through all of it. I could see it happening, so I took him."

Tom felt himself unwinding, a deepening sadness roiling into queasiness.

"Buddy, you didn't do anything with Devon . . . to him?"

Buddy rolled his eyes, "Of course not."

No one said another word. They could hear the ticking of an old clock on the kitchen wall, nothing else.

"Buddy?"

The voice sounded sleepy, high and clear. They all turned to the stairway where Devon stood on the landing holding the railing, his hair tousled, his school uniform rumpled. He looked older, longer than before.

"Hi, Pal," Buddy said, "did we wake you?"

Devon didn't speak, rubbing one eye with his fist, running the other hand through his curly brown hair.

"Look who's here, Devon, come just to see you!" Buddy declared.

Devon turned his head to the couple, their hands folded, sitting still on the couch. He smiled rumbling down the steps straight to Norah, hugging her around her knees, moving up to nuzzle her cheek. He pulled away and threw himself at Tom, tumbling him back against the couch while yelling, "War!"

Tom gathered himself and sat Devon on his lap. "Devon!"

"War!"

"What is it good for?" Tom sang rotely.

"Nothing!" shouted Devon and Tom together. Devon grabbed him close again as they all pitched in, "Absolutely nothing!"

They sat around the card table feeling more than full after consuming all of Buddy's pasta with the special sauce. The talk was raucous led by Devon's nonstop narrative of leaving Long Island, crossing the country in the paths of the first settlers and Lakota warriors, seeing the wide plains and the mountains so steep and high, they almost tipped their car back to the bottom. Everyone sounded paeans of wonder as he spoke, tidbits of noodles punctuating his stories. At length, he slowed down while his audience propped their heads up with their arms on the table. When Devon himself seemed to be falling asleep while sitting, Buddy picked him up and carried him upstairs to bed, detouring twice for their guests to kiss the little boy's cheek.

Norah and Tom arose to put away the leftovers and wash the dishes. As they finished up, Buddy came down into the kitchen.

"Sorry," he said, "he fell asleep before I could get him out of his school clothes. He needs to wear them again tomorrow."

Buddy feigned a shocked expression until he saw their confusion. "He goes to a Catholic elementary school. You know, uniforms and all that."

"Damn, Buddy," Norah said, "How do you expect to stay under the radar sending a black kid out of the blue to a Catholic school?"

"I've been careful," he said, "I grew a beard."

Norah and Tom traded puzzled, skeptical looks.

"You think that's going to be enough?" Tom asked. "They're showing your license photo all over the Eastern seaboard, Buddy. Someone around here is going to see you with Devon at school and put one and one together."

Buddy shook his head, "Not a problem. A friend from far back takes him both ways, calls him her nephew. Everyone knows I can't take him because I work long hours at night driving truck. Which I do not, of course."

"Huh." Norah said, "She's a Black woman?"

"No, but people around here have been very cool about mixed couples for a long time. When I came back, she greeted me as her own son. Her reward, she gets to walk Devon to school."

Seeing Tom and Norah listening in silence, Buddy stood up and left for the kitchen. Waiting for him to return, they moved to the couch. Buddy returned with a bottle and three short glasses. "Limoncello. Not often for me to get a nip with friends."

He poured them each a glass and one for himself. Then he settled down in his easy chair. "Okay, more story, questions later. My given name is Bobby Monahan. My old man was Mike Monahan. He walked out with his suitcase when I was seven, never to return—alive, anyway. Hitching a ride to Vegas, he was dropped off at an oasis for truckers; all-you-can-eat fast food joints, young girls looking for a ride, and cheap-booze watering holes. By the end of the night, Pops had his load on, too pissed to proposition any of the working girls. So, he headed off toward the motel when a trucker jumped his big Mack onto the sidewalk and walloped him."

Buddy leaned forward in his chair, smiling an awkward smile, "Best thing ever happened to us. Red River Trucking Inc. settled with Mom for a hundred thousand. She used it to pay off the house and drank up a lot of what was left. Smoked, too, died a couple years later, cancer. Before that, I cut out to downtown LA where I did not find Jesus, just a bed upstate in a juvey detention home.

"No one wanted me, too big to adopt." He took a sip of the sweet lemon liqueur and continued, "Except Earl Raftery. The director in charge of boys, he was the worst, and untouchable. He wanted me, for a million years. So, when I could I skipped out.

"I changed my name to Rosen, my mother's maiden name and knocked around for some years, lucky to be big and look mean enough to mostly be left alone. But I saw a lot of bad actors do bad things to other kids. I decided to get into social work, help those I could. I got my GED, went to a state teachers' college—higher education was free in Cali those days. Pulled in a social work degree and got an entry-level position fielding a hotline for teens. That crap certainly molded my character, you know, drink, drugs, dumb-ass boyfriends and girlfriends, all clueing me in that I better reboot. I moved east, got my job at Marbury when it was just starting up, and fell deeply in love with the kids."

Buddy raised his hand and stroked his beard absently. "I wanted to help them should any Rafterys show up. And some did. I scared a lot off, most of them. But Terry Able, I knew through the neighborhood grapevine. You know, the southside source of many of Marbury's wards assigned by the borough's family court. I liked living there, poor people but good people, nice people. Also because it was all I could afford."

He sipped more Limoncello. "Any word-of-mouth introduced me to Terry Able and his bosom buddies. Terry Terrific to his boys, Terrifying Terry to everyone else. His crews told all the other dealers to clear out from their corners or face a visit from Dr. Dis-Able. He was big on knives, switchblade, hunting, you name it. Scared the hell out of everybody."

Buddy raised the bottle for more, which was empty. He shrugged, setting it on the floor. "He also could talk some shit. Never got a conviction, not once. Hell, he barely had a rap sheet, just a few arrests when he was just coming up as an enforcer. Nothing stuck."

Buddy stared, lost in the distance. "So silky, a hard guy with a sugar tongue. Worse, he's got short eyes."

He raised his head, "You had that run-in with him, Tom, remember? He took your parking space—you know, the one Gertrude bestowed upon you for good conduct."

Tom shook his head.

"Oh, she didn't? Well, anyway, you did lay into Able, and he doubled over backwards to smooth your feathers. Saving grace for him to be welcome at Marbury."

Buddy leaned in, folding his hands together between his knees. "I never met him before he showed up at Marbury. You know, the way he dressed, like Cary Grant. His new car, no hot Trans Am for him. His utterly affable affect, who could've known? Anyway, I shopped around the 'hood and got the lowdown on his remarkable renovation. Like a phoenix rising from the embers. Call it another veil in his dance with the authorities."

"But this adoption scheme to get Devon," he shook his head back and forth like a horse, "brutally brilliant. Adopt a kid; no one knows what goes on behind closed doors."

"But why, Buddy?" Norah asked, almost pleading, "Why didn't you go to the police. Or come to us, at least."

"I couldn't handle it, and time was running out. That slippery fucking eel was passing every test, every interview. He produced all the documents claiming Devon as his son; the boy's birth certificate, a marriage license to his mother, divorce papers granting her sole custody of their son, and a family court ruling that as Devon's only living relative Terrance Able had full rights to his disposition!" Buddy clenched his heavy hands into fists, "All bullshit forgeries! Terry could take Devon out of Marbury to do anything he wants to our little boy. And after he's done with Devon, he can turn him out like he did a dozen others. After that, they don't make it."

He lowered his head, watching as he squeezed and kneaded his hands. "I couldn't think of anything else, so I scooped Devon up and brought him here." Buddy raised his head again, "And that's that."

They all remained quiet for some time.

"How did you come into this house?" Norah asked.

Buddy shrugged, "My mom left it to me." He gazed around, "It's been empty for a few years, but it's not too bad. My friends kept it up as much as they could. Fix it up, it might be a real moneymaker these days."

"So, this guy," Tom said, "Terry—"

"Terry Terrific, yeah," said Buddy.

"He's still around?"

"Back in New York as far as I know."

"You don't think he can find you here."

"How? He doesn't know my name, where I'm from. He couldn't find me unless he asked Gertrude about me. And he can't do that, he'd blow his whole deal."

"Yeah," Tom said rubbing his chin, "I suppose so."

"Buddy," Norah said, "we have to take Devon back."

Buddy slumped in his chair deflated like a parade balloon. "I guess so."

"It's for his own good," Norah said, "and yours. As far as New York's Finest think, you kidnapped Devon. We can tell them the extenuating circumstances, but it's still a major felony to them."

"So what are you going to tell them?" Buddy asked sharply.

"I have no idea," Norah said. "Maybe a distant relative took him for a visit. I don't know."

Buddy's features tightened. "Fat chance that."

"Look," Tom said, "We'll bring Devon back, tell them we and his relatives got our signals crossed. After that, we button up. Gertrude will back us up and also testify that Terry Able is not suitable after you fill her in. It could buy time for the court to check out his background for real."

"Uh huh. And what about me?"

Tom let out a heavy breath. "Shit, I don't know. You come back later. Stay at my house," he said, then mumbled, "I have a lot of extra room these days."

Norah pursed her lips. Then she said, "We'll figure something out. Just come. You're family, Buddy."

"All right. Enough," Buddy said. "Everyone's beat. Let's go to bed and talk tomorrow. You guys can sleep down here, the guest room's host to all the family junk since I left and came back. One more pile and I'll be booked as a hoarder. Could be a bigger offense than child abuse in some quarters. Anyway, the couch down here is a Castro convertible. The sheets and covers are already on, pillowcases too. The toilet's down the hall. Good night."

He leaned over and kissed them both on their cheeks. Then he went upstairs.

Forty-Two

In bed together, both lying straight, Norah and Tom did not speak. Nor did they sleep; they both knew that the other was awake, too. Finally, Tom broke the silence.

"I have just one question, Norah."

"Yes?" she said, her voice bell clear.

"How the hell did you know I was in Death Valley? Who told you? Only Don and my brother Joe knew where I was going. Gertrude didn't know. Not Mary for sure, she would've fretted to death. So, who? Or did you use a crystal ball?"

Silence reigned in the dark. Finally, she spoke.

"I got a phone call," she said.

"Who? Who called you?"

"Christine."

Shit. Tom felt like crawling completely under the covers. He hesitated. "She told you."

He felt he sensed the air move, but not see her head bob while she said, "Yes."

"And how did she find out?"

"From Don. He didn't know she didn't know. She's good at getting information from people, I guess."

"Uh huh." Good God. "And, uh, did she mention why she told you?"

"She did, sort of. She said she was sorry how things had gone. She didn't realize how . . . how close we were. She said she knew you'd get drunk and . . . and all the rest. She apologized to me. Said she never would have done it if she'd known."

Yup, Tom said to himself, I'm still the asshole here. Fuck me.

"She was really very nice."

I'll bet, he thought. He paused. Then he said, "So, you and your friend detoured all the way to Death Valley to pick me up."

"Yeah," said Norah. "I didn't want to just let you die there," she said, exasperated. "And we were taking the southern route anyway."

Right. That's all. Tom said, "Well, thanks for the effort. You probably did save my life. At least my skin."

"Of course," she said.

Of course.

They both fell asleep, he later than she.

Heavy knocking on the front door woke Tom up. He listened, but he felt prodding among the covers, pulling away, which he grabbed to keep as his own. The hills of Laurel Canyon exercised their fair share of cool evenings.

Propped on his elbow, Tom listened. Nothing. He gave the entire wadded covers a yank just as the pounding suddenly started again. He sat up and sang, "Just a second."

"Somebody at the door?" mumbled Norah. "At this hour?"

Tom shrugged, then realized she missed his gripping the blanket in the dark. "I'll go see," he murmured, pulling on his jeans. Silently straightening up, he felt his way to the door, thinking he would open it just a crack to see who could be there so late. Police maybe?

He quietly levered the latchkey open. Then he gently rotated the knob until it suddenly flew out of his hand as the door was yanked open. He stepped back, bumping into Norah still tucking her nightshirt into her chinos. He instantly steadied her balance behind him, both ignoring the chill air enveloping them from the open door.

Terry Able stepped into the doorway.

"Hello Mr. Weatherly," he said cooly. Resplendent in a black leather bomber jacket and black wool trousers, he continued, "May I come in?"

Tom eyed the silky blood-red scarf at his throat covering a black t-shirt. Tom started to mutter, "If it's it all the same—" when Able slipped sideways sliding inside. Shifting to one side, he started to open the nearest window curtain next to the sofa below *Custer's Last Stand*.

"Don't you folks want to bask in the sunshine?" Terry murmured. "Who knew it'd be so cold in LA? Really effing cold. In the morning anyway. Okay, to the point." He smiled slowly beneath cold eyes. "I'm not alone."

He blew a shrill signal barely below a dog whistle. Sure enough, another figure flitted inside, a man shorter than most, but imposing, especially his heavily engineer boots. A black balaclava cap pulled down low hid his face, also shadowed by brilliant morning sunshine pouring through the door.

"My friend, Julio. Look around, Jules. It looks like a nice place to live." Julio nodded as he sat on the edge of the couch below the painting. Able never wavered from watching Tom and Norah. After a beat, he said, "So, where's my kid?"

Tom started to sputter, "now wait a minute, Terry—"

Norah cut him off, "He's not your kid! Nobody's your kid. Wait until they check your background. Buddy told us all about you, you fucking piece of shit. You'll be lucky not to become some troglodyte's sweetheart in the slam. Except you're so pretty, I don't know . . .." she trailed off.

Goddamn, thought Tom, she kicks ass. He hoped they didn't have guns. Then he remembered; Terrifying Terry liked knives.

Terry shrugged, cocking his head. "Listen; he's my son and I'm taking him home. You can't stop me, I have rights. I know he's here and it's difficult for you to let him go. If you really care for him, you should just sit down on the couch with Julio while I go find him. Otherwise, he might see things not for little boys' eyes before we leave."

"Hello, everybody up? Time for breakfast? And what's all this noise about coming and going?"

Poised at the top of the stairs, Buddy bounded down like a dancing bear in Doc Martens. Wearing his white painter pants, a belt and suspenders, and his red driver shirt, he stopped on the third step and said, "Why, Mr. Able, what a surprise. What brings you here?"

Terry craned his neck and smiled frigidly. He spoke in a saccharine, barely obliging way, "Why Buddy, you grew a beard, I hardly knew it was" you." He stepped closer to the stairways. "But you know why I'm here, Buddy old pal. You know."

"Really? I can't imagine. But I am hungry, and I'm sure my guests are, too." He trotted down and crossed the room in large, fluid steps as he said, "Why don't I whip up a decent breakfast so we all can sit down and sort out everything fully nourished."

He passed by everyone into the kitchen. "Why don't we start with scrambled eggs," he said, turning on a gas burner as he reached with his other hand for a cast iron pan hanging above the stove. Julio suddenly jumped from the couch flashing a knife just as Buddy spun around to smash him squarely on his face with the heavy pan. Julio dropped to the floor loose-limbed as Buddy crouched to fend Terry's knife thrust. The blade skidded off the back of the pan across Buddy's arm, splashing blood like a claret fountain.

Tom tackled Terry low around the waist, slowly slipping down to barely grasp his thigh. Buddy fell back against the counter in the kitchen, holding his pan up with both hands to blunt Terry's furious slashing, drawing slowly closer with Tom tugging his leg. He suddenly jumped back, sending Tom flat on his back with a vicious kick. Holding his blade above his chest, Terry spit out, "You die first mother fucker!" He jerked his knife back posed for the matador thrust when Norah slammed him on his head, shattering the empty bottle of Limoncello. Terry collapsed on the floor.

A half hour later, the Laurel Canyon Sheriff's Officers wheeled the two injured men in handcuffs out to a waiting ambulance. In charge of the detail, Sergeant Miller commended Buddy and his guests for defending themselves so ably and for apprehending their assailants to boot.

"We don't see stuff like this turning out so good," Sergeant Miller said. "You folks are damned formidable."

"Yes, well, we try to keep up with the latest self-defense methods," Norah said, still wearing her night shirt tucked into her pants, a blanket around her shoulders.

"Pretty swell stuff, "the Sergeant said. "Send me the name of your dojo mentor, I'll spread the word."

"You bet, absolutely," she said, pulling the blanket closer around her.

"We'll get these boys booked, and I'll send an officer back later for a full report later. Get yourselves some sleep in the meantime."

"Yessir."

The medics patched up Buddy and Tom, then left. Norah helped Tom get his clothes on as Devon came down the stairs, rubbing his eyes, asleep through the entire fiasco.

"No school today, Dev," Buddy said. "In fact, we've got a big surprise for you. You're going to go back to see your friends at Marbury!"

"I am? With you?"

"Well, no, maybe with Mr. Weatherly here."

"I want go with you."

"No, I have to take care of a few things here, Devon. I'll be back later when I finish."

"Can't you do the things later?"

"I don't think so. It has to do with the police and things. Could be a while. But you can have fun with Mr. Weatherly. You'll be riding in an airplane!"

"I don't want to." Devon wasn't close to tears, but they were inevitable if the argument continued.

"Hey. I'm not flying," Tom said. "I'm driving my car back."

"Oh really?" Norah said. "Now it's your car again?"

"Yeah, well, I do have the pink slip."

"Okay, but I have the keys. I'm driving it back."

"I'll still have the pink slip."

"Let's see how long that lasts." Norah turned to Buddy. "Looks like you and Devon are taking the plane." She leaned down to Devon, "Don't worry, Dev, we're all gonna be back together again at Marbury in just a few weeks. But you and Buddy here can go early and get things ready for us when we return." She stood up, "Right, Buddy?"

His eyes glassy, Buddy said, "Right. Right." He leaned down between Norah and Tom, an arm across each of their shoulders, "Thanks. Thank you so much."

He stood up. "Let's go pack, Devon."

After seeing Buddy and Devon off at LA International, Tom and Norah walked side by side to the Nova in the parking lot.

Tom was not sure if his involuntary shaking showed. He was still scared for his life. He kept seeing and replaying the horror in Buddy's house—the blood, Terry and the other guy's heads, both bashed bleeding everywhere. He hid his shaking hands when they cleaned up the mess. But now leaving, he wondered if he would be shaking while driving all the way back home.

Norah suddenly stopped in the middle of the parking lot.

"God-damn it, Tom, I was scared!" she said, shaking.

He reached over an arm around her shoulders. "Me too, Norah. I'm still scared shitless." She barked a laugh. "So, let's try not to think about it. Let's get in the car and drive back home for a while."

She nodded her head, and they started walking again, her arm through his.

Things would change, Tom reckoned. Buddy would shine off the Laurel Canyon PD. Gertrude would take care of the long arm of the Long Island DA's Office. Buddy would get a slap on the wrist considering the circumstances that saved Devon.

Tom knew, too, that he would still play with his band, but locally mostly, with an occasional trip, maybe, for special reunion gigs and the like. He realized he'd much rather sing "Pachalafaka" with the half-pints than put it all out there for a bunch of lit-up pensioners. Though the grayheads were a lot of fun, too.

Somewhere in the eastern hills of the Rockies, he turned and stared at Norah. Her eyes fixed on the road ahead, one hand on top, one below, she gave him a glance. "Yeah?"

"Do you still love me?" he said.

"Ah, yeah. I suppose so."

"How much?"

"Uh, pretty much."

"Pretty much? That's not calculable. How about infinity?"

"Infinity?"

"Infinity times infinity."

"Gee," she huffed, "you're asking a lot."

"Well, how about it?"

"Eh, so-so," she said, her hand raised flat, tilting it to one side, then the other."

"So, still in the balance."

"That's about right."

He nodded, resting his head back against his folded hands.

They drove on.

Acknowledgments

I started this book about 30 years ago, writing six chapters. Then, I passed them onto our brother Patrick, a professional musician who knew everything about rock and roll including the culture of its performers. I asked him if it rang true; his answer was a roll of his eyes and one sentence: "You have no idea!" Thrilled, I wrote another five chapters and a 25-chapter synopsis. I put it away to write other stories while also working at a university press and raising a family with my wonderful work colleague, work, sweetheart, and mother of our children, Ivey Pittle Wallace. She also read and edited every book I've ever written. Also, thanks to our daughter Molly who creates all the covers for my books. And son Conor, who knows a good joke when he reads one.

We lost Patrick last year, despite the herculean efforts of our sister Ellen to care for him. This book is dedicated to Ellen for her profound empathy and unfailing service to any and all friends and clients in need, her wonderful wit, and her unshakable loyalty and belief in fairness for all.

I also want to thank my brother George for his invaluable objective readings, and my best friend Jim O'Donnell, who has weighed in as well in a gracious, constructive way. Thanks to sister Lucie for her readings and encouragement, and sister Anne for her gracious comments. And grace to Patrick, who I miss every day, as I am sure all of us do who ever knew him.

About the Author

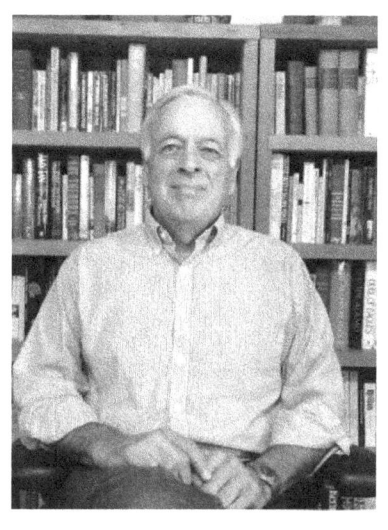

Dan Wallace worked in book publishing for 37 years, most of them at Gallaudet University Press. In 2014, he turned to writing full time. He has written six novels that include *Tribune of the People: A Novel of Ancient Rome* and *Run West: A Novel of the Civil War*, and *Through Noise and Silence*, a speculative fiction story about the future. He has completed three short story collections and also writes poetry and essays that can be read online at his writing exchange *In the Wallace Manner* (inthewallacemanner.com). He lives with his wife Ivey, who is also his editor-in-chief, in the Washington, DC, area.

A New Speculative Novel

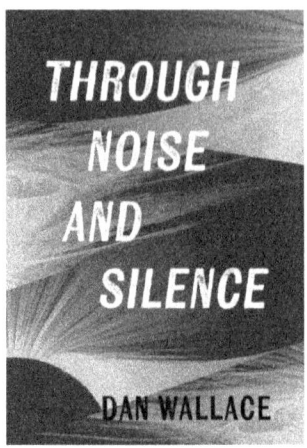

In a world swept by waves of cataclysm and grace, Mick Morris crests them with ease. Founder of the Stanley Institute, he deftly juggles its quantum physics research, commercial development, and government limits with admirable aplomb, now going on for fifteen years. What could possibly go wrong? Mick's daughter Meg soon finds out.

As CEO, she guides the Institute in search of the next, great QP solution to unlock astonishing possibilities in spectacular realities. But obstacles large and small impede her, from mundane office issues to mortal danger both domestic and foreign. She and her stalwart companions Carla and Ev hold their own despite all risks. But their world is running out of time.

Through Noise and Silence travels fantastic pasts and futures on Earth and distant planets. By way of far reaches through the ethos to universes and dimensions unknown, it is a trip well worth the taking.

Through Noise and Silence
ISBN 978-1-73530064-1-7 trade paperback
ISBN 978-1-7353006-1-8 Kindle E-Book
Wylisc Press, Silver Spring, MD
wyliscpress@gmail.com

Historical Novels by Dan Wallace

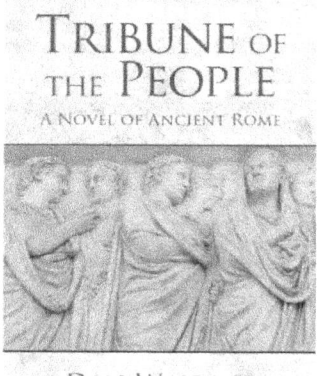

Publishers Weekly—Wallace's epic novel triumphs with a vivid historical account of ambitious elite Roman politicians and generals.

Library Journal— This thoroughly researched novel is as dramatic and gory as any swords-and-sandals epic and demonstrates how educational historical fiction can be. A wide cast of characters including soldiers, senators, slaves, mothers, and wives expand the reader's understanding of life in this time.

Midwest Book Review—A deftly constructed, exceptionally well written, and consistently compelling read from beginning to end, "Tribune of the People" is a truly impressive novel of the old Roman Empire by Dan Wallace. This is the stuff from which block-buster movies are made!

The US Review of Books: Professional Book Reviews for the People— Wallace's epic tale vividly depicts the opulence and grandeur of the ruling classes while simultaneously detailing the sights, sounds, smells, and squalor of those not born to wealth or position. His battle scenes pulse with excitement as he couples the weapons, tactics, and strategies of war with the carnage they wreak. No less compellingly does he describe the deceit and scheming in the porticos of power as well as the intrigue and hidden agendas in intricate familial relationships. RECOMMENDED.

The Historical Novel Society—A most timely novel; the characters are engaging and well-formed and the story well told. The novel gives you a feel for ancient Rome in the last years of the Republic.

Tribune of the People: **A Novel of Ancient Rome**
ISBN 978-1-7335725-0-7 trade paperback
ISBN 978-1-7335725-1-4 Kindle E-Book
Wyliscpress, Silver Spring, MD
<u>wyliscpress@gmail.com</u>

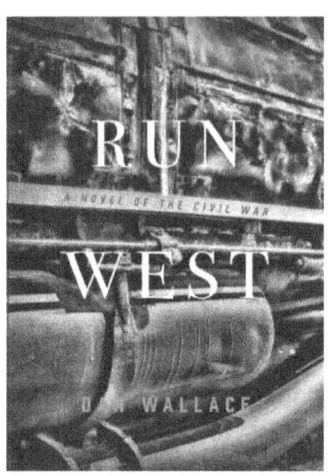

In the winter of 1861, East Tennessee mountain boy Billy McKinney finds himself marching with the Rebels to engage the Yankees at the Cumberland Gap. He never wanted to fight for the South because his preacher taught him that slavery was wrong. Mostly, though, Billy fears getting killed. In his first battle, he charges through a storm of gunfire and cannon shot amid a driving, icy rain. All around him his friends fall, their mouths bubbling bloody webs of agony. Terrified, Billy decides to run. In his mad dash, he meets up with four runaway slaves led by Bev Bowman. They take him along on their flight, though as prisoner or partner remains to be seen.

Run West is a compelling story of survival in a time of anguish and conflict that no one could escape.

***Run West:* A Novel of the Civil War**
ISBN 978-1-7335725-2-1 trade paperback
ISBN 978-1-7335725-3-8 Kindle E-book
Wylisc Press, Silver Spring, MD
wyliscpress@gmail.com

Mainstream Short Stories

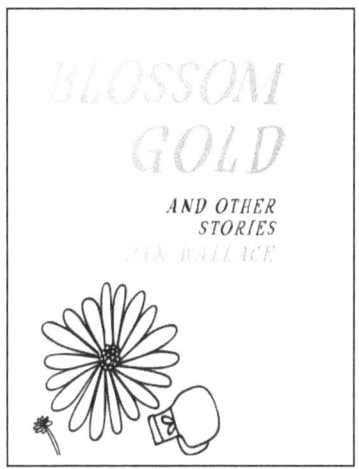

    A young West Virginia girl trained as a boxer by her father strikes up a troubling, long-distance friendship. Hoping to live the dream, a master plumber crosses the ocean to compete for a fantastic prize. In a small city museum, an ambitious curator crosses paths with two aspiring artists at an avant-garde exhibit. Humiliated after dropping a fly ball, a disillusioned boy's love of the game hinges on the actions of an old major leaguer. A young woman considering her tenth school reunion reminisces to decide.

    These stories comprise an array that mine the country's cultural history during the past half century. Each offers vivid characterizations of common people and places as pieces in the puzzle of an ever-changing world. Insights abound in this wide-ranging collection well worth reading through and through.

Blossom Gold and other stories
ISBN 978-1-7335725-6-9 trade paperback
ISBN 978-1-7335725-7-6 Kindle E-book
Wylisc Press, Silver Spring, MD
wyliscpress@gmail.com

City Stories

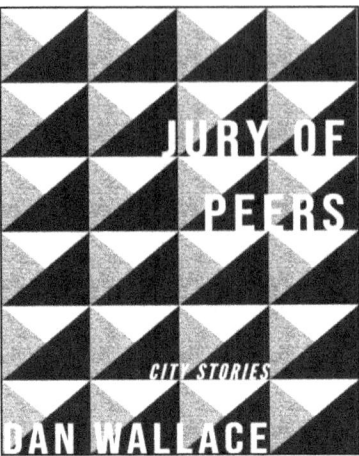

Summoned to jury duty, a divorced carpenter finds himself neck-deep in a Philly mob case. In the high-stakes urban real estate trade, a young agent makes his move to join the heavy hitters. A housecleaner seeks a unique form of justice for her upscale clients only to run into unlikely speed bumps. Tired of his mundane work buying microchips, a computer tech road warrior stops in Las Vegas for twenty-four memorable hours.

These stories and their companions cast stark light on various characters striving to succeed in circumstances singular to life in urban settings. Far removed from the natural world, people are the game and currency is the currency. For many of those shaped by society's strictures, survival defines success. This collection reveals in striking fashion the means an assortment of individuals use to work out their own formulas for success in the city.

Jury of Peers
City Stories
ISBN 978-1-7353006-0-3 trade paperback
ISBN 978-1-7353006-1-0 Kindle E-book
Wylisc Press, Silver Spring, MD
wyliscpress@gmail.com

Science Fiction Stories

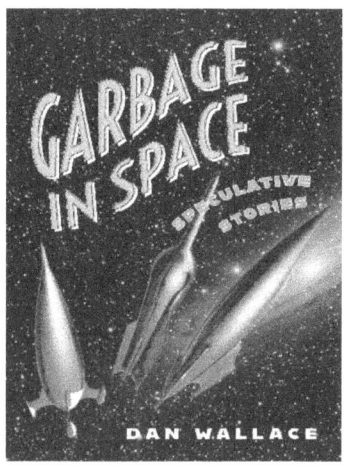

Travel through space with provisional immortals as they panhandle for treasure amid a million iotas of galactic trash. Reserve a front-row seat for truly heroic Olympic feats performed on the Moon. Land on a desert planet where an eternal being chances the immolation of her gray matter forever. Follow a troubled blue-collar worker as he experiences an ultimate epiphany. Join an ambitious researcher who risks his own consciousness by delving into the depths of the permanently comatose. Track the progress of professional sports in ever-shifting environments.

Explore these and other alternate human prospects in this enriching, eclectic collection of stories. Each offers an original perspective on a broad spectrum of the probable and the possible. Together, they deliver an extraordinarily entertaining spectrum of what the future might hold.

Garbage in Space: Speculative Stories
ISBN 978-1-7335725-8-3 trade paperback
ISBN 978-1-7335725-9-0 Kindle E-book
Wylisc Press, Silver Spring, MD
wyliscpress@gmail.com